"Bob Fu has dedicated his life to bringing freedom of religion to the Chinese people. His story is a testimony to the power of faith and an inspiration to people struggling to break free from oppression."

—Mrs. Laura Bush

"The riveting account of a student leader of the Tiananmen Square protests who becomes a literal prisoner for Christ and then escapes to the West. Impossible to put down."

—Eric Metaxas, *New York Times* bestselling author
of *Bonhoeffer: Pastor, Martyr, Prophet, Spy*
and *Amazing Grace: William Wilberforce
and the Heroic Campaign to End Slavery*

"Like John the Baptist, Bob Fu has influenced people from all walks of life, across the nation of China and beyond, and led many to repent and believe in Jesus. Anyone who cares about the persecution of God's household in China and in the Middle East should read this book."

— Brother Yun, Chinese house church leader
and author of *The Heavenly Man*

"This compelling and deeply moving account of Bob Fu's escape from China and his heroic work on behalf of other human rights workers there is likely to become a classic. From the very first page, you are hooked. There are few more convincing narratives of Christian courage under persecution and suffering."

—David Aikman, former senior correspondent for *Time* magazine;
author of *One Nation Without God?*

"Courageous, tireless, well-informed, and effective. Bob Fu and ChinaAid are harbingers of the more just and open China that we pray is coming."

—Dr. Os Guinness, author of *The Global Public Square*

"Bob Fu's story is a gripping and inspiring account of courage and endurance. His personal experience of China's struggle for democracy, religious freedom, free speech, and human rights—particularly coercive population control—makes this an indispensable book, especially for anyone who admires China and its people and who yearns for reform and change. I feel privileged to have had a small walk-on part in what is a story of suffering tempered by hope."

—David Alton, Rt. Hon. Professor Lord Alton,
House of Lords, Parliament, UK

"I will always remember that night in early 1997 when I met Bob and Heidi and baby Daniel at Dulles airport, although I have met many people there over the ⟨…⟩ as we met for the first time. That in⟨…⟩ to many, many others over the year⟨…⟩ Bob and Heidi's experience in Beijir⟨…⟩ d the uncertainty of life as exiles ir⟨…⟩ erful sense of commitment

to helping others who suffer for their faith and more generally for the freedoms of expression and association. They have persevered through many twists and turns of the road, despite the costs. And throughout, they have sought ways to bring God's blessings to the Chinese people."

—**Dr. Carol Lee Hamrin**, senior associate, Global China Center;
research professor, George Mason University

"*God's Double Agent* is a moving testament to the liberating power of Christian faith over the empty ideological doctrine of communism. Every freedom-loving person should read this book. Bob has done Christianity and the free world a great service by sharing his story of spiritual and political liberation. May many millions follow in his path."

—**Dr. Richard Land**, president emeritus,
the Ethics and Religious Liberty Commission (ERLC)
of the Southern Baptist Convention; president,
Southern Evangelical Seminary

"*God's Double Agent* is a page-turner! The incredible growth of the Christian Church in China has taken place in a culture of official atheism and severe persecution. Bob Fu was on the ground and experienced persecution and suffering. He was at Tiananmen Square. The Chinese military opened fire and killed their own university students. His report on what really happened, and continues to happen, is startling."

—**Don Argue**, president emeritus, National Association
of Evangelicals; commissioner, US Commission
on International Religious Freedom

"*God's Double Agent* is an engaging memoir of Pastor Bob Fu, founder and president of ChinaAid, which serves the persecuted church in China. Pastor Fu's story takes us from the hardship endured by his parents under harsh communist policies through his own birth into desperate circumstances and the bitterness he felt growing up. He tells how he was delivered from this bitterness through his conversion to Christianity, immediately began evangelizing others (and was dubbed "the Missionary" during graduate school), and eventually escaped to the United States. Written in an intimate and lively style, this account gives insight into the formation of a tireless advocate for the persecuted church in China, as well as a portrait of his bold, brilliant, and intrepid wife, Heidi."

—**Reggie Littlejohn**, president, Women's Rights
Without Frontiers

"This book is truly one of David and Goliath proportions. Bob Fu may physically be a little man, but in reality he is a giant: full of faith, courage, and tenacity. This is the amazing story of Bob's life spent fighting for freedom and justice both inside and outside of his beloved homeland of China."

—**Mervyn Thomas**, chief executive,
Christian Solidarity Worldwide

GOD'S
DOUBLE AGENT

The True Story *of a*
Chinese Christian's Fight *for* Freedom

BOB FU

with Nancy French

BakerBooks
a division of Baker Publishing Group
Grand Rapids, Michigan

© 2013 by Bob Fu

Published by Baker Books
a division of Baker Publishing Group
P.O. Box 6287, Grand Rapids, MI 49516-6287
www.bakerbooks.com

Printed in the United States of America

Library of Congress Cataloging-in-Publication Data is on file at the Library of Congress, Washington, DC.

ISBN 978-0-8010-1572-4 (cloth)
ISBN 978-0-8010-1590-8 (pbk.)

Unless otherwise indicated, Scripture quotations are from the King James Version of the Bible.

Scripture quotations labeled ESV are from The Holy Bible, English Standard Version® (ESV®), copyright © 2001 by Crossway, a publishing ministry of Good News Publishers. Used by permission. All rights reserved. ESV Text Edition: 2007

Scripture quotations labeled NIV are from the Holy Bible, New International Version®. NIV®. Copyright © 1973, 1978, 1984, 2011 by Biblica, Inc.™ Used by permission of Zondervan. All rights reserved worldwide. www.zondervan.com

The names and details of the people and situations described in this book have been changed or presented in composite form in order to ensure the privacy of those with whom the author has worked.

13 14 15 16 17 18 19   7 6 5 4 3 2 1

Christianity in China has been confined to the history section of the museum. It is dead and buried.

JIANG QING, WIFE OF CHAIRMAN MAO

Rebellion to tyrants is obedience to God.

BENJAMIN FRANKLIN

1

It was midnight. I placed my fingers on the bottom of the window and gently, quietly tried to pull it open. But years of paint had cemented it shut, so I held my breath and gave it a sharp yank. It opened at last—but not as silently as I'd hoped. I prayed that none of the police officers stationed by my building's door had decided to take a cigarette walk around the block and that none of my neighbors were awake. If I was going to do this—and survive—there could be no witnesses.

Heidi, my wife, had just left our apartment on the sixth floor, wearing a silk scarf and different clothing than she normally wore. The agents were used to seeing us as a couple, so she'd have a better chance of slipping past them without me. There were three exits to the gigantic building, but the government had shut down two of them when they began watching us. The only remaining exit was next to a room full of security guards who watched our every move. Whenever I left the building, they sent out an alert and another guard would inevitably pick up my trail. I couldn't remember what it was like to be outside in the open air without surveillance.

If Heidi's disguise didn't work, I wouldn't have much time before the agents would be on their way up to the sixth floor to arrest me—but I wouldn't be there. Heidi had purposely left on the light to mislead the spies into thinking we were still awake and milling around before bed, and I was already on the fifth floor, where I had entered the restroom. Everyone on the floor shared the same bath, and the doors to the restrooms were always unlocked. I looked out the window and couldn't see a thing, but I knew I wasn't getting the full view. My chances of survival would increase with every floor I could safely descend without being detected. I quietly slipped out of the restroom and back into the stairwell, watching the numbers decrease. Fourth floor. Third floor. Second floor. That's where I stopped. The agents were on the first floor, and at this point there was no turning back.

I gently opened the door of the stairwell, looked left and right, and slowly walked down the corridor to the bathroom. I entered a tiny toilet stall and climbed on the ledge of the window, which fortunately was already open. Even though it was August in Beijing, the breeze wafting over the sill sent a chill through me. I placed my feet as close to the edge as possible. The jump was close to twenty feet and though I couldn't see the ground, I knew there was vegetation there to help break my fall. As long as I didn't die or break any major bones, I'd be all right.

After our experience of prison and house arrest, death wasn't the worst option, but now Heidi and I had reason to fight for life. She was pregnant. In China, the government's "one child" policy meant we would be forced to abort our baby because we didn't have the proper permit. Consequently, we weren't celebrating with a baby shower, a new nursery, or by telling our parents they were about to become grandparents. In fact, if we were successful they'd probably never see their grandchild—or us. But we had no choice.

When I looked over the ledge, my glasses slipped down my nose and I pushed them back into place. Using my left hand, I held on to the windowsill, feeling woozy from the height. My legs quivered. Would I be able to do this? What would happen to Heidi and the baby if I died? I took a deep breath, said a prayer, and stepped into the darkness.

As soon as I left the ledge, I forgot all of my ideas about how to fall strategically. The wind rushed over my face, my stomach shrunk, and I felt I'd left my heart back in the building. I flailed my arms and even though I was desperate to remain silent, a yell escaped from deep within me. It sounded like it was from someone else. My glasses flew off and I vaguely remember reaching up to touch my face before everything went black.

2

My life's journey began even before I was born—when my mother's first husband approached her with a shocking request.

"You and the children need to leave."

Really, it wasn't a request. It was more of a demand, a desperate plea. They lived in a small house in the Shandong province of southeastern China, in the lower reaches of the Yellow River. The province is bordered by the Bohai Sea and the Yellow Sea, but their small mud home was inland, next to the wheat and corn fields so they could process—and keep watch over—the food supply. Her husband worked a small patch of land in the commune, where they lived with their two small children.

"Where will I go?" she asked, but she didn't wait for the answer. She knew. My mother shuffled around the house and picked up a few things. She could only take what she could carry, and she had to carry the younger child, just a baby, too.

That's how my mother's marriage ended, which is certainly not the way many marriages do—in the west. There were no affairs, no dramatic confrontations. Rather, the government, led by Mao Zedong, had laid its heavy hand on the villagers and strangled the life out of their marriages. In 1958, Mao performed a gigantic cultural and social experiment called the Great Leap Forward—so named because it was the "great leap" into communism. This meant my mother's husband and all of the other villagers had to give up their private property to live communally. Without personal land, they couldn't farm their own food and had no control over their own food supply. Mao, who introduced his new program by promising his nation, "It is possible to accomplish any task whatsoever," assured everyone he could produce more food through communist techniques. The government built large communal kitchens for the villagers where they would gather to eat every meal. Wonderful weather in the first growing season created much sustenance for the villagers. However, in the following years droughts and floods caused the community grain supplies to run dangerously low. That's when my mother's husband felt he had no choice. "Just go," he told her as she stood there with the kids. "I cannot feed you anymore."

She shuffled through the house one last time, and stole a glance at the bed where she had slept with her husband and kids. The children certainly wouldn't have such comforts on the street. She brushed away a tear. There was no time for such emotion now. The house had no sustenance in it anyway. The large pot that had baked their bread had long sat empty. In fact, the house had been stripped clean of everything valuable, including all metal.

Metal indicated strength, at least according to Mao, who believed a nation with more metal could build more ships, weapons, and buildings. When he ordered that all citizens give up their metal to the state, my mother had dutifully searched through her house for every ounce. She had collected pots, pans, and previously valuable farming tools and taken them to one of the many backyard steel furnaces that had popped up across the countryside. The metal scraps from all the villagers were turned into one large pile of metal, the weight of which was measured and proudly reported to the central government. The reports may have been proud, but the product was pathetic. My family's few valuable earthly goods weren't turned into battleships. Instead, they were turned into an unusable chunk of trash. These large, worthless piles sat in the villages as supposed symbols of strength, but instead they only symbolized the pain, heartache, and inefficiency of the Great Leap Forward.

They also began to symbolize death.

I don't know whether my mother was heartbroken, angry, or terrified—perhaps a combination of all three—but she took the hand of my older sister, put my brother on her back in a sling, and said, with forced cheerfulness, "Let's go for a walk."

For close to four years, she walked from one village to another, asking for food from people who couldn't spare it. Millions of people were dying in the Great Leap Forward, some say close to thirty million. That is double the number of people killed in the holocaust.

When there was nothing else available, everyone, including my mother, ate the bark off trees. But eventually that too ran out, and the once-lush countryside was full of naked trees and no vegetation. When winter came, it was even more difficult. One particularly harsh afternoon, my mother trudged through heavy snow for miles, carrying my brother and dragging my sister by the hand. Fighting for every step, they walked slowly, leaving tracks of despair across the frozen countryside. When my mother finally saw a collection of houses off in the distance, she muttered a Chinese proverb under her breath.

"Even a blind donkey can find its way home because of the guidance of heaven."

Though she was an atheist, she frequently said this proverb when it seemed as if someone were watching out for her and her two children. She'd stayed alive so far because of the kindness of strangers, and she hoped someone in the upcoming village would show her mercy as well. This slight possibility of food was enough to propel her forward through the deep, icy snow.

"Any food to spare?" she asked in the courtyard of a small

house in the village. A kind man offered her a bowl of rice soup and a little bit of shelter from the elements in his courtyard. Though it wasn't much—in fact, it wasn't enough for all three of them—its warmth would help them shake the ever-present chill and possibly help them make it through another night. My mother carefully prepared to offer the broth to her infant son and daughter first. She didn't want to waste a drop.

However, just as the spoon reached the baby's mouth, a rooster came barreling toward them. Mom screamed as the big rooster knocked her down into the snow, biting and scratching at her to drive these unwanted visitors from his yard. After a scuffle, the rooster proved victorious and Mom emerged covered in blood and, even worse, the precious rice soup.

Although my mom and siblings were fighting for life each day, others had it worse. Some people boiled leather to soften it into edible strips. Many of them died as they tried to swallow the leather, and the ones who didn't choke had to ask for help to pry the solid waste from their bodies. People ate mud. Even more shocking, some ate their elderly relatives and children who'd passed away, either from natural causes or murder. In Chinese history textbooks, this time period was known as "Three Years of Natural Disaster," which, of course, hid the government's role in starving its own people. My mother did everything she could to make sure she and her children didn't become just another statistic, a number lost to history.

However, one day she began to cough, like millions of other people who'd become desperately sick because of the paucity of food and the unsanitary living conditions. Her cough got worse and never really went away. Day after day, she struggled for breath and had pain in her chest. Then one day, she coughed up blood. That's how my mother, the only caretaker of two homeless children facing down a famine, realized she had lung disease.

"Even a blind donkey can find its way home because of the guidance of heaven," she said between coughs. For years, she and the children had survived. She continued to believe something would guide her, even though her circumstances had gotten drastically worse. Someone, somewhere had taken her this far.

And she would go farther. Over the next few months, coughing and gasping, she made her way around the same little region, receiving the kindness of strangers. Eventually, she found a tiny countryside village called Shiziyuan, which meant "Persimmon Garden." This is where life changed for my mother in a very unlikely way.

"Any food to spare?" she asked, knocking on the door of a small home. The courtyard was full of fragrant persimmon trees. She was just getting ready to turn around and go to the next home when the door opened.

A tiny, hunchbacked man opened the door. He had only one good eye, which he used to assess the desperate visitors on his step. He was Fu Yubo, the village's bookkeeper.

"This is all I have," he said, offering bread to her and the children. His compassion on the sick woman with two small children was evident. Not only did he give her food, he also gave her a new life. Before long they married and my mother, after several years of living on the street, had a home. She and her new husband soon had children together. First, they had a baby girl named Qinghua, and then on July 12, 1968, they had me. They named me Xiqiu, which means "Hopeful Autumn," because July in the Chinese calendar is the fall.

Additionally, parents in the village gave their children nicknames to stave off evil spirits and bad character. Superstitiously, they believed ghosts roamed the countryside looking for children to haunt. They feared ghosts and demons might take a liking to their kids if they had nice-sounding names. Because of this, they created terrible-sounding monikers for their children. Two of my friends, for example, were called "Ugly Leaf" and "Silly Donkey" to make them as unattractive as possible to the spirit world. My nickname was Pianyi, which is translated as "Cheap."

Everyone believed children would develop qualities that were the opposite of these nicknames, so I imagine my mother wanted me to have a future of soaring wealth and comfort. The indignities of begging impacted her, and she yearned for something better for us. Maybe my nickname would do the trick.

Despite my mother's illness and my father's disability, our lives were so much better. As the youngest child, I was looked after with great care by my parents, brother, and sisters. Our house had a bedroom that we all shared and a sitting room, separated by a small kitchen. The kitchen was always a place of warmth. Mom put flowers around the iron stove. We had vegetables, and flour for bread. After the main meals were cooked, the aroma of freshly baked bread would drift through the small house. We also had a little courtyard surrounded by persimmon trees.

I loved the smell of those trees as much as the smell of bread. They had glossy, broad leaves and bark like the hide of an alligator. As a small child, I would climb those trees and select the perfect persimmon specimens. The yellow persimmons weren't ripe, but the red ones . . . those were ready. I held them to the sun and looked at the sky through them like kaleidoscopes. The sky looked crimson through the ripe, tender fruit. When I think of my childhood, I can taste the sugary and tangy flavor and smell the spring flowers that attracted big honeybees.

Dad kept the books for the entire village. He walked to work every day with his hands clasped behind his back, like a man on a mission, moving so fast I couldn't keep up with him. He worked all day and came home in the evenings, making the equivalent of an American dime per day. He was quite adept with the *suànpán*, a calculating tool used in China for thousands of years, known in other areas as an abacus. His hands moved over the beads like magic. He could add, subtract, and even divide with the beads. Dividing was very complicated but his hands did not falter as he calculated the harvests and determined the amount of food each family would receive. Though he only had six years of education, he was considered a rather educated man. He even read to me in the evenings before I went to bed.

Harvest time was the busiest season for everyone. Because agriculture was collective under Communist law, farmers couldn't grow for themselves. Instead, they grew for the government. The farmers harvested the wheat and the corn and took it to another location to process for distribution. Dad was in charge of distributing the shares of food according to head count and production, and gave families a piece of paper, similar to a coupon, which allowed them to get food like wheat, corn, sweet potatoes, and potato chips. After all of that intense work, the workers gathered to share a meal during the night. Sometimes, because they respected my father, they let me eat with them too.

Dad, because of his position, had the ability to give the poorer families a little extra without being detected. We were poor, but there were people even worse off than we were—much worse.

In particular, the Communist leader Mao hated former landlords, because of their "capitalistic" past. Absolutely despised, millions were murdered or driven to suicide. The few who still lived endured lives of absolute humiliation and persecution. One of our neighbors was known as an "enemy of the people," as the government had labeled him.

Back then, the village children called any older man "Grandpa" as a sign of respect, even if he wasn't actually related. I didn't see any difference between my family and the family of this Grandpa, who didn't seem to deserve the harsh treatment he received. But every morning, when the sun was barely up, I heard the party secretary of the village bark out his name.

"Get up!" he would shout. "It's time to sweep the street!"

After a few moments, I'd hear the sound of the old man's door opening and shutting. He and the other former landlords swept every square foot of the village each morning. My parents were full of compassion toward his family. Every evening, my mother would make a little extra food, wrap it up in a cloth, and hand it to me with a whispered warning. "Don't get caught."

I knew the stakes.

If I got caught, the authorities would destroy my family. Instead of being afraid, however, I was invigorated and perfected my nightly secret food missions down to a science. I would hold on to the food as long as I could, then slip out of my home as quietly as possible.

Casually, I would walk down the road, looking to my left and to my right. If I saw someone near me, I would meander away from my neighbor's home. Sometimes this process would be quick. Most of the time, however, my caution caused me to stroll through the night as I made sure of one thing: that I was utterly alone. Only then would I slide the food under their door with as little motion as possible before scampering back home, my heart racing.

I was never detected.

My parents helped many people in the village, and word of their hospitality quickly spread. Every day, a beggar would knock on our door.

"Pianyi," Mom instructed me from her bed. "Bring food for them—get the best we have." Only the revered people in society, parents and elder villagers, could address me using my nickname. If my friends or peers called me "Cheap," it would be a real dishonor. But when my mom called me that, it was a sign of affection and even hope, especially when her hopes of my future comfort were juxtaposed with the beggars at our door.

Though we scarcely had enough for ourselves, we always managed to have enough to share just a little with a courtyard full of beggars. I served them the best we had to offer and listened to their stories as they ate their food. Sometimes they laughed as they told their tales of woe, but sometimes they wept. Because my own mother had been a beggar, their stories of poverty penetrated my heart. There, in my courtyard, is where I learned compassion. It's also where I learned resistance.

———— • • • ————

Sadly, my parents' generosity came at a great cost. Both of them had true hearts for the poor, but they frequently gave away much-needed food. Financial stress is said to be one of the greatest causes of marital strife. Add disability and an oppressive government into the mix, and things really get hard. At night, my sister Qinghua and I would huddle in the sitting room and hear them arguing through the thin walls. The shrill bitterness scared me. When things got really bad, however, the quarrelling didn't stop with shouts in the night. That's when my mom would wake my sister and me, grab our hands, and say, "We're going!"

Sleepily, we would put on our shoes and trudge out the door, up and down hills, and through graveyards on our way to my maternal grandmother's house. She lived fifteen miles away and was my mom's safe haven whenever she and my dad fought. In the moonlight, our feet sometimes faltered. We tried not to cry. After a few miles, however, Mom's anger would give in to fatigue and she'd kneel down and weep with us. We never made it all the way to our grandmother's house in one night. The distance was too far and our legs were too short.

My mother would knock on the doors of complete strangers in the middle of the night. "Do you have a place for me and my two children to stay?" she would ask. Nothing scared her. Years of begging had created a hard shell around her. Me? I was a different story. I wanted to be home, in bed, with our whole family, in peace. But that was elusive. Oh, we'd go back. After a time, Mom would calm down and we'd begin the long walk home. Things would generally be the same, but Mom struggled. Gradually, it was like the strong survival instincts that had kept her alive during her years of begging on the street evaporated.

Formerly a strong, determined woman, she seemed to have lost the will to fight through her hard life.

A few times she tried to commit suicide. There were no guns to end life quickly, no sleeping pills to pass unconscious into death. Once she ran to a well used for the community's water source, and we had to convince her not to jump. During another bout of her sadness, my sister and I ran around the kitchen, confiscated all the knives from the drawers, and buried them in the backyard.

Her life was challenging. Without any medical care for her lung disease, she never could quite catch her breath. But the worst part was her cough.

"Go down to the garden and bring me a sweet potato," she'd tell me, between heaves.

Absent any real medicine, she felt that somehow a steamed sweet potato seemed to settle her throat.

But even when her coughing subsided, she laid in our bed, called a *kang*, which was made of baked mud and concrete. It was connected with the kitchen stove in the next room. Heat transferred through the bed and warmed the room without having to build a fire. My mom was on one side of the bed, and my father slept on the other. We stuffed ourselves between them. Believe it or not, this was cozy, especially in the winter when the kitchen stove kept us all warm.

Mom, however, was in agony. She'd spit the mucus from her lung infection onto the floor all day. Whenever I heard her begin a particularly bad coughing fit, I would grab a shovel and run to her bedside. My job was to scoop up the spit off the floor to take it outside. And then one day, as my mother's health deteriorated, my dad woke up in the morning with a terrible realization. He was paralyzed.

For two full years, he joined my mom in the kang, not able to work. This left us without an income. We had some food to eat, but we had to ration it so strictly my stomach never felt full. Once

I walked by the community kitchen where people were preparing food for the harvesters. Since my father couldn't work, he couldn't be part of the harvest festivities. That day, an aroma seized me. They were making fritters, long pastries made of special dough. After they're fried, the little confections are light and airy, almost hollow inside. I instantly desired them above all else. Since I was so little, I decided, I could probably get into the kitchen without anyone seeing me. I stood outside the kitchen acting nonchalant. My heart was beating fast, but at the right moment I slipped into the kitchen and found an entire stash of these sweet treats. I ate them like a wild animal, one after the other, hoping I wouldn't get caught. No one noticed, and I walked home with—for the first time in a very long time—a full stomach.

● ● ●

Every few months, the government would set up a projector to show a movie. It was a major social event, because the producers had to cross dangerous mountains and rivers to travel to all of the small Chinese villages. Roads in our impoverished region were challenging to navigate and were only accessible via bicycle or horseback. I don't recall ever seeing a car in my childhood. We rarely had visitors of any kind. That's why everyone, especially the children, really anticipated the arrival of the movies. The movies were usually stories about Communist Party heroes, but we loved them. The movies were advertised for weeks in advance, so the children got up early to put chairs in the best spots. One morning, I woke up early enough to snag a premiere spot for my little chair, right in the front row.

As the sky darkened enough for the movie to begin, I left my sick parents at home and made my way to the movie site. The other kids had the same idea I'd had, and we settled in for the night's festivities. For whatever reason, probably because they noticed my clothes were tattered and threadbare, the other kids made fun of me that night.

"Look at Xiqiu's clothes," one boy in a group of my friends laughed, pointing at me as the movie began. We never had new clothes. Neighbors gave us their old clothes, and our hand-me-downs were mended with obvious patches.

"Are you sure that's a shirt, or is it just some threads trying to cover his little chest?" another piped in.

I didn't listen to them and looked straight ahead, trying to pay attention to the movie. When I finally got to the point where I could tune them out, however, I suddenly felt a warm sensation on my back. They had gathered together and urinated on me.

As I walked home, my sticky clothes clinging to me, my heart ached.

Why did people have to treat us with so little respect? We were already poor and without social status. Why, on top of that, did we also have to deal with such mockery? Poverty, I decided, was the reason we suffered. As long as I didn't have money, people were going to bully me. On that walk home from the mobile movie, I made a decision. I needed to become a millionaire. The fact that I was a urine-soaked peasant didn't deter me. Education was highly prized in China, and after Mao's reign, could be a road out of poverty. If I studied diligently, perhaps I could get into college and make enough money to get rich and support my family.

When I was eight years old, I went to a Communist Party–controlled school where I learned about reading, writing, and atheism. Studying was easy for me because I had a knack for quickly understanding issues and remembering facts. Also, my teachers recognized leadership qualities in me and appointed me classroom monitor year after year. This was a prestigious title because presumably it was always given to the most responsible student in each class who could maintain order if the teacher stepped out, report anyone who dared to break a rule in the teacher's absence, make sure everyone worked, and help out the teacher in the classroom.

I loved the attention.

"Xiqiu." My teacher called me to the front of the class toward the end of fourth grade. "You've been a very good student. You're very capable and eager to work." I tried not to stick out my chest in pride, but this made me feel very special. Then he said something very surprising. "In fact, I'm going to hold you back so you can do another year in my class. You will repeat fourth grade." We were taught to never question the teacher. So when the headmaster visited our classroom later that day, I was silent as my teacher pulled him aside soberly. "Xiqiu has some terrible hearing problems, so he hasn't understood very much academically this year," he said. "I recommend he repeat this grade."

Of course, I could hear just fine. But what made me valuable to the teacher was that I could run errands. Instead of progressing into the fifth grade with my friends, I repeated the fourth grade to essentially become my teacher's unpaid personal assistant. For example, when his mother needed wine, I traveled to town and bartered for it. My teacher was taking advantage of me. Who was I, after all? However, in that culture, it was considered a privilege to work for the teacher and his mother, so I actually enjoyed it. After all, not many fourth graders could barter like me.

• • •

But the joys of school never quite isolated me from the problems at home. One afternoon, I came home and heard my mom coughing. I grabbed my shovel and ran in to her, ready to perform my normal clean-up duty. This time, it sounded different. Her cough was relentless and overpowering. In fact, as I watched her double over in pain, I knew one thing. She was dying.

I can't remember how long it took Qinghua to come home, but it seemed like she'd never arrive.

"Mother is dying," I whispered, as I ran out to meet her in the courtyard. "What do we do?"

Of course, we had very few options. Actual doctors wouldn't come all the way out to our area, and we definitely couldn't afford to travel hours away to the county hospital. Our only source of medical help was a local "barefoot doctor," who wasn't a doctor at all. In fact, barefoot doctors got their name because they were farmers who worked without shoes in the rice paddies and just did the best they could to treat villagers' basic ailments in their spare time.

My sister dropped her books and we ran to our local barefoot doctor's home. "Help us, please," she called from the courtyard. He and his wife opened their door and looked at our tearstained faces and our tattered clothing. With one glance, they knew we weren't good for the bill. The doctor, completely absent of regret or any other emotion, shook his head no. I cried, kneeling in front of the main gate, but the door began to close.

"I offer myself to you!" my sister said, desperately trying to figure out a way to entice them. "I'll work in your fields during harvest time for free! I'll pay you back!" They didn't even acknowledge her offer before they slammed their door in our faces, leaving us to deal with the impending death of our mother alone.

"We can't stay together," my sister said, getting up and dusting off her knees. "I'm going to go find help in the next village. Go home to check on Mom, while I see if another doctor will have mercy on us." The nearest barefoot doctor was three miles away, in my eldest sister's village.

I watched her hurry away as I ran back home to Mom. My heart pounded with every step. But when I opened the gate, I stopped right beside large bales of hay stacked for winter. What would I find when I went inside? Would my mother be dead? If not, how could I break the news that the doctor wouldn't be bothered with her because we couldn't pay?

Overcome with emotion and fear, I stood completely still. Confucius had hailed from my Shandong region more than two thousand years ago, but his philosophies offered no personal god to whom I could appeal. Mao's communism certainly didn't allow for any divine helpers. The only "faith" we had in the village was a collection of superstitions, and we'd tried them all.

For example, when both my parents were bedridden they asked my sister to take a glass bottle and walk ten miles to a mountainous area. There, she took the lid off the bottle, put water in it, knelt on the mountain, and prayed to the gods along with thousands of other people also desperately seeking a solution to their various problems. She burned incense and even money to appease the gods. Then she explained our predicament to whatever supernatural deity might've been floating by.

"Mom has lung disease; my dad can't walk," Qinghua had said. She hoped a god might hear her and, according to superstition, send a sign from heaven by dropping something into the water: a twig, ashes, anything that wasn't there when she arrived. She prayed mightily, and opened her eyes. To her delight, a miracle had occurred—there were ashes floating in the bottle! Quickly, she put on the top to protect the magic water and ran home to my parents. "Drink!" she yelled as she pushed the bottle into their faces.

Of course, as promising as dirty water in a bottle sounds, it didn't have the healing powers we'd hoped. And so Mom tried other superstitious rituals. She had a ritual that consisted of bowing down to the floor, flat on her face, seven times in a row. Then she got up, took seven steps, and did it again. Starting at our home, she'd sometimes make it all the way out to the street, bowing over and over. When she got home, her head would sometimes be bleeding because she bowed so low and with so much passion.

Apparently, the gods rewarded her piety with pain.

It all seemed slightly odd to me. Of course, if you have an open bottle of water near thousands of people burning incense, you might have some sort of ashes fall into the bottle. But I never said, "The emperor has no clothes." I wanted it to work. Faith, no matter what its object, might help a bit.

As I stood next to the hay, however, I knew in my heart that the superstitions were powerless. That's when my mother's proverb came to mind: "Even a blind donkey can find its way home because of the guidance of heaven." After years of hearing her say this, I wondered if maybe—just maybe—there was someone in heaven who might actually be able to guide and protect me.

For the second time that day, I fell to my knees. But this time I wasn't asking a heartless barefoot doctor for help. Right there, beside the hay bales, I called out to my *tian*, which means "heaven," and *laoye*, which means "grandpa," to indicate respect for elder people.

"Heavenly Grandpa," I said, "I'm so scared, and I don't want my mom to die. Please . . ." I wasn't even sure of what to say, but I hoped whoever was up there might extend his hand to help, if I asked earnestly. "Please help my mother."

It was my first prayer.

After getting up, I grabbed my shovel and went into my mother's room. She was in even worse condition than when we left her, so I sat by her side, shoveling up mucus and spit, until my sister came back. When she returned with a barefoot doctor in tow, I cried out in relief.

He rushed to my mother's side, gave her some sort of herbal remedy, and told us how to take care of her. He didn't have much to offer, but we obeyed every one of his instructions to the letter. He was all we had. My mother amazingly recovered and somehow managed to survive this episode.

Deep down, I couldn't shake the feeling that maybe my secret "Heavenly Grandpa" had something to do with it.

3

"We can't afford to do both," my dad said to my mom with resignation in his voice. My parents had been discussing the educational options for Qinghua and me for the past hour, and we were eavesdropping from the next room.

When I graduated from elementary school, the province changed how they schooled children. In an effort to get the brightest students all in one place, they decided to send the highest scoring students in all of the villages to a central location. I was honored to be the only student selected from my village. Not only would this help me on my journey toward wealth and respect, I also was pleased I'd receive a better education than the bullies who had tormented me in my village. The only problem was that this would be more expensive for my family and we simply couldn't afford the cost of the dorm and the necessary food vouchers for daily meals.

"I'll stay here," Qinghua said as she edged her way into the bedroom.

"What are you saying?" I asked, grabbing her arm.

"You're smarter than I am," she said. "And I'm a girl. I can work in the fields to make some extra money while you go to school."

Her voice cracked with emotion as she said the words. I let her generosity wash over me before I responded.

"Will you donate a few food tickets to help my friend get through the school year?" I asked every student I came across when we arrived back at school.

Amazingly, the coupons came in every week. We had enough food for her, and she was so touched by our efforts that she developed a crush on me. I had to spend the rest of the year avoiding her. Her affection made me so nervous!

When I was in senior high, however, another female student in my school faced an even worse situation. She was alone in the world. Both her mom and dad had died, so she was being taken care of by a stepmother and a stepfather. Just like Cinderella, she wasn't treated as well as the biological children of her stepparents. She really didn't belong to anyone, and her family looked at her as a drain on their resources. When she went off to school, they didn't send her any food or supplies. When she came home, they bullied and even abused her.

One day, during her senior year of high school, I saw her crying, holding a tiny bag of crumbs.

"What's wrong?" I asked.

"My stepparents won't send me any food, and I'm hungry," she said. "Plus, they're making me quit school," she said, barely able to get the words out.

It was so close to graduation, it was tragic to take her out of school. Since she wouldn't return home to loving family, school really was the only rope she could grab to pull herself out of her terrible situation.

"Go get dressed in your finest clothes," I said to a small group of my classmates. "And meet me back here on your bicycles. We've got a mission."

Once again, I didn't really have a plan, but I knew I couldn't plead like I did with the other parents. This required strength. As I pedaled to her village and saw her small house off in the distance, an idea came to me.

"Okay," I said as I gathered everyone together for a quick

strategy session outside the house. Thankfully, there was a tall and relatively mature student in our group. I pointed to him. "You are now the headmaster. You," I pointed to a shorter, solemn-looking kid, "are the classroom monitor."

"What?" he protested. "I've never been a monitor!"

"Well, for the next hour you are." I smiled.

I did a fast head-to-toe assessment of the last few in our group. Even in our best clothes, we still didn't look that impressive. "Stand tall," I said to another classmate. "You need to look as old as possible, because you're going to be the school teacher. And you," I pointed to the only guy left, "will be the deputy."

After I assigned everyone a role to play, we rode to her door and forcefully knocked. Her stepparents' eyes were wide when they opened the door and saw this group of relatively well-dressed strangers.

"We are from your daughter's school," I said in a very authoritative tone. The years of being awakened by the Communist Party secretary yelling at my neighbor were coming in handy. "And we need to have a serious talk about your student."

The mother studied me as I spoke, and I wondered if she was onto our ruse. Since it was too late to change the plans, I swallowed hard and continued. "Allow me to introduce the officials who've traveled here to talk to you. Please meet the headmaster, the deputy, the class monitor, and the girl's teacher."

I paused to let the severity of the situation sink in for them. Only a very serious offense would merit a visit from all of these educational dignitaries.

"We have heard reports that she is abused at home and is going to quit school," I said. The stepparents, who were peasants and therefore not used to dealing with the Communist establishment, looked terrified. The woman who'd treated our classmate so severely suddenly held on to the side of the door in what seemed to be fear and intimidation. "Your treatment of her is not acceptable," I continued. "She is your daughter, and she has rights. You cannot starve her by withholding food. If you have difficulty, the school will help," I said. Then, I added an ominous warning. "But if you make her miserable, you will be held responsible."

After a few days, the girl received word from home. Her stepparents had a change of heart and she could finish her education. To make it even better, food started arriving and she could study without the distraction of hunger. I was brimming with joy because we'd saved a friend from a lifetime of poverty. When I told my sister and mother about it, they laughed. "Oh, who will you take care of next week?" they joked. "*Cao xin ren,*" my mom said, which meant, "You take responsibility in your heart." In other words, she could tell that I was burdened by other people's sorrow, so she teased me by calling me "Heart Burden Man."

I was sensitive, but my Gaomi City high school was run like a military school. Every day, for three years, we began at 6:30 in the morning. Dressed in athletic attire, we were made to run laps around the sports field. Only after we had our physical activity were we able to begin our intellectual pursuits. Our headmaster was known as a harsh disciplinarian who really enforced the rules. In spite of this, he treated me with a lot of respect and loved to talk to me about government and world events.

• • •

There was one loud speaker in our whole village, high on a hill, and its sound wafted all the way through the town. It was the Communist Party's mouthpiece, and every morning I'd skip breakfast, run out into the yard, and lean on a tree to hear the news more clearly. Some days, if the wind was blowing, I'd leave the yard and walk toward the speaker until I no longer had to strain to make out the words. Each morning, I practically memorized all of the news. This made me very popular, because I was able to tell people what was going on.

My headmaster had access to a newspaper called *Cankao Xiaoxi*, or *Reference News*, which was the only legal way for government officials of a certain rank to get a glimpse of foreign media. The paper was a digest of carefully selected articles from the *New York Times*, the Associated Press, and the UPI. The government didn't want its citizens to read the articles and start getting crazy ideas about things like "democracy" or "liberty."

One day, I was in my headmaster's office, which also doubled as his living quarters. We were always supervised closely because the headmaster lived right there in the middle of campus. That's when I noticed a copy of *Reference News* on his desk.

"What's that?" I asked casually when he caught me eyeing it.

"Oh, it's nothing," he said, snatching it off the table and sticking it under his bed. From that moment on, I thought of nothing more. If I could get my hands on that newspaper, I would know the truth about what was going on in the world—the real details that the Communist mouthpiece would never relay. Now that I knew he had the newspaper and where he hid it, I waited for an opportunity to get the paper for myself. Two days later, I noticed the headmaster leaving his office and grabbed a friend who was walking down the hall.

"Will you do me a favor?" I asked.

"Sure," he said.

"Okay. Stand right here and keep a lookout. If you see the headmaster, cough really loud."

I could tell my friend was seriously rethinking his offer to help. I patted him on the back and said, "It'll be okay!"

Before he could protest, I disappeared into the headmaster's office. My heart raced as I went straight to his bed. It was made up tightly, and I hoped he wouldn't be able to tell there'd been a disturbance. I slid my hand under the mattress and felt around until my hand landed on the newspaper.

I pulled it out and read the headlines quickly because I knew I needed to get out of there soon. Who knew if my friend was even still in the hall keeping watch? However, the idea of getting news—true, unfiltered, honest news—was too much to resist. I scanned the first page, rolled up the newspaper, put it under my jacket, and slipped out the door.

When my friend saw me, he exhaled the breath he'd been holding the entire time.

"What were you doing in there?" he asked.

"The less you know the better off you'll be."

Seeing the lump under my jacket, his eyes grew wide. "Did you steal something? What have you gotten me into?"

I opened up my jacket and let him see the *Cankao Xiaoxi*.

"You risked expulsion for that?" he asked.

He rolled his eyes and walked off. I, on the other hand, felt like I'd found a treasure. I ran back to my room, sat on my bed, and read the newspaper cover to cover. I memorized every article and was careful not to smear or soil the pages. I was pretty sure the headmaster didn't read it, because the papers never lost their crisp crease. However, I didn't want to take any chances.

The next day, I casually walked the hall outside of the head-master's office and slipped in while he was at lunch. Once again, I lifted his carefully made-up mattress and slid the newspaper back into place. It was as if nothing had happened.

Once I had of taste of true news, I was never again satisfied with the Communist propaganda. Every week I was at school, I visited the headmaster's office, stole his newspaper, memorized it, and returned it. I could name most of the world leaders, where they governed, when they were visiting China, and who they were meeting. I could even regurgitate what was going on in England, America, and Cambodia. Gradually, as I became more and more certain that he never opened his papers, I got more bold. I began cutting out clippings that detailed how other countries ran businesses. I was especially interested in restau-rants and the way the West ran them so cleanly and proficiently. One day, I thought, I'd run a restaurant too—American style.

During my second year of high school, one article really got my attention. While sitting on my bed one morning, I read that tens of thousands of Chinese university students were protesting in Hefei City's main square. They did a sit-in at government offices and carried banners that demanded, "Give Us Freedom" and "Long Live Democracy." The Chinese government wasn't sure if they should crack down on the protestors or let them speak.

I stuffed the paper into my jacket and ran to my class. My fellow students were already memorizing English vocabulary when I burst into the room.

"Listen to this," I said, pulling the headmaster's paper out. "There are protests in Shanghai!" I read them the whole editorial about this major event. "Can you believe it? Students are demanding freedom and democracy on the streets!"

A girl in the back of the class got up to sharpen her pencil. Someone else sitting in the front row yawned, reopened his book, and went back to his work.

With all of this news bouncing around in my head, I was brimming with ideas—some of which were probably wild and crazy. However, I really wanted a way to host a conversation in our school. There had to be some students who cared about world events who would join me. Over the course of the year, I took notice of people who seemed to care about international issues. When I found enough people, I gathered a group of likeminded students, from both younger and older grades, and made a proposition.

"I want to start a school newspaper," I said. "All you'll need to do is write and edit the articles. Leave the rest to me!"

Surprisingly, they did. Within a week, I had several high-quality articles—and absolutely no way to publish them. After all, China wasn't a hotbed of free speech and my communist school certainly had no reason to permit, let alone facilitate, such a publication. That's when I remembered that two of my old friends from elementary school worked for the government township. Every township had a secretary's office to help process messages from the leader. And every secretary's office had typewriters.

I practically ran to the township office, carrying my stack of articles.

"Look at all these," I said to my old friends. "Can you help me get these published?" Perhaps needing to add a little excitement to their jobs, they took on the challenge. Somehow, they convinced the township secretaries to type the articles, format them, and even print them out on some very old-fashioned paper.

I named our school newspaper *The Green Leaf*. I was the executive director, another student was the editor-in-chief, and my friends from elementary school were the "publishers." I like to joke that *The Green Leaf* was my first nonprofit organization, one that I managed to get completely funded by communists.

However, we weren't concerned about only politics. Since our school was located in the capital of the county, we had the chance to go to the theater to see movies. One memorable movie was a romance film that, by today's standards, probably would've been rated PG-13. The headmaster didn't want us thinking about romance, so he absolutely forbade us from seeing it. This, of course, made us want to see it even more. But our history teacher seemed very progressive and modern, so we figured she might be willing to help us.

"This movie ban is a little heavy-handed," I said aloud in class, hoping she could hear me. When she didn't correct me, I approached her privately after class.

"A bunch of us want to see that movie," I whispered. "Are you willing to help us?"

"Next Tuesday night, the headmaster has an off-campus dinner he has to attend." She smiled as she whispered back. "He won't even be on campus."

Consequently, on Tuesday night we wore dark clothes and

headed out. When we got to the school gate, it was locked for the evening, so all of us climbed over the wall, saw the movie, and climbed back over the wall undetected.

Sometimes my extracurricular activities impacted my studies, but I always made excellent grades. My biggest assignment was my senior thesis, which was supposed to detail my future occupational aspirations. Did I want to become an astronaut, an engineer, or a physician? Well, the senior thesis gave me the chance to research various fields of study, explore my options, and ultimately declare my intention. I rode my bicycle through several villages and interviewed all types of people: doctors, farmers, and workers. Ultimately, my thesis was simply a report of my findings of how things worked in the villages. In my hometown village, for example, I discovered that everyone had been experiencing electricity problems. During the day, when they needed electricity, it was off. Before they went to sleep, when they didn't need power, it was on.

Those are the types of problems I thought should be documented, and hopefully fixed.

"What's going on with the electricity?" I asked several villagers.

"It's on one minute and off the next," a frustrated farmer told me. "But it's almost always off during the Spring Festival." This season, of course, is when family members living away from home come back to celebrate. It's the busiest time for airports, train stations, bus stations, and stores as people bustle to get to their families for the festival.

"That's the worst time to be without electricity," I said.

"That's why it goes out," he said.

"How long does it take to come back on?" I asked.

"Oh, it comes back on immediately," he explained, shaking his head. "After we bribe the utility officials."

I was aghast. Corruption in a state-run industry? As I heard this, it struck me. People who had authority, even a relatively insignificant party secretary or an electricity official, acted like they were upper class and treated anyone they considered beneath them condescendingly.

"How much does it cost to turn the electricity back on?" I asked incredulously.

"One tractor load of eggs."

As I child, I hated being despised by everyone above me in the social structure and was on a perpetual search for equality. As I stood there listening to this tale of bribery, I wondered, *Could it be the problem is not poverty, but corruption within the system?*

• • •

This new information would be great for my thesis, but I wasn't content to merely get a good grade. I also wanted things to change, to put an end to this injustice. I didn't know it yet, but bribery was very common in China. Anytime local officials were in charge of permits and approvals, they expected cash or gifts to help speed up the process. But as a naïve high school student, I was convinced the government would be horrified to learn of this corruption.

"Dear Party Secretary," I wrote. "In our village, we don't have electricity. I've learned the city electricity company turns the power off when the village needs it the most, and then demands one tractor of eggs to turn it back on. Please investigate to find the wrongdoer and put an end to this corruption."

Of course, this was just one of my findings. By the time it was my turn to present my thesis to the class, I'd talked to people from all walks of life and made policy recommendations for agricultural, medical, and industrial reform. I stood at the front of the class and read from my big stack of papers, which included about thirty proposals for cultural change.

"I know these plans can't be accomplished now," I said in closing, much to the relief of my bored classmates. "But these things *can* be accomplished with reform over time. In order for it to be fulfilled," I paused for dramatic effect, "I need to be the first democratically elected Prime Minister."

My friends laughed at my unbridled ambition.

"I mean, in twenty years or so," I hedged.

My classmates, who had all written papers about being doctors or teachers, began calling my thesis my "State of the Union" address.

"Here comes Prime Minister Fu," they laughed when I entered the room. This was particularly amusing to them because my family name means "deputy," or "vice," as in "vice president." A Fu could only be second-in-command, not a true executive.

I laughed along with everyone else, but after witnessing and experiencing terrible poverty as a child, I realized the only way to get rid of inequality was to become someone very important and powerful. If I had power I could truly help the underprivileged by working to eradicate systematic corruption. My mission changed from becoming a millionaire to becoming a high-ranking Communist official. Power, I reasoned, was even better than money when it came to making lasting change. For example, who created social ranks? Who classified people? I knew in my heart that if I were important, I could help the poor.

But my idealism and naiveté posed problems.

A few days after I read my "State of the Union," I was called into my headmaster's office. Normally, because of our close relationship, he greeted me warmly. But this time he had a very sober look on his face. Had he found out about our late-night movie excursion? Did he know I was stealing his newspapers? We weren't alone. Another grim-looking man was waiting there too.

"Hello," the man said, sticking out his hand very formally. "I'm the party secretary of the city electricity company."

Uh-oh, I thought. *I'm in big trouble.*

He was holding my handwritten letter, outlining my complaint of corruption. I was terrified.

"We received your accusation that our officials received bribes in order to provide electricity," he said in a cold, even tone. "And so, I've come here to . . ."

In my mind, I filled in the blanks. . . . *to punish me? To tell me to stop spreading lies against the Communist government? To suspend me from school?*

". . . to address your concerns."

The headmaster looked at me with an amused look that conveyed, "You troublemaker!" When I saw his affectionate glance, I knew I would not get in too much trouble. Still, I could barely breathe as the party secretary continued.

"I admit," he said, "that there may have been some irregularities around the Spring Festival in your village. Perhaps some part of the company has problems. But I want to assure you that we didn't receive any tractors of eggs."

I couldn't believe it. This was the number-one guy—the party secretary of the city—right there with me in the headmaster's office. After I got over my initial fear of reprisal, I was incredibly proud that my high school letter received all that attention. After all, he seemed like a respectable, honorable man. He even talked to my other classmates about the integrity of the electricity industry, which made me feel like that important person I'd always wanted to be. The flattery went straight to my head. As a high school student, I was able to get this Communist official to explain himself and to hold himself accountable to the "little people." That moment verified my life's calling: I'd rise within the Communist Party and fight corruption. I'd work against inequality using my prominence and power.

As he said goodbye, he shook my hand, thanked me for my concern, and smiled reassuringly. Though he didn't say as much, I got the message. Though I'd forced their hand on this issue, my relationship with the government would be respectful and amiable as long as I understood who was ultimately in charge.

It wasn't me.

4

"You got in! You got in!" My classmate slammed on his brakes, causing a cloud of dust to rise up around his bicycle. He hopped off and ran into our courtyard, shoving a piece of paper at me.

"You got accepted!"

In June, at the end of high school, the graduating seniors sat down over the course of several days to take the *gaokao*, the dreaded college entrance examination that determined our future.

"Here are your scores!" my friend said to me. A low score meant I'd have to stay in my village and be a farmer forever— permanently residing in the lowest class. A high score meant college, maybe even in a big city. I always dreamed of a more urban existence. Beijing, with its university life, tall buildings, opulent palaces, and political power, held a definite allure. Plus, college meant government food coupons, a salary, and an immediate bump into a higher social strata. I grabbed the paper and looked over it quickly until my eyes landed on the number.

Of my forty classmates, I'd ranked thirteenth. *Not terrible*, I thought. *Well above the national average.* I lowered the paper and considered what this meant for my future. While my classmates had crammed all year for the big test, I was more interested in creating newspapers, sneaking out to the movies, and fighting the electric company. Perhaps I should've studied more, but I had scored high enough to get into a four-year college. Each student had to submit a list of three universities, ranked in order of preference. Through a rather mysterious, opaque process, the government assigned a college that determined the destiny of a student. Since the College of International Relations was in Beijing, I had listed it as my top choice of college.

"No, no, no," my headmaster said to me, taking a pencil and marking through that college's name. "You're too much of a troublemaker to go there. Why don't you become a teacher? It's nice and safe."

Later, I realized he was just trying to protect me. Apparently, the College of International Relations, managed by the Chinese Ministry of State Security, was where the intelligence personnel were trained. In other words, it was the Communist Party equivalent of a CIA school. Though I heeded my headmaster's advice about that particular college, I definitely didn't want to become a teacher. Teachers were paid very little and weren't respected. I needed an important job, an impressive title, and a big paycheck. And so I ended up putting law school at the top of my list, journalism second, and management third.

It took several weeks to find out which direction the government had chosen for my life. When the news finally arrived, I was the only student in my class to get into a four-year university. This alone would've been a huge honor for most students. However, as I glanced down the form in my excitement, I realized I didn't get into my first, second, or even third choice of school.

"How could this happen?" I asked my mom through tears. Her health had been gradually deteriorating over the years, which made college all the more important. "I didn't even list this school as an option!"

"It says they accepted you to study in the English teaching department," she said, reading over the paper to see what had upset me. Liaocheng Teacher's College had accepted me, which meant the government was forcing me into the very occupation I didn't want. "That's better than being a typical school teacher, right?"

"Barely!" I said. I was too distressed to admit that teaching English was actually more prestigious than teaching other subjects. "I might as well be working in the fields!"

I ran to my room, locked the door, and flung myself facedown on the bed. During my self-imposed exile, I went on a hunger strike.

"What am I going to do?" I cried. Should I stay another year in my village and try to take the exam again? Maybe if I took the exam more seriously, all the extracurricular activities wouldn't distract me.

Later in the day, I overheard my mother talking with my sister in the yard. "I'm worried about Xiqiu," she said, her voice full of sorrow and concern.

It seemed like just yesterday when my family was discussing how to afford to send me to school and Qinghua had volunteered to sacrifice her education for mine. She was smart. Would she have done better on the test if she were in my shoes? Maybe my family had bet on the wrong child. But after an entire day of feeling sorry for myself, I realized my dramatic reaction was worrying my parents too much. Finally, I was able to gather myself.

With resolve, I emerged from my room, and said, "I promise you that I'll go to the teacher's college, but I won't stop there. I'll go on to graduate school. And with a higher degree, I'll make more money."

My mom seemed relieved to see my resolve and helped me pack my bags for my journey to Liaocheng City.

"You'll get to Beijing," she assured me. "You must simply do it in a different order."

"When I get there," I said, as I folded clothes and placed them neatly in my suitcase, "I'll make sure to take you to Tiananmen Square."

"I'll remember your promise," she said.

● ● ●

My new college was situated north of the Yellow River, the longest river in Asia. No matter how beautiful it was, however, it was located right there in Shandong Province, the area I'd never been able to escape all my life.

"I'm Xiqiu," I said, extending my hand to one of the other male students on the first day of classes. I selected a desk in the middle of the class—close enough to hear my teacher and back far enough to still keep an eye on everything. As I met my new classmates, I learned they were from all over the province. Some seemed excited to be there, others were anxious to get to their studies. The guys, I could tell, were checking out a group of female students who were gathered at the front of the class.

Girls generally made me nervous, so I didn't introduce myself to them. In China, dating didn't start as young as it does in other places, because parents wanted their kids to concentrate on learning, not romance. That meant my life had been free from the drama of turbulent high school relationships. I didn't have much experience talking to women, which was just fine with me. University officials, after they welcomed us to the campus, promptly warned us that dating was frowned upon. In fact, we weren't supposed to pair up, because it would be a distraction to our academics.

Still, the guys were already evaluating the female contingency of our classroom.

"Who's that?" a guy to my left asked. He was pointing to a dark-eyed, athletic girl in the second row.

"Oh, that's Bochun Cai," his friend responded. "But don't get your hopes up. I heard she has a crush on a hometown guy who got sent to a different university."

I didn't pay attention to all the romantic maneuvering, but I did evaluate our room pretty quickly. Some students immediately introduced themselves to others, while some simply unpacked their backpacks and sat quietly waiting for the teacher. Some were laughing with people they'd apparently already known from high school, while others seemed mortified at being with a group of strangers. Unlike other areas of study, the English students had all of our classes together, so this group of strangers would soon be my circle of friends.

I hope we get along, I thought, as the professor came into our class and smiled.

"Welcome to the English literature department," he said. He was dressed very casually, like he'd just come from a beach—which, I soon learned, he had. Bryan Harrison was an American teacher from California. He was tall and had a kind face.

"The first thing we're going to do is to select an English name for each of you," he said. "This will help you guys familiarize yourself with English names. And it will help me remember who you guys are."

The students laughed.

"Let's face it. I won't be able to remember a roomful of Chinese names. Your names sound just as foreign to me as my name, 'Bryan,' sounds to you."

Everyone giggled at the sound of his name. We wouldn't call him "Bryan," of course. Since he was going to give us English names, we'd give him a Chinese name. In China, we acknowledge people's age in order to revere our teachers. Later, as we got to know him, we'd tease him by stressing the "elder" part, because we knew Americans had an irrational desire to be seen as young. Since he was only in his twenties, we used the Chinese word "Lao," which was an affectionate but more familiar word. It was more like "Hey, ol' buddy" than the stuffy terms of respect we had to show our Chinese teachers. Bryan loved his new name, "Lao Wu," and passed around a hat full of tiny slips of paper that had English names on them. Soon it was my turn to draw one.

"Yo-seph," I laughed, as the word clumsily fell out of my mouth.

"Joseph," the teacher corrected me. We hadn't yet gone over the sound associated with the letter J.

"Yo-yos-yoseph," I fumbled. "These English names sound ridiculous. I'll never learn how to pronounce a name like that!"

I passed the hat to the classmate sitting next to me, who drew his piece of paper.

"Bob," he said, and burst into laughter. These names sounded so foreign to our ears.

"Bob?" I asked. "Now that's an easy name to say."

"Want to trade?"

"You'll be Yoseph?"

"I'll be Joseph."

That's how I went from Xiqiu to Joseph to simply "Bob"— a slip of paper out of a hat and a last-minute trade with my friend. My Chinese name is pronounced "She-Shoe." Changing from Xiqiu to Bob would definitely help English speakers say my name. Of course, I had no idea that English names had meanings or connotations. Bochun, the girl in the second row, drew her slip of paper and read it aloud, "Hi-dee."

Everyone giggled. "Heidi," she said, a little more certainly.

Armed with our new, ridiculous-sounding names, we were on our way to teaching English.

As soon as I got settled into my academic life at college, a few other things fell into place. First, I was appointed classroom monitor, which was an even greater honor at the university level. Second, I was the vice president of the Student Union, which was under the leadership of the Communist Youth League of China. Mostly, that meant I'd be tasked with organizing student activities and recording the other students' attendance and grades.

Of course, I also decided, once again, to start a newspaper.

Not only did I want a platform for all of my many ideas, I loved hearing other people's ideas and starting campus-wide conversations. I soon approached Heidi with the idea of the paper and asked her to write articles for it.

"Why are you naming it *Ugly Stone?*" she asked, confused at the title.

I'd selected the quite peculiar name simply to get attention. I could tell by her reaction I'd chosen wisely.

"I could really use a writer like you," I said. At this point, I hadn't really hit it off with Heidi. Though she was nice, I was too involved in all of my extracurricular activities to be bothered by the notion of romance.

"How much do you pay?"

"I *might* be able to get you a free copy of the paper."

Heidi's first article was a social critique of a country that still had a lot of potential despite its recent hard times. She named the article something provocative, like "A Starved-to-Death Camel Is Still Bigger Than a Horse." That article showed me Heidi was a girl who could write political commentary.

Many of the English students didn't study much. Quite simply, teachers weren't going to be wealthy, so why spend so much time in the library? Every year, however, the college chose three students from the graduating class to be government officials instead of teachers. I hoped to be one of those students, so I made sure I earned high enough grades to impress the university and created many activities to gain new friends.

Joseph was a trusted ally and friend. As the class monitor, I'd frequently ask him to assist me in various tasks, and he reliably was able to obey orders and perform tasks on time for me. This allowed me to have enough time to plan chess tournaments, dancing parties, and basketball games.

Lao Wu would join us in our sporting activities. He loved to play basketball and baseball, and the students enjoyed hanging out with him during the athletic competitions. He lived in the foreign expert regiment building on campus, so he could easily drop by our activities. And he invited us to stop by his place too. He had an open door policy . . . or as we liked to call it, an open fridge policy. He was the only professor I'd ever known who allowed students to drop by his apartment and grab whatever we wanted from his refrigerator. Once, we dropped by his house when he wasn't there and helped ourselves to his pantry. We ate all of his bananas, and the next day he pretended to be angry. He was so laidback that we knew he didn't really mind. College, to me, was less academic and more social.

● ● ●

Of course, more than anything—even free food—I cared about international issues. In fact, I'd promised my parents I'd go beyond this paltry teaching degree. At night, even though I was just beginning college, I'd sit on my bunk bed and read huge textbooks on international relations for hours, preparing for graduate school. I even got hold of a Chinese translation of *Perestroika: New Thinking for Our Country and the World* by Russian leader Mikhail Gorbachev, the man with the famous birthmark. I'd developed an intense appreciation for this world leader because of his systematic reform thinking. The book was a rare opportunity to be able to really read, understand, and process his thoughts. I remember opening the book like an American child might open Christmas presents, eager and anticipating. The first line grabbed me.

"We want to be understood."

I read in amazement as Gorbachev criticized Soviet society, wrote that the economy couldn't create useful goods, described the demoralized Soviet people, and claimed the Communist Party propagated dysfunctional social systems.

One beautiful autumn afternoon, I was walking through the campus on my way to class when someone touched my arm.

When I looked up, I was surprised to see the president of the university, Zhang Ming.

"So, what do you think of *Perestroika*?" he asked, glancing at the book I carried.

I stopped in my tracks, intimidated so much I could neither move nor answer. The president was a well-regarded expert on diplomacy. With a forty-year age gap between us, what could I possibly say to him that would matter?

"I know Gorbachev shouldn't trust Reagan," I said, trying to sound confident. The Chinese propaganda department had told me all my life that the United States didn't want China to be great, so I figured this was a safe response.

President Ming's eyebrows narrowed. "Do you think his democratic socialism would actually work?"

Apparently, he was writing a paper about his various philosophies on international affairs, and was very interested in conversations that might help him hone his ideas. He'd stopped the right guy. After years of memorizing news clippings, I had an opinion on just about everyone and everything. We stood on the sidewalk and talked in depth about Gorbachev, my palms sweating the entire time. As I shuffled to class after our conversation, I replayed the conversation in my head. Did I say the right things? Did he think I was ignorant?

But the next time I saw him on campus, he noticed me.

"Xiqiu," he called out. What? The president of the university knew my name? "Drop by my office later. I'd love to hear your thoughts on Afghanistan."

"Definitely," I said, with as much poise as I could muster. But as soon as he was out of sight, I ran back to my dorm, scanned over my textbook to make sure I knew everything there was to know about Afghanistan, and went back to knock on the door of his office.

Several assistants worked busily in the reception area. His chief of staff looked at me suspiciously. "How may I help you?"

"President Ming asked me to come by." Even as I said it, the very notion seemed improbable. Why would someone of such a high status want to confer with me?

The chief-of-staff walked over to an appointment book and glanced over the entries then back at me. "Is he expecting you?"

He walked down the hall, disappeared into the president's office, and came back with a more welcoming countenance.

"Right this way," he said, bowing slightly and motioning for me to follow him.

We walked down the hall and came to a perfectly decorated room.

"Your guest has arrived."

President Ming was sitting behind a large desk. "Please sit," he said, gesturing to the sofa. He wasn't a big man, but his dignified presence filled the room. His forehead had a few deep wrinkles, evidence he'd spent his whole life thinking seriously about the issues of the day. I'd heard that he was beaten up pretty badly during the Cultural Revolution and that he'd suffered from health issues ever since. The sofa was made of old elm wood, with a carving of a dragon in the center of the backrest. I moved a red silk pillow and sat down next to his desk.

"Tea?"

I felt stiff and nervous. Why would the university president be interested in my thoughts? But the special treatment was nice. I knew having a good relationship with the university president might mean my future could be brighter. The administration had so much power over the students' lives and destinies. For example, if I developed a good relationship with the president, perhaps he would select me to work in the capital city in my province.

"I'd love some tea," I said.

We instantly connected. Even though President Ming was known to be a very sober man, our conversation that day was frequently punctuated with laughter. I was shocked to discover

I could hold my own with him, and he seemed to be delighted to have a like-minded conversationalist. I could tell I was helping him hone his own philosophies, but I made sure to defer to him. After all, he was the expert.

From that point on, I became the only student in the college who could walk right into the university president's office, sit down, and have a conversation. It made me feel very important, and I dreamt of getting a high-paying government job. All of my family's hopes rested on my shoulders. I wanted to do everything I could to continue to earn favor within the administration.

And if I couldn't earn it, I'd buy it.

● ● ●

Bribery is an age-old Chinese custom, and it's especially common during a season called the Moon Festival. The morning of the fifteenth day of the eighth month in the Chinese calendar is when the moon is at its most round. That day, during my freshman year, I got up early and rushed through the campus. I didn't want to run into anyone I knew.

The Moon Festival was one of the most important holidays in China, when families united under the full moon to exchange gifts. Usually, the gifts were "moon cakes," or delicious round pastries filled with salted egg, lotus seed-green bean, sesame, nuts, sugar, ham, or egg yolk. Interestingly, these moon cakes were also a popular way to bribe government officials—when they weren't made of baked goods. Some were made of solid gold, while others had money or silver baked into the confection. I bought a very nice moon cake of the bribing variety to make sure the deputy party secretary of the English department took notice of me during this time of gift giving.

Before I left the dorm, I took one last look at the moon cake. It had a lotus flower imprinted on the top and looked quite nice in the beautiful box I'd selected. I carefully shut the box, tucked it under my arm, and headed across campus. Bribery was so common before graduation that students coordinated their calendars to avoid potential awkwardness. Each dorm would have a certain hour to deliver bribes so they wouldn't run into each other. I didn't have much money, but my "special" moon cake for the party secretary was worth about twenty dollars. I held the box like it was a bag of money stolen from the bank. After all, I'd never done this before. I approached the administration building, took a deep breath, and scurried up the steps.

The deputy party secretary's office was located at the end of a long corridor, and I looked at the floor as I shuffled down the hall. I didn't want to make eye contact with anyone. When I came to his office, I paused as I looked at the door. Was I really going to do this? Was I going to offer a bribe?

Ever since I was a little boy, I talked to myself when I was anxious, and I did so now, without forethought. "Oh, you aren't worth anything," I said. "Why would you think you could get ahead this way? You're just a peasant, so why fight destiny?"

"Is someone out there?" a voice said from beyond the door. I assumed it was an assistant who must've heard my mumbling. As I opened the door, I wasn't sure what to say. I'd planned on seeing the party secretary and handing him my moon cake with a wink or some sort of sign. I wanted him to know that my moon cake was more than just a moon cake.

However, since the deputy party secretary was nowhere to be seen, I had a wrinkle in my plans. I couldn't very well introduce myself to the assistant, explain that this was a special moon cake bribe, and leave. Absent any sort of plan, I simply said, "Hello. Here's a moon cake."

Only after I handed him the cake did I realize he was not an assistant after all. Apparently, the deputy party secretary shared an office with a deputy dean who believed the moon cake was for him. And so, to my everlasting humiliation, he took the cake, thanked me, and I left.

I had just bribed the wrong person.

Even though that didn't turn out well, I still hoped the administration would look favorably upon me when the time came. I didn't want to be a teacher, no matter how much the government seemed to be forcing me down that path. If they selected me when I was a senior, I could be a government official and make enough money to help my family, justify my sister's educational sacrifice, and get my mother good medical care.

● ● ●

One day, however, a school official with a very sober face came into my dorm with a cable.

"Xiqiu," he said. "May I come in?"

I slowly opened the door. I could tell by his softer voice that this was not about school business. "Your mother has been admitted to the hospital and has lost consciousness. She's in critical condition," he said.

I didn't move. Did I hear him correctly? Was the death of my mother, the event I had feared all of my life, actually imminent? Fear and grief seized me, but I managed to stand up, grab my backpack, and run out the door. First I took a bus, then a train, and then I walked. I had to travel fourteen hours to get home and every minute I was desperately hoping I could see my mother before she died.

"You made it," my father told me when I got there. Immediately, I felt relief. I could tell by my father's slumped shoulders and heavy countenance that I didn't have long. "We told her you were coming, and I think she was just holding on to see you."

When I walked into her hospital room, she was unconscious.

"Mom!" I called out. "I'm here. Mom!" Her eyes didn't open, but then her hand squeezed mine ever so slightly.

"Mom?" I said, taking her hands in mine. "It's me, Xiqiu. I'm back. I'm here."

I could tell she was listening. "I've been studying well," I said. "And I can't wait to take you to Tiananmen Square."

She didn't respond.

"Mom?"

It was too late for any real conversation, and I felt helpless. Her life was slipping away too quickly for any last sentiments.

Then, to my surprise, she opened her mouth, just barely, and mustered up the last remaining energy she'd expend on earth to spell out a word.

"P-i-a-n-y-i."

My childhood nickname. No one had called me that in so long. My mother used to call me in for dinner from the persimmon trees by shouting "Pianyi!" She used it when talking to me soothingly before we all went to bed. She used it when reprimanding me for mischief. She used the word, "cheap," as a talisman against the poverty that had so defined our lives.

But that was the last time I'd hear it come from her mouth. After she spelled out my name, she breathed her last.

"Mom?" I said one last time, but she never answered. She had lived fifty-seven years.

My sister and I spent a little more time with her body before we called out to the others that she'd died. Afterward, we all left the hospital and went home. It was the same little house I remembered from my childhood, but it felt oddly vacant without my mother's presence. There was the courtyard, the sitting room, the stove on which many aromatic meals had been made. And yes, there was the kang, the place she'd spent so much of her life. My little shovel was propped up beside her bed.

When I saw that shovel, I wept. Next to the kang was a hole in the floor. I'd dug it so gradually—cough by cough—over her many years of infirmity, I was surprised when I really looked at the hole.

It was three feet deep.

5

"Read this letter," Heidi said to me, handing me a piece of paper covered with Chinese lettering. She looked as though she had been crying.

"For me?" I said, a little confused. Heidi had become a good friend and an excellent writer for the newspaper, but we'd never had conversations of a personal nature. She was smart, and could hold her own against any male student.

"Sadly, it's for me," she said, looking away so I couldn't see her eyes fill with tears. I felt slightly panicked when I saw that emotion. I immediately wanted to fix it, to do anything to stop the tears. "Remember the student I liked? Well, I broke down and told him of my affection."

"And this is his response?" I asked.

She nodded, almost imperceptibly. "Just read it."

It was an act of trust. As I read the letter, which basically explained that a relationship between the two of them wasn't possible, my heart softened toward Heidi. Suddenly, instead of looking at the girls sitting near the front of class, I began to see only one girl.

Over the course of the next few weeks, we started talking more.

"I think you're very gentle," she told me. "Very down to earth."

It was against university rules for students to date and against Chinese law for students to marry. But suddenly, I thought of nothing else.

In China, people don't date one person after another until they find that almost magical "soul mate." Usually, we would have only a few serious dating relationships before getting married, so dating was a very sober undertaking for us. I began to feel Heidi was my destiny, so I tucked the adoration I felt for her into my heart. There, in privacy, it grew.

"I'm going for a walk," I'd tell my roommates on the way to meet her downstairs.

For weeks, we'd arrange clandestine meetings across campus, hoping no one would notice we were always together. Having a forbidden romance was pretty invigorating. There was nothing quite like meeting Heidi's eyes across class and knowing we shared such an intimate secret. I did tell one person, however. In one of my regular letters to my father, I mentioned I was very interested in a girl named Heidi. A few weeks later, I received a note back from him.

"Dear Xiqiu," he wrote. "Thank you for your letter updating me on all that you're doing at college. I encourage you, of course, to pay attention to your studies and not to get distracted by extracurricular activities."

"Extracurricular activities" was apparently my dad's euphemism for dating, and he seemed willing to tolerate it if I kept it within the right balance.

I figured we weren't the only ones with a secret romance. Occasionally, I'd notice a couple walking around the school's racetrack together. If they walked slowly, I knew they weren't there for the exercise. Sometimes I'd see people holding hands in the quad. At night, under the cover of darkness, couples nuzzled on the steps of the library. In fact, one day, we were all called to a meeting by the party secretary of the English department.

"Apparently, some of you are ignoring the very reasonable

rule that dating is not allowed on this campus," he sternly announced. "In fact, recently campus security discovered several lights knocked over. These lights—which are very expensive, by the way—were put there to make sure our campus is safe. Yet, for the sake of *kissing* in the quad . . ." He said the word *kissing* with such distaste that one might have thought he said *defecating*. "Someone took it upon himself to break our campus lights."

He paused and looked around the room to intimidate the kissing criminals.

"And so, I'd like to take this opportunity to remind everyone of a simple fact," he said, straightening his back in indignation. "Dating is not the purpose of college."

The university made sure the lights were back up within the week, and the campus police began walking around with flashlights, hoping to stem the raging hormones on the library steps and in other dark corners of the campus. Eventually, the students realized we had the upper hand. After all, there were so many covert relationships the university couldn't punish everybody. Gradually, people began holding hands in public. Then, a few weeks later, people came out and simply announced their relationships.

"Really?" I said, when my roommate told me he was dating a beautiful girl in the Chinese lit department. "You hid it very well!" I didn't admit my surprise was mainly due to the fact that I assumed she'd find a more attractive mate.

When Heidi and I told our friends that we were dating, their mouths dropped open too. "You?" Joseph said. "And you?"

Apparently, we had hid our affection very well, because people were shocked. The person who was the most shocked was Heidi's dad, who used to be a teacher too but had been imprisoned for five years during the Cultural Revolution for a crime he didn't commit. While in jail, he lost his job teaching at a government school. Even though all criminal charges were dropped after the revolution, it was too late. His reputation was forever marred and he was damaged beyond repair. In China, children bear the responsibility for their parents' care, so his hope for the future of his family was placed squarely on Heidi's shoulders. He hoped Heidi would marry someone who could make some money.

"Dear Bochun," he wrote, after she revealed our relationship in a letter home. "I urge you to find someone else. Someone who can work in the capital city of our province, bring home a nice paycheck, and be respected in our community." We were walking to class together as she read it aloud to me. "That way our family can have a better future."

"He doesn't have much confidence in me," I said, though I understood why her father placed such an emphasis on having a good reputation. "But I promise I'll go to grad school, focus on international relations, and make a good living for us."

I smiled as I assured her that I could pull it all off. However, the number of people who were already depending on my future salary was growing. My dad, my sister, Heidi, Heidi's parents, and possibly her siblings. And that was not including any children Heidi and I might have.

And so, I continued to focus on my international studies during the evening, after doing all of my other English homework. I developed a friendship with a Chinese literature student named Bruce, who was the son of a political leader. Because of his dad's position, he was more interested in government and could speak more intelligently about it than most people. I enjoyed his company, so I told him of my future plans for grad school, and we spent many hours discussing world affairs.

• • •

In 1988, we got to see some political affairs being acted out right there in China. A nationwide outcry against the poor treatment of teachers erupted all over the country, and students began protesting the widespread government corruption.

"Why won't the government help the teachers?" I asked Bruce one day while we ate lunch in the cafeteria. "Aren't the teachers the guides of the souls of children?"

"I don't know," he responded, thinking while he chewed. "But they don't have the resources to teach. The whole nation—even the party secretary—admits teachers are paid too little. Want to orchestrate our own protest?"

"You organize the protest route," I suggested. "I'll try to come up with some catchy slogans." We stayed up late, organizing friends from the dorm to help, and thinking of ways to get our message into the community. The next morning, I went to the university's propaganda department to get the permit.

"We'd like to submit our plan for a protest," I said at the counter.

"You want to do what?" he said, looking at the signs we'd made, which were leaning up against the wall. "You can't walk around with those. We'll solve the problem within the system."

"The system," of course, was communism. Though I hadn't joined the Communist Party yet, I assumed I would one day. We used to say, "Join the party in order to change the party."

"This *is* 'within the system,'" I argued. "Everyone agrees with us," I said. "We are a teacher's college. Don't you think we should stand up for teachers? My professors agree with us, as does the president!"

"If you keep at this," he said, lowering his voice in a menacing admonition, "you'll face some real repercussions."

With slumped shoulders and dashed hopes, Bruce and I walked slowly back to our dorm.

"I don't understand," I said. "We had it all planned out. It's not like we were advocating for the overthrow of the government."

"Maybe we should," Bruce said, with an impish grin on his face. "Want to try to fight this?"

That was the last conversation I ever had with my friend.

Within days, Bruce was "persuaded" to switch to another school. The school had told his dad, the political leader, that his son was out of control. He feared that his son was jeopardizing his political future, and so—just like that—he was gone. I was left confused and alone. *Shouldn't we fight for what's right? We're all future teachers, so why can't we unite?*

I tried to understand the propaganda department's concern, and figured that the party official was simply confused on how to deal with the unrest. The protests went on for a while, which I followed in the news. Then, on April 15, 1989, the editor of the official school newspaper ran up to me on campus.

"Hu Yaobang is dead!" he said. Yaobang was the former Communist Party secretary who supported the 1986 student movement. My mind flashed back to high school, when I had read news of the story in my stolen newspaper.

"What happened?" I asked.

"It's mysterious," he said. "No one knows exactly, but he died right in the middle of a high-level Communist Party leaders' meeting!"

"What were they discussing?" I asked.

"What else?" he said. "The education budget."

"He must've sided with our teachers!" I said. I envisioned him standing in front of the group, passionately arguing for the rights of teachers. I imagined the hardliners fighting back against his rhetoric and him dropping dead of a heart attack.

The whole nation was shocked over news of Yaobang's death, especially students. Spontaneous demonstrations of mourning caught the government off guard. After the 1986 student protests, he'd been ousted and had become something of a disgraced icon of reform. Completely bereft, I left my friend and went to be alone in my dorm. There, in the silence of my room, I got out a pen and paper and thought about the legacy of Hu Yaobang.

The words flowed out of me until the sun went down outside

my window. By the time I finally turned off the light to go to sleep, I'd created a poignant tribute to the man who'd inspired so many students in China.

"Here," I said the next day, when I saw my friend again. "For your consideration for publication."

He took the poem from me, read it silently, and swallowed hard. "It's perfect," he said, fighting emotion. The official newspaper had a large distributorship beyond the school, and I smiled when I thought of all the people who'd read my tribute to the fallen leader.

The next day, the editor came to my dorm with a proof of the following day's newspaper, used to catch typos before the school made the official copies.

"Look," he said, holding up the proof of the paper. "Your poem will be front page, above the fold!" I grabbed the paper and admired the amazing placement. I read my poem again, this time aloud, enjoying the way the words rolled off my tongue. The poem was an imaginative interpretation of Hu Yaobang's love of education and the circumstances that surrounded his death. It ended with a simple line: "We should all do more."

That night, as I drifted off to sleep, I made plans to get several copies of the paper off the stands to show my friends and family. At midnight, however, a harsh banging on the door jolted me from sleep. I jumped out of my bunk bed, stumbled in the darkness, and flung open the door. My friend the editor stood there with a look of horror on his face.

"What have you gotten me into?" he asked.

"What do you mean?"

"We're in big trouble," he said. "We printed our newspapers and they're already ready to be sent out to the school and other cities. But someone in the administration read your poem and recalled them all! We have to redo all of it!"

"Because of a poem?"

"Yes," he said, exasperated. "I don't understand it, but apparently they didn't want to portray Hu Yaobang in such a positive light."

I rubbed the remaining sleep from my eyes. Was this a dream? Would a teacher's college really not let me honor the life of an education reformer? And why would they take such draconian steps to stop me?

"And there's not enough time to do another print run of the paper without it," he finished.

After he left, I tried to go back to sleep, but the trepidation in my spirit wouldn't let me. I pulled the covers up to my chin and looked at the ceiling. Why would the administration consider a poem so dangerous?

Without any real answers, I decided I'd try to snatch a copy in the morning and get advice from the university president. Surely, this was some weird oversight or miscommunication. I laid there all night, nervous about what seemed to be a strange tightening of control over the students. When the morning finally came, I jumped down off my bunk bed, threw on some clothes, and headed down to the newspaper rack.

Another student, wearing jogging attire, was standing next to a completely empty newspaper rack. All of the copies had been destroyed during the night.

"Look at that," he said. "I wonder why there aren't any papers today."

A lump caught in my throat as I responded.

"I honestly don't know."

After that moment, I was shocked, confused, and more than a little angry. After Hu Yaobang's mysterious death, some students had gathered at Tiananmen Square to try to get the government to reassess his legacy and to honor the man's life. One week after his death, there were one hundred thousand students gathered there for his memorial service. But this spontaneous public mourning had turned into a nationwide protest for political reform and against all the Party corruption. The students held hunger strikes and demanded government accountability and freedom of speech and press. Though some of our American professors were nervous about the unrest, no one else really seemed to give the events in Beijing much thought. It didn't affect *their* grades, after all.

• • •

One evening, as I walked into an auditorium filled with studying students, I got so frustrated that I made a rather rash decision. I reached for the light switch and turned it off.

The lights flickered, then went completely dark. I heard a few gasps coming from the now dark room.

"Do I have your attention?" I yelled into the dark auditorium. "Why are you so numb?"

"Turn the lights back on," a guy in the back of the room yelled. "Unless you're going to take my exam for me."

Some students giggled.

"I'll turn them back on, after you hear me out," I said. "Don't you know the Beijing students are already acting for our country's future? And yet, you sit here? You, who still have the luxury of studying. But how can you just sit, with your books open on your desks like nothing is going on in the world?"

No one spoke, but I could tell by the silence that the students began listening. I flicked the lights back on. "You're so concerned about your grades and your future, but you aren't willing to fight for it. Come on, everyone. Let's go!"

Amazingly, a student in the back of the auditorium got up. Then, another. And another. Pretty soon, a large number of students followed me right out of the room and out into the campus. This time, I didn't care about a permit. We were advocating for the right things, and I wasn't going to be stopped because I didn't have the right piece of paper.

"Anti-corruption!" we yelled as we walked down the streets. As we marched, our numbers swelled.

"Xiqiu!" I heard from a side street. When I turned around and saw the man from the propaganda department running toward me, I was ready to defend myself. After all, he had previously admonished me in an ominous tone, threatening me. Dread filled me, but I tried to push it out of my mind. They couldn't make me disappear like they had Bruce. After all, there were even professors walking alongside us!

"You can't stop me," I said, preemptively. "What we're saying is good and right."

"We don't want to stop you," he said, a little out of breath. Behind him, a guy carrying two portable speakers emerged. "We want to join you!" The student protest in Beijing seemed to have softened the whole nation. There was something about the peaceful protest that penetrated the very essence of the nation.

We took the loudspeakers and continued our march, drawing even more people out of the dorms and classrooms. Students from all levels and disciplines joined me. Even more teachers followed.

"Look!" someone yelled, pointing to a university car following slowly behind the parade. "It's President Ming!" The president of the school, my friend and ally, waved out his window at me. It made me walk even faster and shout even louder. After all, I knew he'd be on our side.

"Higher wages!" we yelled.

The campus the next morning was electrified by the protests. People began to skip classes in solidarity with the Beijing students. One friend hung a bedsheet from his window with the word *freedom* written in his own blood.

It was meaningful and exciting to be a part of something that was larger than us. "There are a lot of people fed up with this system," I remarked to my fellow student union leaders a few days later as we gathered to plan our next moves. "Our student union really helped enact change." However, deep down, I was secretly proud of myself, thinking I was the true catalyst behind the movement.

"What should we do next?" one of the leaders asked. "What's our next move?"

"Actually, I think we should disband," I said.

"Are you sick?" the union secretary asked. "We just successfully created the first protest at Liaocheng Teacher's College!"

"But our group is Communist school–approved," I explained. "And we're ushering in a new day! Now we advocate for freedom!"

"Should we not protest?"

"No, we should," I said. "But only after we disassociate ourselves with the Communists."

"Well, I agree we should reorganize into a new group," another leader said. "But we'd have to figure out a new name."

"And we can't leave it up to Xiqiu," another said. "No offense, but you named your newspaper *Ugly Stone*."

That's how we became the descriptive yet not creative "Supporting the Democracy Independents Union," and everyone was happy. With a newly democratic group, our next move was to put our loudspeakers in dorm rooms to blast our messages into the campus. I was in charge of the news media and all broadcasts. Another student was in charge of the donations. The whole school rallied, and I couldn't help but enjoy the fact that they rallied around me.

Of course, they were truly passionate about what was going on in the nation. However, at lunch, everyone gravitated to my table. When people saw me on campus, they warmly greeted me and sometimes gathered around me to receive updates.

"Xiqiu, what's the latest on the protests?" someone would ask. "Are you heading to Tiananmen Square?"

It was a fun time of life, both at the university level and on the national level. The national party secretary, Mr. Zhao Ziyang, was sympathetic to the Beijing students and in an amazing turn of events ordered the newspapers to report honestly on the unrest. The Communist Party's mouthpiece began to present points of view that differed from the official government message. Students' views about the protest were reported fairly on the front page. Other articles praised the Beijing students' courage.

This was the only time in the eighty years of Communist Party history when there was real freedom of speech and press. Giddy with our newfound freedom, we began to believe one day we could be free from hatred, violence, corruption, and fear.

The joy spilled out into everyday life. Shop owners, construction workers, and other citizens greeted the protesters warmly and sent food out to us when we marched. An owner of an ice cream shop sent ice cream treats free of charge. In Beijing, even a group of thieves decided not to steal anything for a time to show support of the protestors. The police were busy with Tiananmen Square, so ordinary citizens stepped up to direct traffic. Miraculously, drivers slowed down, yielded the right of way, and did all they could to preserve the peace. Bicyclists who got in wrecks didn't curse each other, as was customary. Even the newspapers reported that these accidents resulted in friendly exchanges in which people greeted each other and left without argument or blame. "It's okay," they'd say, leaving the scene. "Everything's fine."

It was like someone who'd held on to our arms so tightly suddenly let go, and we were lighter with the newfound freedom. We walked more confidently, we smiled, we debated issues with intellectual honesty. In record numbers, people spoke out against the Communist Party. Others expressed support for it. Some even advocated for anarchy. Everyone's opinion was fully respected and discussed.

Life, with freedom, felt fuller and more robust. I remember thinking the flowers in the garden were particularly vibrant and the aroma of cooking rice was more pleasant. Freedom seeped into everything.

Sadly, it lasted less than two weeks.

"I hear rumors," said Joseph, "that the government is going to declare martial law."

I dismissed his words, even though his father was a government official. After all, why would the Communists do that to peaceful protestors? It just didn't seem right. But the government couldn't agree on how to handle the unrest, and consequently began to retighten its grip on the media. Suddenly, the newspapers went back to printing the same kinds of filtered propaganda and life settled back down into its gray, listless state. Though Zhao Ziyang was still compassionate toward the students, he was branded a troublemaker.

By late May, the students at my college had pushed the protests into the back of their minds. Life returned to normal. Even though we'd called for a boycott of all classes, I noticed some students showing up there. As the vice president of our new democratic student group, I called a meeting to discuss the situation. "These students who are so apathetic to the plight of the protestors are wrong."

"Well, what are we going to do?" someone asked. "Go around with a megaphone and ask them to fill the streets again? They've already done that, and they're ready to study and work on their futures."

"This is their future," I said. "We have to make them see that this affects their future as much as whether they get into grad school."

We talked for a bit more when an idea came to me. "Does anyone have access to a great deal of tape?"

That afternoon, we went to a classroom and closed its door, then taped it shut. "Attention, everyone," I said. "This is what we're calling the new 'conscience seals.' Whoever dares to break this seal," I explained, "has no conscience. We need to be in solidarity with the Beijing students by continuing to participate in the classroom boycott."

We went from class to class, and—once again—caused all of

the classes in the English department to be shut down. While this was another incremental victory in the fight for freedom, Liaocheng Teacher's College wasn't where the real battle was being fought. Our president, professors, and students were all philosophically on board with the Beijing protestors, though our distance from Beijing lessened the urgency. I'd heard the students at Tiananmen Square had grown exhausted from the weeks of living in hot, humid conditions. They'd become weak from hunger strikes and weary of fighting the government.

Suddenly, my efforts there in Liaocheng City didn't seem enough. I didn't want to sit idly on my hands while my fellow students were mounting the largest peaceful protest in China's history. And so, at the next student union meeting, I asked a simple but life-changing question.

"Anyone want to take a trip?"

6

"Tickets, please," the conductor asked, glancing at me and then across at Heidi.

I reached for my wallet. It was going to be a long ride, but I figured it would go pretty fast. Our sudden trip had the intoxication of a road trip and the joy of a mission trip. Not only was I participating in a national shift in our country, I was doing it with people I cared about deeply. "I need to buy two tickets," I said.

"Destination?" he barked, looking down at the roll of tickets he carried in his hand.

"Beijing." I nodded to the other rows of my friends, who were talking quietly. About twelve of us had left the comfort of our dorms. After riding the bus for five hours, we looked a little crumpled and tired. But now that we were on the train, we were invigorated once more. "My friends and I are going to join in the protests."

"Let me guess. Tiananmen Square?" he asked. He had the air of a man who'd seen everything and was generally unimpressed. At the height of the protests there had been a half-million students there, but many of the students had grown tired and left. "We believe in freedom and democracy," I said. Part of me worried the conductor might charge me double. Instead, as I looked at him, I detected a smile. I knew he was on our side when he waved off my money and went on to the next row. "No tickets needed."

For the next eight hours, the countryside flew by our windows and I became lost in thought. It was my first trip to Beijing. I smiled as I remembered the day I worried my mother by pouting over not getting into any of my Beijing school choices. I wished I hadn't put her through so much anxiety, though I was still deeply disappointed at being forced into a teacher's college. So far, everything was going as planned. For now, I had to concentrate on getting good grades, establishing strategic relationships, and studying international affairs every night for a couple of hours. I'd figured out a way to exist in the system, and maybe even beat it. Even though both the train car and my mind were crowded, I drifted off to sleep, lulled by the sound and the gentle rocking of the train. I awoke when my friend Sam reached over and nudged me.

"Xiqiu," he said. "What is that?"

He pressed his face against the glass, and I wiped my eyes to see what had his attention. There, on the border of Beijing, we saw a long train filled with soldiers wearing camouflage and carrying heavy weapons. On the back of the train there were tanks covered with military green blankets. They appeared to be preparing for a strike.

"That doesn't look good," he said, under his breath. "I've heard they were going to declare martial law."

"Oh, that's just a psychological threat," I said.

"Maybe we should go back."

"Not after we've come this far!" I encouraged him. "They know these trains are full of students going to protest and they want to dissuade us before we even get there."

By the time we arrived at the train station, we'd pushed aside our fears and had a very deep hope that something good might happen in Beijing. We stretched our stiff legs, got our backpacks, and made it to the place the entire world was watching: Tiananmen Square.

Thanks to Chairman Mao, Tiananmen Square was one of the largest city squares in the world. Approximately the size of nine football fields, it was full of tents and makeshift student villages. People walked around carrying signs that read, "Hunger strike to survive!" and "Democracy."

"Look at that," Sam said, almost to himself. Heidi, our other friends, and I looked and saw a statue of a woman holding up a torch that stood between the Monument to the People's Heroes and the Tiananmen Gate. She was the "goddess of democracy," and towered about thirty feet in the air, directly facing a large photograph of Mao.

"It's like they're having a silent confrontation," I said. Though she was just made of plaster, we longed for the everlasting freedom she embodied.

We stood and took in the whole scene for a few moments before we found a nice little area with enough space to accommodate our group. The Square was full of tents, some donated by a sympathetic computer business. These looked almost military-like, simple, utilitarian, and olive green. Others seemed to be thrown together, made with red, white, and blue striped plastic. All of them were aligned carefully in little rows, and everything was ordered and calm. We unpacked our belongings in our tents and placed our university flag over our encampment. The scene almost looked cheerful and festive.

When we got settled, we immediately began walking around shouting various slogans. It was easy to be engulfed by the excitement and the energy. We made fun of the senior Communist Party leaders, using their names and mocking them at the top of our lungs. "Anti-corruption! Freedom! Democracy!"

We cheered, we marched, we sang songs of freedom. Occasionally, someone would approach us holding small baskets of food. "Would you like a bread roll?" People came from the city to give the protestors all kinds of food and other items of necessity. Vendors handed out snacks to those who weren't on hunger strikes. Water was more difficult to safely acquire. We got ours from an emergency management system that ran water out of the ground.

"Does this taste strange?" Heidi asked, frowning, after gulping down a cup.

Over the course of a few days, the atmosphere changed. It began to feel more ominous. The air was foul, full of the collective perspiration of thousands of protestors and rotting trash baking in the sun. The portable toilets were overflowing. Tension grew. Every night, before we bedded down, the loudspeaker in the Tiananmen Square called for people to come to different corners of the street.

"We need thirty students to block tanks over there," the voice pleaded. One day, we noticed troops amassed near the People's Great Hall.

"Something's going to happen," Sam said to me, worry filling his voice. But none of us believed there'd be a real crackdown. We knew the military had made a decision to find the best time to conduct a military strike. The military vehicles, so far, had all been blocked by students.

"What's the worst that could happen?" another friend asked.

"Yeah, maybe one day the soldiers will penetrate into the crowd and possibly grab us," I said. "But surely freedom is worth an arrest."

Even as we brushed off the fears, some in our group grew afraid.

"We heard the Communists have won over some old party loyalists," our friends said. "This protest isn't going to last forever. If we end up on the losing side of things, it will be bad for us."

"No, no, no," I said, sensing a weakening of resolve. "We're doing good things here—not bad things. We aren't calling for violence. We are peacefully protesting," I said. "As long as we have the chance, we should continue."

Heidi, who hadn't felt quite right since drinking the water, agreed with me. But she was also nervous. A natural rule follower, she was apprehensive that the military was planning a move. Seeing so many likeminded, passionate, principled people, however, filled us with joy and hope. I'd lived long enough to realize that true change could only be achieved through democracy. I really felt this was a moment in which China would—must—change, no matter what the military threatened. In spite of the less than perfect conditions, I could've stayed there forever.

However, on the morning of May 29, I woke up, looked at Heidi, and noticed that she was pale and listless.

"We have to get you out of here," I said.

She could barely respond.

Though I was upset over leaving the protest, my love and concern for Heidi far outweighed any apprehension I had about our departure. We said goodbye to our friends and began our long journey to the hospital.

"Stay strong," I called out to my friends as I left. "Stay strong," I whispered to Heidi as I walked her to the train. The only way to get her medical care was to take her on the train, then the bus, all the way back to the hospital near our college. I assisted her, worried that the water she drank might've been contaminated. She was dehydrated but couldn't keep liquids down. I held her hands, negotiated the transportation system, and finally checked her into the hospital. My heart swelled at seeing her so ill. I feared she might die, and when the doctors finally examined her, I could tell her situation was pretty dire.

Thankfully, we'd done the right thing. The doctors confirmed that she had a very serious intestinal problem due to the unsanitary water from the Square. We'd gotten her medical treatment, even if it meant leaving our friends to carry on without us. Heidi was released from the hospital after only a couple of days, and she was revived and refreshed. I wondered if there'd be time for us to return to the protest.

Six days after we left, on June 4, we were in the center of campus, next to a loudspeaker the independent student leaders had set up. It was a bright, sunny day, and students played sports around us. Others had brought picnic lunches and ate happily on the grounds. A radio station from overseas called the Voice of America emanated from the speakers.

"Breaking news," said the voice on the radio. "The Chinese military has gone into the crowds of protestors. Many have been killed."

"I don't believe that," I said to Heidi. "The military wouldn't fire on its own people."

Another student said, "I heard the protestors turned on the soldiers. Don't listen to that American propaganda." He pointed to our radio. "The government wouldn't kill innocent students."

For hours, we heard rumors and desperately tried to figure out what had actually transpired. Then I noticed our friend Sam emerge into the quad, out of breath. He was wearing no shoes, and his hair was mussed and pressed down on his face. When he made it to the center of the school sports field, where all the students gathered, he fell to the ground and covered his face with his hands.

"What happened?" we asked. "What did you see?"

We wanted to believe in the ideas of democracy. We wanted to believe in China. We wanted to believe that our government would protect students who only wanted to strive for a better future.

But as we looked at Sam, his body crumpled in grief and fear, we knew everything was about to change. Because covering his shirt was confirmation of the radio program's report.

Blood.

"They really killed people," he said, gasping for air through his sobs. "They really did it."

Apparently, after we'd left, the government had classified all of the protestors as "counterrevolutionaries," enemies of the nation.

"What happened?" I asked, gently trying to pull his head up from the grass.

"They almost killed me. I had to crawl over dead bodies," he sobbed. "There were fires everywhere. I didn't know what to do, so I just ran. I ran so fast I lost my shoes."

"That's not what the government is saying," a student from the crowd said. "They said the counterrevolutionaries turned on the peaceful soldiers and attacked them."

Sam moaned at this, and began to tell his story again and again, to all who would listen. "They killed, they really did it!"

As images of tanks facing down unarmed students were broadcast around the world, China clamped down on the media. The time of a relatively free media was over, and information was more tightly controlled than ever. Initially, the state media outlets reported on the massacre sympathetically to the student protestors, but the government moved in quickly to rectify the reports. Those responsible for the sympathetic broadcasts were removed, as were two China Central Television news anchors who got choked up as they reported on the deaths in Tiananmen Square. Several editors sympathetic to the students were arrested, journalists were fired, and foreign correspondents were sent back to their countries and blacklisted from ever coming back to China.

The campus, reeling from the massacre, went into shock. For a couple of days, students milled around, compared notes, and comforted each other as the death tally rose. The official tally never was officially settled and figures vary from several hundred to several thousand. It was such a substantial blow to the students in our nation that we suddenly had a new language to connote time: there was before the incident on June 4, and after it. The students stuck close to campus in the immediate aftermath of the massacre, but classes were canceled due to the boycott or the shock of the tragedy. After a few days most people packed their bags and went back to their respective hometowns, since nothing was going on academically. Gradually, the campus became a ghost town, and I couldn't wait to get home to tell my dad all that happened. Maybe he could help me make sense of it all.

• • •

As I was leaving, I noticed one of my American teachers, a guy named Dan from San Francisco, sitting in the courtyard.

"What are you doing?" I asked, sensing he was listless from being so far from home and without students to teach.

"Just watching everyone skip town," he said, smiling.

"Why don't you come with me? I can show you around my hometown and we can think about setting up a summer English camp for high school students there."

It didn't take much to convince him. He threw some clothes in a bag and we jumped on a train. When we arrived, however, he caused quite a commotion.

"*Yang guizi!*" the villagers called out, using the sarcastic and affectionate nickname Chinese people call all foreigners. It meant "foreign devil." Dan was tall, had brown hair, blue eyes, and fair skin, and was very obviously not from around there. Because he was the first *yang guizi* to come to our peasant village, he was treated like a panda in the zoo. No matter where he went, he was encircled with villagers asking him the same three questions: Where are you from, how old are you, and are you married?

"Let's have some fun," I said, pulling him aside after detecting this pattern.

"Oh," Dan said. "Suddenly, the student has become the teacher!"

After a little coaching, Dan dazzled the villagers by preemptively telling everyone he met three pertinent facts.

Every time someone came up to him, he said, "*Wo shi meiguo ren*" (I am an American), "*San shi sui*" (I'm thirty years old), and "*Guang gun*" (I am a bachelor). Actually, the last was a local saying that means, literally, "I am a piece of single stick," but the notion was communicated: he was available. This caused quite a stir, because the villagers were amazed at the single foreign devil who could speak fluent Chinese and also read their minds! In spite of the grievous circumstances of our return home, his presence in my village was a fun—if temporary—distraction.

A week after we'd arrived, however, a police car pulled up to my home, stirring up a cloud of dust.

"What's going on out there?" my dad asked, peering through the window at the somber-looking officers who banged on our door.

I looked at Dan, who'd broken out into a complete sweat, and then rushed to the door, hoping perhaps they'd come to the wrong house.

"What's the matter?" I asked, shocked at the grave expressions that met me when I opened the door.

"You." One of police officers pointed to Dan, who was standing behind me. "You have to leave this area voluntarily."

"What's so 'voluntarily' about it if you're forcing me out?"

"You obviously have a choice. You can leave voluntarily now, or stay here and face serious consequences."

"Could we leave in a few days?" I protested. The journey had taken us a great deal of time, money, and effort. Plus, there was no reason to go back to a desolate college.

The officer opened his mouth, as if he was about to explain the tense political environment, then thought better of it. Instead, he simply said a cold, harsh, "No!"

Another officer said, "In fact, you must go now, without delay. We can give you a ride to the train station in the county headquarters of Gaomi County."

"How far away is that?"

"Fifty miles," the officer responded. "So, let's get going." They gave us about three minutes to grab our things before placing us in their police car. To our surprise, they "asked" us to sit on the back box of the car where criminals were forced to sit. Dan's presence in the village had caused so much commotion independently of any sort of scandal. However, when we were whisked away like hardened criminals, the villagers stood along the main road terrified, wondering what we'd done. My family believed we were being taken away to prison, but the officers did take us to the train station.

"Don't come back," the officer said to Dan as we got on the train to go back to the university.

● ● ●

When we arrived back at college, we walked through campus a little shaken. My entire life, I had wanted to help better my nation. At first, I believed being wealthy would help me have enough influence to meaningfully change things. Then I began to think that reform would only occur through government influence. If only I could become a leader in the Communist Party, then I could issue changes that could make things more equitable and fair. After being faced with communism's corruption, however, democracy seemed like my only hope of reform. But if my own nation's government would turn their tanks on their own citizens—what hope was there?

Dan grabbed my arm, and stopped me right there on the sidewalk next to the campus's official message board.

"This isn't good," he said, pointing to a newly posted white sign.

"The Communist Party has made a decisive decision to crack down on counterrevolutionaries," I read aloud. "We urge these leaders of the illegal organization to surrender."

"Isn't that you?" he asked. "You're the main leader. They're going to arrest you!" Dan and I both were a little rattled after our incident with the police.

"Don't jump to conclusions," I assured him. "It just says I need to surrender. If they'd wanted to arrest me, they would've done it back home."

And so, I scurried off to find if the other student leaders were still around or if they'd gone home. I found about six others, and we made the trek to the police station, walking slowly as we tried to figure out what would happen. Would we be arrested? Would we be interrogated? Would they try to deny the truth of what some of our group had seen with their own eyes?

"So what *did* you see?" I asked the others to make sure I understood the basic outline of the story. As they had done when I was there, the students had set up barricades to block the tanks from entering the square. At about 10:30 p.m. on June 3, the army fired live bullets at the protestors. Later that night, after midnight, they completely broke through using tanks and armored personnel carriers. Many people were killed. Reports from the government were that no one had died. I knew for a fact that Heidi's graduate school advisor had an eighteen-year-old son who was at the protest. He was shot to death on his mother's birthday. I also knew that a tank pushed over the goddess of democracy statue, its hand and torch breaking off when it struck the ground. We knew the military had been watching the protests, but we never anticipated this. Not an actual massacre.

"Looks like they're ready for us," a friend said, nodding to a sign that read, "Illegal Organization Leaders Surrender This Way."

In spite of the grave circumstances, we nervously chuckled. That was not the kind of sign we saw every day.

Obediently, we followed the markings, and I tried to calm myself. I was in a better position than most. First of all, I wasn't even there at the time of the massacre. Second of all, I had acted in accordance with my school's administration and our student body. I'd defied no one locally, and I hadn't done anything wrong. After all, we were simply advocating for truth.

"Sit down," a policeman barked when we walked in. "What have you done?" he said to our group collectively, without waiting for a response. I'd come in ready to defend myself, but apparently the police were not interested in negotiating.

"You all need to register as counterrevolutionaries," he explained. First, he took our fingerprints, and I felt like a criminal. Then he slammed a form in front of each of us. "Fill these out."

I picked up the pen, and began to carefully fill in the blanks— my name, age, hometown, parents' names. It was the first time I'd filled in a form since my mother's death, and I felt a pang in my heart as I wrote her name on the piece of paper. *What would she think of this?* I wondered. For a couple of silent hours, we were left with these forms staring at us in the face. We were forced to write general descriptions of how we were involved in the protests, when we started, and why. Finally, the agent came back into the room, collected our papers, and told us to stand.

"Go back to your school," he said. But I had a feeling this was far from over. "Your administors will give you further instruction."

The walk back to school was like a funeral procession.

"What have we done?" a friend lamented.

"What if they yank us from school?" another asked.

I almost tripped over the sidewalk when I heard that. The thought had never occurred to me. Getting removed from school would be devastating. After all, my family sacrificed so much for me. They placed their hopes on me alone. Had I just placed my entire family's future in jeopardy?

The grim-faced deputy secretary of the Communist disciplinary party met me at the administration building. "I'll be watching you," he said. "This is your special agent from the Public Security Bureau." He pointed to one of the other two men. "And this is the director of the investigation." They wore plain clothes and were of similar height. Their eyes were dark and seemed to stare right through me.

"Our job is to monitor your progress," he said. Only the next day would I begin to understand what this "monitoring" would entail. The next day, my interrogator showed up at my dorm at around eight o'clock in the morning. "Let's go," he said.

I assumed he'd take me to the English department and watch me sit there during class. Perhaps my activities would be restricted, but I'd still generally be living my normal life.

However, we didn't head toward the English department.

"Here's your area," he said, opening the door to an empty classroom with one desk and nothing else but paper and a pencil. "Write your confession."

"For how long?" I asked.

The officer looked at his watch. "You only have until six in the evening," he said.

"That's ten hours!" I said.

"You have a lot to confess," he said. "Write what you've done, with all the details. Where did you go? When did you start your insurrection? Who are your witnesses? What happened when you got to Beijing?" Then he smirked at me and slammed the door shut.

But I knew he was standing on the other side of it.

I took the paper and positioned it correctly on the desk, trying not to panic. Why was I not allowed in class? What would Heidi do when she noticed I didn't show up?

"My name is Xiqiu Fu," I wrote, tears filling my eyes. "And I'm an enemy of the Chinese people."

7

I slammed the button on my alarm, pulled down my covers, and yawned. Another morning. On a normal day, I would brush my teeth, grab a bite to eat, and head off to see my friends in the English department. However, registered counterrevolutionaries weren't allowed that privilege. Instead, I walked to my solitary room for more confessions.

"You haven't told us everything," the deputy said, when he saw me. His clothing was pressed perfectly. Not one hair was out of place, and his general air of perfection made him look like he'd just stepped out of an expensive catalog the Communists used to order deputies. His only imperfect feature was his bottom row of teeth. Now that he was angry, he snarled a bit when he spoke, revealing that they were crooked. He tossed a notebook on my desk, which caused my pencil to fall to the floor.

"Good morning to you as well," I said.

"Start all over again," he said, "but this time don't leave anything out."

I couldn't believe my ears, but I tried to shake it off. "How long should I write today?" I asked, forcing a nonchalant smile.

"How long will it take you to start telling the truth?"

I was told I needed to eat lunch at my desk, which further stripped me of time to spend with my friends. I hadn't gotten a chance to tell them all that had happened, and I knew they were worried.

"And dinner?" I asked.

"Do I look like your babysitter? I don't care what you do between six and eight," he said, before beginning to walk out of the room. "But meet me at the back of the classroom in the English department so I can check your work."

I suppressed a smile and simply nodded. I didn't want him to know he'd given me a gift. Since I'd registered myself as a counterrevolutionary, I'd been in exile. Being able to see my friends at dinner would allow me to tell my story and, honestly, to revive my spirit a bit. My friends had become my family while at college, and I couldn't wait to talk to them to start processing the massacre and its aftermath.

I picked my pencil up off the floor and started to write, including as much detail as possible. This time, for example, when I told the story of going to Beijing, I included a bit more.

"We got on the train," I wrote, "but the conductor didn't make us pay for tickets. I did not get his name, nor do I remember anything remarkable about his appearance . . ." And so, I began again, scrawling out my life on paper. The minutes eked by, and I—once again—filled the empty pages with minutiae. I wrote about the people who gave us food, the contaminated water, Heidi's sickness, and the train ride home. When I finished writing the story of Tiananmen Square, I couldn't think of any more details. I glanced at my watch. Only noon? I began to write in slightly larger letters, hoping to make it look like I'd written more text. I also searched my memories for specifics the government might find interesting. A second straight day in that room made me feel slightly claustrophobic. So, when the hour hand on the clock finally crawled all the way to the six, I grabbed my backpack and practically ran to the cafeteria.

It was only about a five-minute walk, and the air felt crisp on my face. Being threatened by the police had sharpened my senses, and I felt so thankful to be out of that room and out on the gorgeous campus. I passed a dorm and walked through the quad, which was decorated with beautiful flowers along the walkway. As I was admiring the rows of scarlet and yellow flowers, my eyes looked past the flower beds and landed on two men standing slightly off the beaten path. Their arms were folded, and they were standing completely still, like statues of intimidation. I recognized them immediately from the police station, and a chill ran down my spine. I knew I was going to be watched, but I didn't expect it to be so obvious. So intentionally intimidating. I put my head down and continued quickly to the cafeteria.

"You'll never guess what I've been through," I said to my friends who were already eating at our regular table. I wanted to let the whole story spill out, to explain my unexpected absence from class, to ask what news and gossip I'd missed. I sat down in the empty seat next to Joseph and simply said, "Wait 'til you hear this!"

To my surprise, he physically recoiled when I sat by him, like I had a terrible sickness he didn't want to contract. The others looked down at their trays, and then at each other. No one asked me what happened or where I'd been. No one even looked me in the eye. Collectively, they all stood, gathered their food, and left the table. They moved so quickly and without a word, like they were geese flying in formation to a more hospitable lake.

"They forced me to register as a counterrevolutionary." I kept talking as I watched my friends gather their things. Slowly, I realized what had happened. They already knew. Now that I was "an enemy of the people," I was an inconvenient and possibly dangerous friend. The last to gather her food was a girl from the English department who sat with Heidi in the front row. I caught her eye, only for a moment. She didn't say anything, and she didn't even smile. But her eyes were full and deep. It seemed like she was trying to convey, in that one glance, "hang in there."

While I tried to collect my thoughts, I picked up my drink and took a sip. Not only was I trying to figure out what to do, I also wanted to look busy. I felt very conspicuous sitting there all alone in my humiliation. Was it my imagination, or was the whole cafeteria staring at me? I took a bite of rice to look casual, hoping my emotions would not betray me. Had I begun to cry—if one tiny tear had managed to escape—I wouldn't have been able to stop. I would've sat there in front of all of my friends and simply wept. With much effort, I tried to look calm. I took another bite of food. Then another.

"Is this seat taken?" I heard a familiar voice. Heidi smiled at me as she placed her tray on the table across from me.

"Are you willing to take the risk?" I asked, though I'd never been happier to see another person.

When she smiled, I melted in relief. While she ate, I told her everything that had happened. I talked so much that she finished her meal before I'd even taken another bite.

"Well, you may already know this, but there's been a great deal of criticism of you."

"Among our friends?"

"On TV, in radio, in the newspaper," she said. "It's like a marathon of criticism about you and the other student protestors. Also, your teacher got up and made a speech about how you were dangerous. He said you were no longer qualified to be a class monitor."

I chewed silently on my chicken for longer than I needed as I processed this news.

"I know it meant a lot to you," she said. "I'm sorry."

"It'll be interesting to see who replaces me."

"You haven't heard?" she said, while her finger traced the outline of her napkin.

"Already there's a replacement?" I asked. "So soon?"

"Joseph," she said very gently, letting the news sink in slowly. "He accepted the position yesterday."

I looked across the cafeteria, to Joseph surrounded by all of my old friends. He was talking and the people around him were laughing. I bit my lower lip and forced a smile. "Well, that explains it."

"If you ask me," she said, leaning in across the table, "he's a real jerk. He used to be your right-hand man, and now he thinks he can fill your shoes?"

"My main concern," I said, trying to be magnanimous, "is not being the monitor or in student leadership. The main thing I want is to get a degree." My voice broke a bit at the word *degree*, and I cleared my throat. I'd looked so contemptuously at my teaching degree, seeing it as merely a stepping-stone to my real passion. Now that it was in danger, however, I wanted nothing more. "My family would be devastated if I showed up back home and became a farmer." I didn't add what really burdened my heart as I sat across the table from Heidi. I also knew if I didn't get a degree, I'd never be able to provide for a wife.

"Also," she began, before hesitating. I could tell she was nervous to tell me even more bad news. "President Ming made an open speech rebuking the student leaders of the protests. He said they disturbed the peace, were instigators, and were sowing social turmoil."

"But he was on our side," I said. "There has to be some sort of mistake."

After dinner, I headed to the English department classroom where students gathered to study. I felt a surge of emotion when I saw my old desk. Heidi sat in the front row, as usual, and I walked to the back of the room, as usual. What was not usual was the tall, perfectly starched deputy waiting for me in the corner. He nodded when he saw me, and motioned to a chair in the very back of the classroom. I was separated from the others to discourage me from talking to anyone, which, of course, was an unnecessary precaution.

In the very recent past, I would've been surrounded by friends and acquaintances. Known as a leader, I was a big man on campus. People sought my advice and my company. I was invited to all the afterschool parties. When there was a study group, I was the first to receive an invitation. Now the other students backed away from me, avoided me, and pretended they'd never known me. I had social leprosy.

"Sit," the agent said. I sat silently as the agent graded my paper and corrected grammatical mistakes. He marked every error, then handed me the paper and some ink to fingerprint it. I wasn't technically a prisoner, but I felt like one. The real purpose of this game, of course, was that he was looking for evidence to use against me, to determine if I was a threat to the government or if my friends were threats. And he was going to make me sit there, day after day, until I either remembered some amazing details or fabricated them.

● ● ●

Welcome to my new life as a counterrevolutionary, I said to myself the next morning as I walked slowly through the campus to start yet another day of forced confessions.

I wasn't looking forward to sitting in that room again. I'd already written all that needed to be said. They were simply trying to wear me down, to get me to confess to things I didn't do, to incriminate friends who weren't guilty.

On the way, however, I passed a newspaper stand and slowed down to check out the headlines. After all, my news addiction didn't stop just because of my punishment. In fact, the news seemed even more pertinent, even more urgent.

I stopped and opened a box, pulling out a newspaper with a very curious headline. "Those Who Make Chaos and Disturbance Should Be Killed."

Killed?

I put the paper down and glanced around to make sure no one was watching me. I suddenly felt guilty, like I was reading someone's mail and had just read something atrocious about me. "Those Who Make Chaos and Disturbance Should Be *Killed*." Yes, I'd read that correctly. *Killed*.

I forced my eyes over the rest of the article, which was neither impressive nor particularly well written. Though it covered the entire top half of the newspaper, it was simply a regurgitation of the standard communist propaganda. It claimed we student protestors had turned our backs on all the nation had given us, that communism was the only way to achieve peace and prosperity for everyone, and that we were selfish, violent, and a detriment to society.

I folded the paper and was about to toss it into a metal garbage can next to the sidewalk.

You'd think the writer would at least try to make more creative arguments against me, I thought. *This is so boilerplate!*

But just as I was about to throw it away, I read the byline. It stopped me dead in my tracks.

Joseph wrote this?

I tucked the newspaper under my arm and walked briskly back to my room. How could my friend turn on me in such a dramatic fashion? Not only did he believe I should die, he had advocated for my death in a newspaper. I unlocked my dorm room door and lowered myself into a chair near my desk. Joseph had been my friend and confidant when I was planning extracurricular activities. If my buddies were advocating for my execution, what were my enemies planning? Suddenly, I started breathing faster, like I couldn't quite get enough air into my lungs. I jumped up from my chair, ran to the window, and closed the blinds.

My room and my life grew darker. Every day was the same: forced confessions, lonely dinners, and back-of-the-room isolation. It went on for an entire week, then two.

Then three.

After a month, I began losing count. The days ran together

into an amorphous blob of forlorn, uneventful days. I confessed to things I barely remembered and admitted to positions I'm not sure I believed. But even with the additional confessions, the government didn't relent. In fact, their grip tightened. A few times a week, my two agents showed up to follow me down the sidewalk, or passed by as I was washing clothes, or stood near me as I ate dinner. I didn't hold my head up high, but I didn't want to let others see how wounded I really felt. I began to wonder if the agents were following me to keep tabs on me, or if they were going to seize me and put me in prison. I felt like I was always looking over my shoulder.

If I just had the chance to explain myself, things might be different, I thought. After all, the whole campus joined in on the protests.

"I didn't mean any harm by leading the protests," I said to the deputy one day, in the most reasonable voice I could muster. "In fact, have you talked to the president of the university?"

"Why would the president of the university defend a student like you?" He sneered.

"Because we're friends," I assured him. Even as I said the word *friends*, hope swelled in my chest. "Just talk to him and you can get all the information you need."

"In the meantime, write your confession." He pointed to the paper.

"For what?" I asked. I no longer tried to hide my incredulity. "How can I confess to something I never did? I didn't burn any tanks. I didn't hurt anyone!"

"Oh, you did plenty wrong," he said. "All you've given me so far is description. I need to see sorrow."

"For what? I'm sorry you're treating me like a criminal."

"There's a reason I'm treating you like a criminal," he snarled, revealing a glimpse of his jagged bottom teeth. "For one, you could start by saying you were misled and that you damaged the country by your misguided efforts."

I rubbed the bridge of my nose, and then my eyes. Trying to reason with this agent was getting me nowhere. I needed an advocate, someone who could testify that I was one of the good guys.

"Will you talk to the president?" I asked, before adding a conciliatory, "Please?"

"Get to work," he said as he disappeared into the hall.

"I was misled," I wrote, but it seemed the pen didn't want to move across the paper. "I did something terrible for the country. I boycotted class."

Along with everyone else in the nation and with the permission of the president.

Even as I wrote this so-called confession, I began to feel hope. If my special interrogators talked to the president, they'd soon realize I was no "enemy of China." I actually had its best interests at heart. I was a friend.

When I awakened the next day, the same thing happened. I was forced to skip class for another day of writing my confession. I was warned to be more forthcoming, and I scoured the recesses of my brain to find some pertinent yet obscure fact that could win me favor.

No detail, however, satisfied them. Instead of being a human being, I was a warning to others, like a memorial on the side of the road at the scene of an accident. *Don't let this happen to you.*

Another week passed, and another. After two months, I was no longer desperate; I was invisible. People didn't even notice me. I had been removed so thoroughly from their lives I wasn't even a consideration. My friends, the ones with whom I had laughed and conspired, no longer even looked my way. I was a ghost, an apparition people were vaguely aware of but preferred didn't exist. Occasionally I'd make eye contact with someone. It may not seem like much, but it was the most affection I received from my friends. I began to live for those very infrequent looks.

Incrementally, hour by hour, my future slipped away. With

every missed class, I got a little more behind. At night, I still studied for my eventual goal of an international affairs postgrad degree. But even as I studied every page, I knew this goal was becoming more and more elusive.

One morning, the deputy came into my room with a splotchy, red face.

"Quit lying to me!" he yelled, as a vein stuck out of his forehead. He was so mad I could see his entire bottom row of teeth. They were more crooked than I imagined, all of them pointing in the wrong direction. "You still aren't telling me the truth."

"I've given you all the details," I said. "Why are you accusing me?"

He opened up a notebook with all of my many confessions. "On this day," he said, pointing to a page, "you were broadcasting an anti-China news organization from the loudspeakers."

"I've never done that," I said. "In fact, I wasn't the person who chose what to broadcast. I had other things to do. I assigned that task to others."

"That's not what your friend told me."

"What friend?" I was exasperated.

He told me the name of his informant, and I couldn't believe my ears. The person who had made up stories against me was the same guy who was so passionate about protesting that he wrote the word *freedom* with his own blood on a bedsheet.

That's when I realized that except for Heidi, every single friend and follower had turned on me. Presumably, they gave false stories to lessen their own punishment.

"I won't confess to that," I tried to say in the most reasonable voice I could muster. "Because I do not want to lie to the government. Did you ever talk to President Ming?"

"Sure," he said. "He wants you to come by for tea one day soon."

My eyes grew large.

"You and the Queen of England."

I averted my eyes from him and looked at the floor so he wouldn't see my disappointment. I breathed out slowly, in an effort to calm myself. After all, if I obeyed and did what I was told, I would be reintegrated into the college and could salvage my reputation.

• • •

One day, I was meandering around the campus, on my way to another dinner alone at the cafeteria, when I caught the eye of my old friend, William. He worked with me on the *Ugly Stone*, but never got as intensely into the protests. I was ready for him to look away, like everyone else. Instead, he slightly nodded to the garden behind the English department as he walked briskly toward it.

Was that an actual interaction? I wondered. I'd been so separated from everyone else for so long, I felt like I might have lost my social skills. Was it even an invitation? I slowed my gait and looked for my agents. By this time, I had gotten used to them showing up in odd places, stalking me, watching me. Sometimes they stood off the sidewalk and simply watched as I walked by. Other times they fell into line behind me, causing me to fear that they'd grab me at any moment. Occasionally, they were nowhere to be seen, but I felt their presence lurking, threatening. I scanned all of the sidewalks and pathways around the garden, but couldn't see anyone. *Is William setting me up?* I wondered, but I had to take the chance. After I circled back around, I casually strolled into the garden, looking to my left and my right.

Chinese gardens are designed in mazes, so one doesn't see all of the beautiful flowers and stone architecture all at once. This meant, of course, it was a perfect place for a discreet conversation. Once I was sure there was no one following me, I meandered around a small pond and over a bridge. Then, behind a blossoming plum tree, right next to a wall of pink lotus flowers, I saw William.

I would've been just as shocked had I turned the corner and seen a dragon. The fact that a friend of mine would actually dare to talk to me in public was a miracle.

"Xiqiu," he said, as soon as he saw me. "I know you've been through so much, but I wanted to tell you about a conversation I overheard."

"Why are you risking yourself to tell me?" I asked, looking around.

"Let's just make it fast," he said. "I was working in the administration office today, as a favor to my Chinese lit professor. You know, making copies, filing papers, and the like. I noticed the dean of the English department walk into President Ming's office."

I knew President Ming would somehow figure out a way to save me, or at least to mitigate some of this unreasonable punishment. After so many weeks of confinement, I really needed an advocate, someone to vouch for my character. He was my only hope.

"I wasn't paying attention at first," William said. "But I could tell they were talking about grad school recommendations." During that time, there was a two-stage process for acceptance into graduate schools. First, students had to earn certain grades. Second, the undergraduate institutions had to submit letters of recommendation from both the department and the university level.

I breathed a big sigh of relief. Graduate school was my only hope for a real occupation. As I spent day after day in my isolation, however, I feared my future was slipping away. If I knew my future was secure, I would be able to tolerate the days of seclusion.

"Wonderful news," I said. "I was worried my enrollment process would be interrupted because of the trouble I'm in."

"You misunderstand," he said, his voice lowered to a whisper. I had to lean forward to hear him. "They started yelling. As I went to get more copy paper I heard President Ming raise his voice."

"About me?"

"Yes," William said. "The dean of the English department wrote you a recommendation, but President Ming was not happy about it."

"How could you tell?" I asked.

"Because he said, 'How could you recommend this trouble-maker? Are you trying to sully the name of this college? Of me?'"

"Troublemaker?"

"Yes, Xiqiu," he said. "The president said, 'Bob Fu will damage the whole country!'"

"But President Ming is my friend," I managed to say. "He participated in the protests with me!"

"He *was* your friend," William said, very kindly. "Now he's working against you."

"In what ways?"

"He told the dean to withdraw his recommendation for you."

I shook my head, as if there was something covering my ears that prohibited me from hearing correctly. Surely, I'd misunderstood. Certainly, after all this work and so much effort, my life wasn't going to end up in the poverty of the rice paddies.

"That can't be true," I said, my voice raised.

"Why would I risk my own academic life to tell you a lie?" he said sternly, putting his hands firmly on my arms. "Get yourself together, Xiqiu. I just wanted you to know that President Ming is against you. You need to know that."

I couldn't speak. After a moment, William dropped his hands from my arms and apologetically said, "I have to go. Don't follow me."

I watched him disappear into the maze of the garden, without thanking him for his courage or friendship. Instead, I stood there, gobsmacked.

As the sweet aroma of the lotus flowers wafted over me, I ran my hand through my hair and tried to think. What options did I have left in life? No matter how much I tried to improve my lot, I was a peasant, a son of a beggar. Without a degree, I could neither support Heidi nor provide my family with much-needed relief from their lives of poverty. I'd be a farmer. I'd be ashamed.

Rage began to build in my chest as I thought about all the hours I had spent preparing for grad school. I used to dream of going places, of cultural reform, of defeating corruption, of conquering inequity. And yet, there I was under the cruel foot of injustice. I wasn't sure of anything, except one inarguable fact: life as I'd planned it was no longer a possibility. I was dishonored.

I gasped when the thought fully took hold of me. I never quite understood why people would decide to commit suicide. It felt desperate and wrongheaded. But as I stood there by the blossoming plum tree, I reached for a branch and broke it off. I'd kill myself, I decided.

But I wasn't dying alone.

8

I walked through the campus as a man on a mission, one foot firmly in front of the other as I went down sidewalks filled with students lugging backpacks. Left foot, right foot, left, right. I was in a rhythm, like a soldier marching off to war, though I was hardly a soldier. But this was definitely war.

I felt numb. Hazy. As a kid, I wasn't the type of boy who caught bugs and dissected them. I didn't kill small animals or throw rocks at birds. In fact, I wasn't sure how to kill anything. But the government was forcing my hand. I could learn.

The first step was obvious. I needed to go to President Ming's house, scout out the property, and figure out the best way to proceed. I didn't necessarily want to make a big public spectacle out of his death. Out of *my* death. I simply wanted a chance to see him one last time, to explain his betrayal, and to blow us both up.

His house seemed like a fine enough place to die. Tucked away in a little compound reserved for high-level university executives, it was relatively secure. I knew that, because he'd invited me there in the past—back when we were friends, when we'd talk about politics and world events over tea, when I thought I was securing my future by impressing him. Just a few months ago, I would've fought anyone who dared speak ill of President

Ming. I thought he was a brilliant reformer, an independent thinker, and a thoughtful scholar. How was I to know he was a communist thug willing to let me suffer a lifetime of indignity to save himself?

I approached the area of the university where the officials lived, and didn't really fear getting caught. After all, I had no weapon, no ill intentions for the evening. I was simply on a fact-finding mission. And as far as I could tell, no agents had followed me.

In my head, I prepared the words I'd say if I ran into him.

"You aren't worthy," I said, practicing out loud. "You are a cheater. Honestly, I don't even think you're human!" Hearing the words gave me a little jolt of energy. I couldn't wait to be able to deliver my lines to his face. I was going to condemn him, maybe even curse him.

It was dusk when I approached his beautiful villa, which was larger than the other academic domiciles. It was tall and stately, about two or three stories high. I walked all the way down the street, past his house, then turned back toward it. No one was milling around outside. Perhaps everyone was finishing up dinner. President Ming would probably still be at work and my special agent didn't expect me back at the English department until eight o'clock. I had one hour. My plan was simple. I would go around to the back of the house, find a window, and check out the lay of the land. Usually Chinese architecture follows the same basic pattern. The home's center has an area for a shrine to the deities and ancestors. On its two sides are bedrooms and "wings" of the building for younger family members, the living area, the dining room, and the kitchen. However, I wanted to make sure there were no surprises. If I was going to deploy a suicide bomb, I wanted to make sure my plan would work. I only had one chance, after all.

I glanced at my watch, then back up at the house. Instead of walking by it again, I walked around it, vaguely aware that what

I was doing was dangerous. If I was caught sneaking around the home of the president, however, what was the worst that could happen? Would I lose my academic standing? My degree? My future? I almost laughed. The government had overplayed its hand. The Communists should've left me *something* for which to live.

I crept around the home until I found a window covered with a carved window screen. I took a deep breath, stood up on my toes, and peered through the window. Through the opening, I saw a hallway. A red rug on the floor. A small table with a jade bowl sitting on it. No one seemed to be home, but this was getting me nowhere. I took a step back from the house and noticed a back door. It was red, with a dragon-headed doorknocker on it. I placed my hand on the brass knob, which was cool to the touch. I pulled on the door, and to my surprise, it opened. I looked into the silent house, and then I looked around me. No witnesses.

When I stepped into the house, I felt a strange combination of pure hatred and complete excitement. I'd been cooped up with my special agent, some pencils, and a stack of never-ending paper for so long. Now that I had decided to die, I finally felt alive. I placed my foot on the slate tiles of the hallway. My shoe made a sound, and I paused.

Was I right about the home being empty? I took another step and paused to listen. Nothing. I took another step. Then another. And so I made my way through the hallway toward the kitchen, one step at a time. If the president was home, he definitely could've heard me—either my shoes clicking on the tile or my heart thudding in my chest. But I couldn't control either of those things. I'd started realizing just how few things were in my control.

The hallway led to the kitchen, which was open and clean except for some tomatoes sitting on a butcher's table in the middle of the room. One was cut with a knife, which was lying beside the food and a dirty plate.

My feet were suddenly glued to the floor and I strained to hear sounds indicating another person's presence. Was President Ming's wife there, nibbling on food instead of preparing dinner because her husband was working late? I scanned the rest of the kitchen. An empty wine glass sat beside a copper vase holding chrysanthemums that should've been thrown away a week ago. A few dead petals had fallen from the flowers and piled beneath it.

I was somehow both completely numb and exceedingly invigorated as I left the kitchen—and heard a loud crash. I froze again. My first inclination was to assume I'd unintentionally hit something, knocking it to the floor. However, the sound had come from the living room, which was about ten feet from where I stood as still as a statue. Had the agents followed me here? Were they setting up a trap in the other room?

After the crash I heard a gasp, and then laughter. It was a man, definitely President Ming. Though he was generally a serious and sober man, we had shared many good times in his office. I would've recognized his throaty laugh anywhere.

Instead of feeling fear or trepidation, I felt relieved. It was like I'd walked into his house and heard the sound from times past, when things were less serious. When I had more life in front of me than behind me. Instead of running away, out the door and back to my security agent, I put my hand on the living room doorway and peered around it.

There, sitting in a chair, was President Ming. His eyes were partially closed, his head tossed back in a complete belly laugh. A bottle of wine was between his legs, and a glass was on the floor, completely shattered. All of the rage that had built up in my heart against the man was temporarily halted. It's hard to hate a man who's giggling.

"Xiqiu," he slurred. If he was surprised at all that I was in his house, I couldn't tell. When he said my name, it reminded me of the first time he called to me on campus. Inexplicably, even in those weird circumstances, I felt honor that the president of the university knew my name. "What are you doing here?"

I walked into the room but stayed near the doorway.

"Wait," he said, holding up a finger. "Let me guess. You've come here to . . . protest something." He absolutely cackled at this, and I noticed an empty wine bottle on the floor next to the broken glass. My anger rose again.

"You're mocking me?" I said. "You used to be on my side!"

"Well, your side is now the losing side," he said, leaning over and picking up shards of glass. For the past few months, I had hung my hopes on the asinine idea that this man would be my advocate?

He got up out of his chair and headed toward me. I thought of the knife on the butcher block in the kitchen, but didn't move from my spot. When he got to me, he stuck his finger in my face, just an inch from my nose.

"You are such a troublemaker," he said, little drops of spittle hitting my face. "The Communist Party has nurtured you for years. Why do you go and do these offensive things to the nation that's given you so much?"

"You betrayed me," I yelled. "I was loyal to you, and you turned on me!"

"What do you know of loyalty?" he barked, his jovial mood completely gone. Beads of perspiration had formed above his eyebrows. "China has taken care of you like a son, and all you've done is try to destroy her. You are an enemy, an agitator, and you will pay for your treachery."

I was livid, but I suddenly wanted nothing more than to get out of there. "No, you will pay!" I yelled. I turned away from him and ran through the house. By the time I reached the back door, all I heard was chortling from the living room.

"I will pay?" He laughed. "I will pay?"

As I scurried back to campus, I didn't feel humiliated or even fooled. I felt betrayed by a person I had believed to be a true friend and ally. He mocked me because he knew I'd always wanted to right all the wrongs in the culture. Of course, I couldn't do that with my life.

But in my death, I was satisfied to be able to right just one wrong.

9

In the pre-internet age, English literature majors were at a serious disadvantage when it came to figuring out how to build bombs. Had I paid more attention in high school chemistry class, perhaps, I could've known the basic science, how to mix this chemical with that to make the perfect, deadly mix. However, my academic specialty provided precious few clues on how to get the job done. Shakespeare killed his characters in rather gruesome ways—smothering, stabbing, beheading, hanging, plague. Too messy. I needed something faster that could take both President Ming and me out at once.

I began to dream about death and murder all the time. During the day, I looked out for the agents, dutifully sat in my isolated room, wrote my so-called confession, and dreamed about revenge. Sometimes an hour would pass, and I'd look down at my paper and find it blank. Instead of scurrying to fill the page, I'd simply start again. I no longer cared enough to give the impression of effort. Without college and post-graduate options, I no longer had any incentive to please my deputy. In fact, I no longer tried to impress anyone. In the evenings, as I sat in the back of the class while my papers were graded, I laid my head on the desk and cried.

One day, as I sat in the back of the classroom, something

unexpected happened. The guy who sat in front of me, who'd drawn the English name "Jack," finally turned around and spoke.

"Here," he whispered. "This might help you." He laid a booklet on my desk. It was a biography of a Chinese intellectual.

I looked at the cover, and then flipped it over. "Why would *this* help?"

"I don't know," Jack said, a little exasperated. "Lao Wu gave it to me."

"Thank you," I said, touched by his compassion, even though I didn't see the use of it.

"Maybe it will help you stop being so . . . weepy."

Reluctantly, I flipped through the pages of the booklet, which was the story of a Confucian scholar from the Western Zhang village near Linfen, Shanxi Province. He was known far and wide for his wisdom, but when he was alone, he was sad and very depressed.

I can identify with that, I thought as I turned the page. Though I wasn't really in the mood to read a new book, I didn't have anything to do as I sat there in silence waiting for my papers to be graded. Plus, I found it interesting that Jack would think this might be a solution for me. I readjusted myself in my chair and began reading about this tortured scholar.

His name was Xi Zizhi, and Confucianism and the Chinese classics couldn't calm his troubled soul. When he was thirty, the sorrow took its toll and his health deteriorated. At one point, his wife and friends dressed him in his finest clothes, laid him on his bed, and waited for him to die. He didn't, much to his own chagrin. One day, his friends suggested opium might brighten his mood. The drug provided an immediate—yet short-lived— relief. The temporary thrill was replaced by a deep depression, even worse than he'd had before.

"This is a terribly sad story," I said, hitting Jack in the back with the pamphlet. "Why would you give me this? Do you want to make me cry even more?"

"Lao Wu said it was inspirational." Jack shrugged.

I reopened the book and started reading again. By the time Xi realized opium wasn't going to solve his problems, he was already addicted. His health began to deteriorate at an even faster rate. In 1877, when his province was hit by a famine, two British missionaries from Hudson Taylor's group went to a nearby city to offer assistance. Thousands died from starvation, suicide, and disease, so the two missionaries brought food, money, and a new religion. When the famine finally ended, the missionaries used a very clever way to get the community thinking about this new faith. They conducted an essay contest in their newspaper, asking people to answer the question, "What's the most effective way to get rid of an addiction to opium?" This got Xi's attention. He knew a thing or two about opium, and he desperately needed money to buy more of it. He decided to enter the contest four times, under four different names. He won three out of the four prizes.

Reluctantly, he and his brother-in-law went to one of the missionary's houses in Pingyang to collect his money from a Mr. Hill. He'd heard all sorts of rumors about the missionaries and their new religion.

"As daylight banished darkness, so did Mr. Hill's presence dissipate all the idle rumors I had heard," he said. "All sense of fear was gone; my mind was at rest. I beheld his kindly eye and remembered the words of Mencius: 'If a man's heart is not right, his eye will certainly bespeak it.' That face told me I was in the presence of a true, good man."

I stopped reading for a moment, and rubbed my hands over my face. When I was a child, I'd heard of people my father described as being of the "Jesus religion." In fact, there was an old, abandoned church where they'd met in a nearby village about two miles from my home. I remember walking by it for the first time and saying, "Oh, what is this?"

Though it was beautiful, it was deserted and one of the walls had fallen in. My friends made fun of it, but I never went in. It seemed dangerous and very mysterious.

"Some foreigners used to be there," they told me. Of course, anything related to foreigners was infinitely fascinating. As the Chinese term for foreigners, *yang guizi*, literally means "foreign devil," the first Christian church I ever saw was automatically related to devils because it was related to Americans. We went near it and looked at it with as much curiosity as if it had been a spacecraft from another planet.

I smiled as I thought of that old building, perhaps the only smile I hadn't faked in months. I put the book down and stretched as I looked at the backs of my classmates. They were working diligently while I was reading about an opium addict. *This is how far I've fallen*, I thought.

Nevertheless, I turned the page and kept reading. Xi took his prize money, and even began working for the missionaries, translating the New Testament into Chinese to use as religious tracts. When he got to the story of the crucifixion, he fell on his knees and wept. He felt he'd finally found the answer he'd been searching for his entire life. It wasn't found in Confucianism or the Chinese classics. Mysteriously, it was found in the story of a man named Jesus, who had been punished and killed by the government for something he didn't do.

A chill came over me and I looked up from the book. I felt like it was written specifically for me, like it was whispering deep truths to me with each new page. There were so many beautiful sentences in it, phrases I'd never heard used together, and ideas I'd never contemplated.

I reached down into my backpack and grabbed a notebook I used to use for my English studies. I opened it, drew a dark line after my old English notes, and wrote, "Notes from the Xi Zizhi Book." Then I began to copy some of the beautiful sentences I'd been reading.

I copied a couple of pages of the quotes and then went back

to the book. I was eager to discover what would happen to Xi after he converted to Christianity. After all, he was a drug addict. Would Christianity be enough to help him finally escape both his sadness and his addiction?

"I tried to break it off by means of native medicine, but could not; by use of foreign medicine, but failed," I read. "At last I saw, in reading the New Testament, that there was a Holy Spirit who could help men. I prayed to God to give me His Holy Spirit. He did what man and medicine could not do; He enabled me to break off opium smoking."

A tear trickled down my cheek, and a student sitting a few rows in front of me turned around at the sound of me sniffling. When she saw me, she rolled her eyes and turned back around quickly. My crying in the back of the classroom was no longer interesting. This time, however, I was not crying from the desperation that had become my constant companion. Instead, I cried in relief. There was hope. His name was Jesus? The Holy Spirit? How did they relate to the "Heavenly Grandpa" I'd prayed to in my youth? I jotted down some notes, wiping the tears from my eyes so they wouldn't land on my notebook. I was so overcome with emotion and confusion, I couldn't write quickly enough to get back to the story.

After Xi believed, he was so much of a changed man that he changed his name to *Shengmo*, which meant "conqueror of demons." He stopped using drugs, he set up gospel drug prevention centers, and he helped rescue hundreds of thousands of people.

I was in awe. This man had created real, lasting change—not just for himself but for others. That's all I had ever wanted to do. When I was a poor elementary school kid being ridiculed, I wanted equality and respect, and I figured the only way to effect change was to become wealthy. When I was in high school, I wanted fairness and equal opportunity for all people, so I figured the only way to pull that off was to become prime minister. When I made it to college, I wanted democracy and freedom. By this time, I figured the force of my own ambition and personality would be enough to transform my community into a better place.

But none of my grand plans worked. In fact, the people I had supposedly changed had betrayed me! That was the real reason I felt so desperate. That was the real reason I'd been scheming on the best way to kill President Ming and then myself. Nothing changed. It *never* changed. My life, my nation, and my community were going to be the same forever. And it didn't matter how much I tried or how much inequality, unfairness, or injustice existed in this world. I'd never see anything actually change.

Up until that moment, I had thought, *Wow, I am the man who can lead China. I'm a good guy, a righteous man who can lead people in a better direction.* But the beautiful sentences in the book I'd been reading had penetrated me to my core. Suddenly, I felt the weight of the darkness in my own heart.

I shut the booklet, laid it on my notebook, and glanced at the deputy secretary who was still grading my work. Just the sight of him—this Communist official—pierced my heart. I'd proclaimed to everyone that I was against corruption, but I had also previously tried to bribe the deputy party secretary. I thought I was working for freedom, but I had also sealed the classrooms in my college, forbidding others the liberty to choose whether to join us. I was for fairness, but I had stolen food as a very young child. I was for kindness, but I had decided to murder someone.

Reading the book was like taking a bright light and shining it on my life. The invisible man had become visible, and I didn't like what I saw. I wasn't a righteous leader; I wasn't even really a good guy. In fact, I was days and maybe one chemistry lesson away from committing murder.

I looked at the clock and realized my time in the classroom was coming to a close. I'd spent my entire time reading and copying the "beautiful sentences" into my notebook.

"Do you need this back?" I tapped Jack on the back. "Or can I keep it for a while?"

"I don't want it back," he said, waving me off. "I don't believe in that stuff."

• • •

The next morning I scurried through campus. The sun had already been up for an hour, but the dew still stubbornly clung to the blades of grass like tiny crystals. In a plaza near a fountain, dozens of students were beginning their day with tai chi and qi gong, moving together like a flock of geese as they stretched a new day into being. Two students lugged heavy backpacks into a teashop as the store owner swept the steps, preparing for the day.

"Lao Wu," I said, knocking on the door of his apartment in the foreign expert regiment building. The foreigners were a privileged group of professors because the university provided a laundry service as well as cooks for them. Their building was also nicer than the others, newer, and with more accommodations.

"What's gotten you out of bed so early?" He smiled as he opened the door. "Come to see if I had any more bananas?"

He was dressed but his hair was mussed, and he held a steaming cup of coffee.

"I'm sorry I came so early, but I need to talk to you," I said.

He motioned toward his couch, and I plopped down onto it. "I need to talk to you about the biography of Xi Zizhi."

His voice lowered like we were suddenly in a library. "Oh? Where'd you get it?"

As an American, he'd signed an agreement not to evangelize the students, though he was allowed to answer any questions honestly. Because the students were interested in all things American, Lao Wu created opportunities to arouse curiosity among the students about Christianity. He hosted Christmas and Easter celebrations and always discreetly answered any questions that came up.

"Jack gave it to me last night," I said. "He said you gave it to him."

"Oh, right," Lao Wu responded. "I remember giving that to him. Want some coffee? I made a fresh pot." He jumped out of his seat and disappeared into the kitchen area. I'd never talked to him about Christianity because I'd bought into Karl Marx's theory, which I had been taught my entire life: religion was the opiate of the masses.

"He thought it might help me."

"It might help you do what?" Lao Wu asked, cautiously.

"To be happy, to be less depressed!" I exclaimed.

"So, you're saying," he prompted, "it worked?"

I laughed when I responded. "It worked! I've seen the light!"

Lao Wu came out of the kitchen and handed me a cup of coffee. "What exactly do you mean?" he asked when he sat back down. "Tell me about this 'light.'" He took a sip of his own coffee.

"I believe in Jesus!" I gushed. "I feel like the birds are singing just for me. I feel like God Himself is putting His arms around me. I feel joy where there used to be only sorrow."

Lao Wu's eyes narrowed. He'd known me for over a year, but he'd only seen me raid his pantry and play moderately good defense on the basketball court. I'd never shown an interest in spiritual things.

"Well, that certainly is interesting news," he said, noncommittally. I suppose he wondered whether I had actually undergone a conversion to Christianity or if I was some sort of spy working for the government.

"How do I sign up?"

"You mean, how do you join Christianity?" Lao Wu laughed in spite of himself.

"Yes, how do I formally become a Christian?" I asked, very earnestly. "To join the Communist League, you have ceremonies. First you join the youth party, and then you're sworn into the Communist Party. Is there some sort of ceremony?"

"Let's don't get ahead of ourselves," he said, still very calm. "Why don't you write down what you're feeling? Just take a moment to reflect on what happened as you read the book."

Lao Wu flashed a wary smile, but I didn't really notice his hesitation. Because I wasn't familiar with Christianity, I didn't understand the inherent dangers that came with being a Christian in China. I simply knew I'd been bitter, sad, and ready to commit murder. Then, after I believed in Jesus, I wasn't.

"Great idea," I said as I grabbed my satchel and stood up. As I walked toward the door, I noticed bananas sitting on his counter. I grabbed one, peeled back the skin and took a bite, then looked at Lao Wu.

"May I?" I said, my mouth full of the fruit. I'd never had such exotic fruit in my hometown growing up.

"Sure," he said, as he opened the door for me.

"When I'm done, I'll come right back!"

I walked across the campus, my head spinning with thoughts of my new faith. Even though I'd made that journey many times, the stroll felt different now. I wasn't alone. A loving God was aware of me.

"Good morning." I beamed at my two special agents whom I noticed lurking behind a bush next to the building. They'd been waiting for me. "How are you today?"

They looked completely shocked that I would acknowledge them. They were supposed to immobilize me with fear, but they didn't have that kind of power over me anymore. When I arrived back at my room of confinement, my deputy was already there waiting.

"Glad you finally decided to make it," he said. "Quit delaying, and get in there to write your confession."

"Sure!"

The deputy tilted his head, completely baffled at my quick agreement. I slipped into the room, got out my stack of paper, and began writing. I would have plenty of time to write my so-called apology for my time as a student protestor. But first, I had to write something else.

"Last night, while reading a book, I believed in God," I wrote. Even as I wrote the sentence, my heart felt like it was going to leap out of my chest. My pencil flew over the paper, recording all of my many thoughts about my whole world, now that it had become more vibrant. Suddenly I had become aware there was a supernatural power, and that knowledge had miraculously replaced the hatred and anger I'd previously harbored against so many people. I smiled as I thought of the Communist special agent standing outside my door. *He just doesn't know about Jesus*, I thought, as I continued to write. Even the animosity I had for President Ming disappeared. And I even felt compassion for my former friend Joseph, who had publicly advocated that I be killed. As I finished my first page, I realized I was humming.

The guard knocked on my door and barked, "What are you doing in there?"

"Sorry!" I said, and continued scrawling out my spiritual thoughts. Pretty soon, I'd need to continue my forced confession so my agent would have something to grade. I'd been under surveillance for three months now, but a joy bubbled in my soul that couldn't be quenched by any government guard.

When dinnertime came, I almost sprinted to the cafeteria to find Heidi. I couldn't wait to talk to her about my conversion. When I came through the door, my eyes found her. She was sitting at the table where we usually sat, alone. She waited for me every night, in a solemnly sweet ritual.

"Hello!" I said warmly as I sat down beside her.

"What happened to you?" she immediately asked. She was used to me oozing around the campus, head down, shoulders slumped.

"You won't believe it," I answered. "I am a Jesus follower."

She looked at me blankly. "Really?"

"Yes, I feel like a mountain has been removed from my chest," I explained. "Instead of sorrow, I feel joy."

"Are you sure it's 'joy' and not a fever?" She laughed. "I can take you to the infirmary, if you like."

I could tell by her sarcasm that she'd rather talk about anything else. But I persisted. "I've never felt better in my life!"

"Religion's for the weak, the vulnerable," she said, more seriously. "You're much smarter than that."

"I read this book," I said as I pulled it out and laid it on the cafeteria table. "It's about a man whose life was changed. He used to be sad and depressed too, but then he believed in Jesus."

"Don't you see?" Heidi said, with as much gentleness as she could muster. "People who are full of angst are not strong-minded. This man was weak, so he accepted this crazy religion." She looked at me like I was sick, lying in a hospital bed and clinging to a false hope of recovery. "You don't have to follow his path."

"But I have so much love in my heart now," I explained. "I don't feel any bad feelings toward President Ming or Joseph."

"Why not?" She practically spat out the words. "They ruined your life!" Implicit was the very distinct message that they'd ruined her life as well. After all, she and I had grown closer over the past few months, even as my other friends moved away from me. "The President has no backbone, and Joseph is an opportunist. The smoke over Tiananmen Square hadn't even blown away by the time he had betrayed you, taken your position as a student leader, and advocated for your death in the newspaper!"

"These guys also need to find a new life in Christ. God can help them," I said. "He can save them too."

"Xiqiu, listen to me." She slammed her hand against the table, and the water in my glass rippled. She picked up my book. "You are an intelligent man. You don't need this kind of intellectual crutch, and you don't need to love people who want you dead."

"So . . . you're saying you'll read it?" I asked, with a sly smile.

"You believed in Jesus last night, and already you're an evangelist?"

Reluctantly, she dropped the book into her backpack.

"Let's just eat," she said, rolling her eyes, and we ate our meal in silence.

• • •

The next day, I knocked on the door to Lao Wu's home after one of his classes. When he opened the door, he motioned for me to come in. "I was expecting you." He smiled.

"I wrote it all down," I said, plopping five pages onto his coffee table. "Just like you asked."

Lao Wu sighed, put on his reading glasses, and picked up the papers. I felt nervous as he turned the first page, then the second. Were my feelings enough to justify a conversion? Was I, as Heidi claimed, simply being emotional because I'd gotten so lonely? But by the time my teacher flipped over the last page, he looked up at me with tears in his eyes.

"So, can I join?" I asked.

"Sure," he responded, as he knelt down on the floor. "The first thing is to ask for God's help—for God's guidance."

"Oh, right," I said. "We need to ask for a directive from God." I understood what I needed to do, but I didn't have the right language to wrap around my ideas.

I spoke of spiritual things using the only language I knew. Because communism demanded we ask for "directives," or authoritative instruction, from our government, I wanted a directive from God Himself. I wanted to be saved.

There, in his apartment, Lao Wu led me in a prayer.

"God," I said. "This is life to me. I want to become a follower. I want to become Your child."

I remembered one of the beautiful sentences in Xi Zizhi's book.

"If anyone is in Christ, he is a new creation, the old has gone, the new has come."

The "Heavenly Grandpa" I prayed to years ago was the one who made new creations.

10

"In the final analysis, character is more important than reputation," I wrote in my new journal. Not only did I copy the "beautiful sentences" from the little booklet Jack had given me, I also wrote down thoughts and new ideas from my devotionals. "One's reputation may be good when one's character is not. The opposite may also be true."

I used my new theology like a sword, or—considering my lack of knowledge—like a chopstick. Maybe even a toothpick.

I didn't have a Bible, so I relied on Lao Wu's English translation. I desperately wanted to share the gospel with everyone I knew, but it was hard to tell my Chinese friends about this new gospel that I could only read in English. Of course, that didn't stop me. In the most basic terminology, I told people about Jesus.

Though people weren't scurrying to hear my spiritual thoughts, they did notice a change in my demeanor. I used to hang my head low and avert my eyes when my old friends passed by. When they treated me like I was invisible, I simply disappeared into the background. Now that I no longer felt the shame of that punishment, I walked tall, shoulders back, head high.

"What are you smiling about?" a student asked when I walked into the English department. My deputy hadn't arrived yet, so I had a little time before I'd be forced to sit silently while he graded my work. "The last time I saw you, your head was down on the desk and you were crying."

"Yeah," another student said, "I think I failed my test because your sobbing was such a distraction."

I walked to the chalkboard, picked up a piece of chalk from the tray, and wrote "JOHN 3:16" right in the middle of the board. "I want everyone to know I became a Jesus follower." I tapped on the board with the chalk, and a little cloud of chalk dust tickled my nose. Only about ten students had gathered in the class early, but all ten stared at me with blank looks. Eventually, they all looked back down at their books and study materials in silence. "So, if anyone wants to go to church with me," I added as I walked back to my desk, "I'm going on Sunday!"

A few minutes later Heidi, who still sat in the front with all of the girls, walked back to my desk. She had a funny look on her face, and I figured she might be finished with dating me. After all, it hadn't been the easiest road.

"I'll go to church with you," she said, with a very sly smile.

"You want to do opposition research?"

"Not quite," she responded, her eyes looking down at the floor. Then she looked up, smiled, and said, "I'm a believer too."

She gently placed the biography of Xi Zizhi on my desk and walked back to her seat. Apparently, Heidi had read the book. As I watched her very calmly settle back into her seat, I wanted to scream with joy! God didn't let her be my persecutor for very long. I'd never known a Christian, yet suddenly I was dating one. I *was* one!

I kept living my normal life of forced confessions and surveillance, but my sense of drudgery was replaced by elation. During the days, I tried to memorize some of the English translation of Lao Wu's Bible, and at night I'd pray before dropping off to sleep. One night, however, I got out a pen and paper to do one last thing.

"Dear Dad," I wrote in my next letter home. "I just wanted

you to know that I have become a Jesus follower." I had no idea what he'd say or how he'd feel, but I couldn't wait to tell him. My only regret was that I couldn't tell Mom.

* * *

The next morning, I went to the campus post office to mail the letter and pick up my campus mail. I thumbed through the stack on my way to the garbage can. But I stopped when I noticed an in-campus letter from the English department. I stopped, slid my finger under the seal, and opened a request from the deputy dean of the English department for an in-person meeting.

I left the post office and headed to the administration building, wondering what would require a meeting. Was I being reinstated to my classes? Or had I done something else wrong? Normally, one would call, make an appointment, and meet him at a scheduled time. However, my mind began racing as soon as I read his letter. I couldn't wait for normal protocols. After all, I was a social outcast. How much worse could my reputation be? When I got to his office, I knocked on the door, let myself in, and held up the folded letter.

"I came just as soon as I received this," I explained.

"Yes," he said, peering over his glasses and looking at me very intently. "Please." He motioned to a chair sitting alongside the wall.

I walked over and lowered myself into it without a word. The last time I had a conversation with him, he was helping me plan the student protests. Now he was stopping me from getting into grad school.

"Tell me," he said, in a very caring tone. "Are you okay?"

It felt as if he were asking me a trick question. Why would he suddenly care about my well-being? "Yes, sir," I responded. "I'm fine, actually. Thank you for asking," I said, trying to make my voice light and unconcerned, but my back stiffened in the chair.

"The reason I asked is that you've always been a very good

student. You have always been a class monitor, until now, of course. You were a very effective student leader, and you made wonderful grades."

I didn't move as I waited for the bad news. Surely, he was simply warming me up to lower the hammer on me. My mind raced. What could he possibly be taking away from me now? I exhaled slowly and tried to calm myself.

"Thank you," I said. "I've been very pleased with my grades." *Back when I was allowed to earn actual grades*, I thought.

"What I'm trying to say is that the university isn't going to deal too harshly with you." Then he smiled and walked over to my chair. "Everything is going to be okay for you. Don't fret."

I ran my hand over my knee, rubbing out an imaginary crease. For three months none of my classmates except Heidi would be seen talking to me. Occasionally, someone would glance at me sympathetically. So I was a little perplexed by the sudden concern of the deputy dean of the English department. It just didn't make sense.

However, I could tell by the quick pat on the back he gave me that the meeting was over. He shook my hand and sent me on my way. I walked back to my dorm, trying to process the purpose of the meeting. If he were really concerned for me, he could've asked the surveillance agents to give me some space. Or, even better, he could've let me attend classes again. Surely it wasn't just a little pep talk. As I pondered the interaction, I saw Joseph and some former friends around the corner of a building. He was laughing, as if someone had said something terribly clever.

"Joseph," I called out. He stopped, completely stunned. It was the first time I had spoken to him in public for months.

"Aren't you still under surveillance?" He laughed. The people in his group stifled laughter. "Or did your special agents finally get sick of you?"

"Listen," I said. "Something strange has happened. I think the deputy dean just gave me a pep talk."

"Come here." He pulled me aside, away from the ears of the group. I could tell I'd piqued his interest.

"I was told he needed to see me," I explained. "But when I got there, he encouraged me and my school work."

"Don't you get it?" Joseph asked.

This was our first real talk in months. Before Tiananmen Square, I was the leader and Joseph was my faithful assistant. He helped me plan activities, he took orders, and he even switched English names with me so that I could be the more easily pronounced "Bob." Yet here he was, condescension dripping from his tongue. He acted like he would rather be doing anything in the world other than talking to me. His group of friends—who used to be my group of friends—waited for him as we talked.

"Everyone is talking about you now," he said.

"What are they saying?"

"That you're strange."

"So, now I'm not an 'enemy of the people,' I'm just odd?"

"More than odd," he stressed. "You changed too much, too fast. You went from depression to laughter."

"I became a Christian," I beamed. "I've changed!"

"Well, they think you're," he paused a moment, then looked back at his group of friends, "mentally disabled. People are saying the university put too much pressure on you and then," he held up his hand and snapped his fingers, "you lost it."

I wanted to speak harshly to Joseph, to remind him of the days when the campus was talking about me because they supported me as I led them in a just cause. But when I looked at his face as he criticized me, I knew he was simply relaying the truth. Joseph let out a little chuckle. "Listen, I bet the deputy dean was just making sure you weren't about to kill yourself. That's all."

When Joseph said the words, "kill yourself," perspiration formed immediately on my forehead. *How close I came*, I thought, as I watched him walk away.

When I got back to my room, I pulled out my little notebook and began writing down my thoughts. "Many times in history, good people have been harmed by fake statements, slander, and false accusations. Their reputation was bad even though their character was good. In reality, the only thing we can control is our character, so that should be my primary concern. An active hatred, animosity, or a simple misunderstanding may soil my reputation. I want a good reputation, and for the most part it would seem a good reputation follows good character." I paused a second, as I thought about my predicament. "So my primary concern must always be character . . . what I do even when nobody's looking."

When Sunday came, I realized I'd invited half my class to go to church with me. I got dressed in my best clothes and walked to the government-sanctioned church. Lao Wu and some of the other American teachers worshiped there, and I couldn't wait to see what a real Christian church was like.

"I'm heading to church," I announced to a group of students sitting in a restaurant near the student dining hall, reading newspapers. To my surprise, a few people actually put down their morning paper and joined me. Later, we passed another restaurant, where I noticed a few other acquaintances. "Would you like to go to church with us?" I asked. "It could change your life, like Jesus changed mine."

Sure, I was the not-so-flattering talk of the campus. But by now I was used to being unpopular. By the time we got to the government-sanctioned service, there were about ten students who probably went to see what kind of "happiness spell" had been cast over me. Part of me wondered if they went to the church with me for a deeper, culturally significant reason. Students across the nation were grieving after the Tiananmen Square massacre, which set them both politically and emotionally adrift. They'd been taught Marxism was the only way to peace and prosperity, but had lost faith in it when those students lost their lives. Those tanks didn't force China's brightest and most culturally engaged students back into conformity. Those tanks set them on a course to find truth.

Much to my delight, some of the students who went to church with me that morning gave their hearts to Christ. I couldn't believe that these people, many of whom had pretended I didn't exist, now believed in God. This, of course, made me even more enthusiastic about sharing the news about Christ to my friends. The next weekday night, I went to the English department with a plan.

"Jack," I said to the guy who sat in front of me during my nightly grading. "I appreciate you giving me that book."

"At least you're not crying all the time now," he said, barely turning around.

"Want it back?"

"I'm not interested," he snapped.

"Well, let me tell you about the message in the book. It's really good news."

That's how Jack became a believer. The students who'd attended church with me told others about Jesus too. Many students on the campus believed in Christ. In fact, so many students from all areas of studies became followers of Jesus that this period of time was known as the Liaocheng Revival. We were considered to be one of the first generations of Chinese Christian students.

• • •

I was reveling in the goodness of the gospel as I walked back to the dorm from the English department that night when someone grabbed my arm.

I whipped around to see who'd gotten me. For so long, I'd been terrified of the special agents lurking behind every shadow. During my months of seclusion, the university didn't even let me go home to see my family. It was a pretty scary and demoralizing time. But when the fall semester arrived, I was allowed to go back to the classroom. This allowed me to relax a bit. I didn't look out for the agents, or think of them as much. On rare occasions, I'd catch a glimpse of them off in the distance. They were always just staring, like dogs waiting for the command to attack. They scared me, of course, but I had no other choice than to just keep going and live my life. And thankfully, after a while, they seemed to disappear.

Until now. The hand wrapped around my arm firmly so I couldn't pull loose.

"Stop it," I yelled, looking up to see one of the agents who'd been assigned to me. It was the older, thicker one, the one who looked like he could snap my spine with one hand. Behind him stood his cohort, smirking like a cat who had finally caught his mouse. I knew my life would somehow end up like this, getting snatched without committing any real crime. I'd feared this moment for many months, and yet as I stood in their grip, calmness overcame me.

"Xiqiu," the thin one said very sternly. He hiked up his pants, which were already too high on his waist, and revealed shoes that were disturbingly shiny. "We need to talk to you about your recent behavior."

"What do you want to know?" I asked, looking around to see if I'd have any witnesses. We were standing beneath a tree near the sidewalk on the way to my dorm. They'd caught me just as I was about to go into my building.

"Did you write some sort of Bible passage on the blackboard in the English department?" he said, through impossibly thin lips.

"I did," I said. "I became a Christian!"

"Don't you know that's illegal?"

"There are state-run churches," I said. "Why would it be illegal to join one?"

"Well, you're a university student," he said. "Don't you know the Communist Party forbids students from converting?"

I sighed and the agent released his grip on my arm upon seeing my resignation. There were so many government restrictions I'd need a chart the size of the Beijing phone book to keep up with them all. Why would I pay attention to rules governing, of all things, Christianity? I'd never cared about it before. I took a handkerchief out of my pocket and wiped my forehead.

"Christianity is a danger to national security," the older one said. "It's the party's policy that all university students be socialists."

"But this isn't about politics," I said. "It's a spiritual decision. Do you know the gospel?"

"No!" He put his hand over my mouth for a moment. "And I don't want to know. You shouldn't share Christianity with me, and you shouldn't share it with the other students."

"Honestly," I said, plaintively. "I didn't know."

"Religion and politics are always intertwined," he scolded. "Do you realize you were a counterrevolutionary student leader and now you're going around asking other people to join you in illegal religious activities?"

I swallowed hard, trying to maintain my composure.

"You could lose your student status if you don't stop." He sneered. "You'd be farming potatoes for the rest of your life."

Both agents turned their backs to me and began walking away. After taking a few steps, the thin one turned around and added, "And if you don't stop, there's no telling what else could happen to you."

11

"I don't want to be a potato farmer," I said, sitting in Lao Wu's home with the other new Christians the next morning. I took a sip of hot tea and scalded my tongue, but that didn't hurt as bad as the thought of going back home without a degree. "Did you know telling people about Jesus is illegal?" I set the mug back on the coffee table and flopped back into the soft cushions of the sofa. The small living room was packed with wide-eyed students, including Heidi, Jack, and about a dozen other people. We'd begun meeting every week for Bible study, but this felt different than when we'd hung out there in the past. It felt dangerous.

"It's not technically illegal," Lao Wu said, moving a gigantic bowl of popcorn and picking up the newspaper it had been sitting on. "The authorities are just panicking."

"I'm panicking," Jack said.

Lao Wu traced his finger over the newspaper before landing on an article just below the fold. "Listen to this." He put on his reading glasses and cleared his throat. "In Beijing, students now comprise over 25 percent of government-sanctioned Three Self Patriotic Movement churches."

"It doesn't feel like we're an epidemic," said Heidi. I looked at her, sitting in the apartment listening so earnestly to Lao

Wu. Gratitude overcame me. I was thankful to have someone like her in my life, and even more thankful that she had also come to know the Lord. But in the back of my mind, I worried I wouldn't be able to make a high enough salary to provide a nice lifestyle for her. Even though she came from a peasant village like I did, she deserved more than that. She was kind, beautiful, smart, and courageous. Every time I looked at her, however, I worried if I could take her as my wife considering all the problems I was facing.

"Reports indicate more Chinese students are becoming Christians than joining the Communist Party," Lao Wu read.

We sat for a moment in silence. It seemed both shocking and perfectly natural that this religion—so foreign and unknown— was spreading like a fire through the various campuses. "So, it's legal to be a Christian, but illegal to talk about it?" I asked.

"And doesn't the Bible tell us to spread the good news?" Heidi asked. "Just like Jack told Bob?"

"Hey," he protested. "I was just trying to stop Bob's blubbering."

"We just need to be careful," Lao Wu said, his sober tone quieting the room. In silence, we felt the gravity of our situation, and one by one we bowed our heads. "Let's pray."

From that point on, our college Christian group went "underground." Though we still told people about Jesus, we didn't do it in such obvious ways. We attended church, but we didn't go in one large group. Instead, one of our members went through the halls of the dorms on Sunday morning, knocking on the doors of the Christian students. We had a special knock, a rat-a-tat-tat, which alerted our friends that it was time to attend worship. Instead of attending the more popular late services, we worshiped during the early morning. Three knocks meant to meet down by the riverside instead. Also, we didn't publicly use the word "God" or "Jesus," but instead referred obliquely to "father" and "brother." In fact, we stopped using the phrase "Bible study" altogether. We began calling our Bible study groups by three repeating letters. Our guys' group read the Bible together, so we called ourselves "BBB." The ladies focused mainly on prayer, so we called them "PPP." Also, we no longer walked directly to Lao Wu's apartment for Bible study. Instead, we took a back way into the foreign expert regiment area and climbed over a wall to reach his place unnoticed.

We did all we could to spread the gospel. Once when we were at church we saw our friend Craig, who was a dear Australian missionary friend. He was always trying to connect us with others to make sure new Christians received good teaching, theology, and support.

"There's a new Christian I'd love for you or Heidi to call," he said, slipping a business card into my hand. "He works at a travel firm, and I don't think anyone at his agency knows of his faith. So be discreet."

"When am I not discreet?" I asked. He looked at me and laughed.

And so we gradually spread the gospel from one person to another. Even though we had to sneak around, my new faith made my college life full of joy and gladness. I wasn't completely sure how my dad felt about my newfound religion, as he never really addressed my Christianity in any of his letters. Even though I kept him updated about all of the activities of our Christian group, he always responded in the same way as he did when I told him about Heidi. "Just make sure your main focus is on academics," he would vaguely respond.

Though I took that as tacit disagreement, I obeyed my father. As college came to a close, I had pretty good grades, though it didn't really matter. No matter how much I studied, the Communist Party in the university conspired to keep me out of graduate school in international studies and I was unsure of my future. Excitement—and anxiety—permeated the atmosphere of the campus as academic life began to wind down. Students jockeyed

to find the best possible positions for themselves after graduation and went through back channels to get good jobs back in
their hometowns. Mainly, I regretted I'd have to leave the close
bonds of fellowship with my new Christian friends and Lao Wu.

• • •

"What are you going to do after graduation?" a friend asked
me one day close to the end of school. "Do you know whom to
bribe to get a good job?"

"Bribery's not for me," I responded. I'd tried it before I'd
given my life to Christ, but even then it had felt wrong.

"I'll keep you in mind if I ever need to buy some potatoes."
He laughed.

"I don't want to be a farmer, but I don't want to be a teacher
either." For as long as I could remember, my goals were pretty
simple: get my degree, go to graduate school, and make money
to send home to my family.

"Oh, that's right. You're a troublemaker so you can't get into
grad school," he said. "Why aren't you rushing around? You have
more to lose than anyone else by not angling for a better future."

"My future's not dependent on bribery or the whims of a
university," I said. Though I knew this last-minute maneuvering would affect paychecks for the rest of our lives, I didn't feel
compelled to rush around. For the weeks leading up to the end
of school, peace surrounded me, even though I didn't have a
clear directive.

"Okay," he said, chuckling. "Well, I've got to go deliver five
bribes this afternoon!"

I walked back to my dorm with a heavy, confused heart. I
knew God was all I needed, but I wasn't sure what that meant
for the next steps of my life. I also didn't understand why God
would shut the door to graduate school when that's all I'd ever
wanted to do. A large stack of international textbooks sat on top
of my bed, and I plopped them onto the floor as I made room

for myself. I'd studied these books on my own time, preparing for graduate school. It felt a little like it'd been stolen from me.

"Lord," I prayed aloud while burying my head in my pillow. "What would You have me do?"

I listened, but all I heard was the sound of people laughing outside my dorm room. A dog barked off in the distance. Friends chatted as they walked by my door. Life, in other words, was going forward as per usual for everyone but me. I sat up in my bed and looked out the window at all the happy people living their lives. Off in the distance, carrying a stack of papers, was the dean of my English department. I looked again. He was walking toward my dorm.

Hurriedly, I slipped on my shoes, ran my hand through my hair, and bolted down the stairs. Certainly, if anyone knew a good path for me to take, he'd know. He was very open-minded and had been supportive of the students' movement. However, after the massacre, he had to follow the official line. Behind the scenes, he'd invited me to his home and tried to persuade me to give up. "If we invited Gorbachev, Thatcher, and Reagan over here, do you think they could manage China as well as the Communist Party? Could they win the popular vote in China? Don't think of a Westernized China because we have our own historical tradition," he'd said.

But even though he thought I was too idealistic, I could tell he knew I'd been wronged. I ran down the stairs two at a time until I reached the main floor with a thud. Then I tried to slow down my breathing and walked sedately in his direction.

"Oh, hello!" I said as I neared him, acting surprised. "What brings you over to the dorms?"

"Everyone is filing last-minute recommendations. I got behind, so I'm hand-delivering some," he said. "What's next for you?"

"I can't go to graduate school to take the exam," I began. "Because of my . . . problems."

He gave a pained half-smile and placed his hand on my shoulder.

"Sorry, Xiqiu. I know how much you really wanted that post-grad degree."

"I heard there's another program, a double bachelor degree," I said. "Do you think I could qualify?"

His eyes were instantly filled with compassion and pity. "Well, the People's University of China recruits people with your academic background, but there's no way you could pull that off. It's one of the most prestigious universities," he said, clearly straining to keep incredulity out of his tone. "Which means it's also one of the most *exclusive*. You have to compete against other students nationwide just to take the exam."

"That's what I'd like to do," I said.

"It's not a matter of what you'd *like* to do," he said, much like a parent trying to protect me from unrealistic expectations. "You need to focus on what's *possible* for you to do."

"So . . ." I said, with a sheepish grin, "if I managed to pull it off, you'd give me a letter of recommendation?"

The dean laughed out loud. "Listen," he said quietly, after he collected himself. "I know you've gotten a raw deal here, but that doesn't mean you can expect a miracle. Students across the country have been studying for years to take this test, and they only select a few."

"But if I did . . ." I smiled, prompting him to relent.

"All right, sure," he said, tossing his hands up in the air. "Don't forget I warned you."

Few things clear the mind like desperation. As soon as the dean gave me this sliver of hope, I ran back up to my dorm room, packed my bags, and headed to Beijing. I had a friend there, who offered me a bunk and a quiet dorm room. Though my chances of succeeding were certainly improbable, at least I had a small window of opportunity. All I had to do to score well on the exam was to master English, Chinese literature, international relations, and political science. In four weeks.

No matter, I told myself. Education wasn't the most important aspect of my life anymore, and I trusted that God could help me get through this. If I was successful, I would get my bachelor's degree in law, which would be a nice continuation of my years of self-study and would give me the chance to do something to help change China's policies in some way. It would also help me make enough money to support my family back home. Though time was of the essence, I rolled out of bed every morning, got on my knees, and prayed for a couple of hours. I spoke openly and freely, laying my fears at God's feet, praising Him for revealing Himself to me through that booklet, and asking Him to show me mercy for my future goals and dreams.

Only then would I turn my attention to studying. Since I was already pretty strong on the other three subjects, I decided to focus on Chinese literature. Of course, this was no small task since China's prose, poetry, philosophy, and history spans over three thousand years. However, there's an ancient Chinese proverb that says, "One step at a time is good walking." So every day I took steps, memorizing until my head was so full of facts I thought it might explode.

One afternoon, I squinted my eyes and shut the book I'd been looking at for hours. The lines on the pages were running together. I got up, stretched my legs, and cracked the window open just a bit. I needed some air, a chance to breathe. *How can I compete with people who've been studying this stuff for years?* I wondered. No one regarded me as the student with the highest IQ. I was the troublemaker and the naïve idealist, not the scholar. "God, help me," I muttered under my breath as I walked to the mailbox for a distraction.

I got a stack of mail from the box and laid the letters on my friend's desk. But there, on the top, was the familiar handwriting of my father. That tiny piece of home caused tears to fill my eyes. I wiped them with my sleeve and opened the envelope.

"Dear Xiqiu," I began reading as I sunk down into a

comfortable chair away from all of my books. "Much has been going on here in our area." He told me of the weather, the local gossip, and any local construction. Then he added, "Also, I met with Zhou, and we've been having some interesting conversations."

Zhou was a legendary elder Chinese individual, about eighty or ninety years old, who had always been perceived as a wise and mysterious practitioner of feng shui and Chinese fortune-telling. As I sat there in that chair, however, it dawned on me why he was so famous. He was using parts of Deuteronomy, Proverbs, and other parts of the Old Testament to tell people things about construction and how to live. Since no one was familiar with the Bible, they believed he had access to age-old truths of which they'd never even heard.

Which, in a very real way, was true.

Was my father telling me he was now my brother in Christ? I folded the letter and placed it into one of my textbooks. *I'll get this out when I'm feeling down*, I thought as I got back to studying. Instead of feeling sorrow and stress as I had just minutes ago, I felt peace and joy.

● ● ●

When the day of the test finally arrived, my mind seemed to be completely blank. After so many weeks of cramming, would any of the information be there when I needed it? I got out my pencil, turned over the paper, read the first question, and breathed a sigh of relief. I knew the answer. I wrote out my response as neatly as I could before moving on to the next question. Thankfully, I knew the answer to it too. And the next. My pencil flew over the papers, one by one. It felt very supernatural, almost surreal, because I knew how to best answer every single question. It was almost like I had a photographic memory, because I could easily retrieve the necessary information from pages I'd read about Confucianism, Daoism, and Mohism. Plus, I already knew all the international studies answers because I'd prepared for that portion of the test since childhood. I tried not to laugh in delight or cry in relief as I wrote. And when my results came back, I knew God had delivered me.

"I was accepted," I said to the dean, after bursting into his office. "The college only accepted eighteen students, and I was number three!"

He leaned back in his chair and threw his head back in disbelief. "How did you manage this?"

"It was the Lord's grace," I said. That had to be the only explanation.

"Well, I'm sorry I doubted you, but no one else in our college got accepted," he said. "And they'd been studying for years!"

As news spread across the campus that I'd been accepted into this prestigious program, people marveled and said it was a miracle.

I was thrilled to tell the news to Heidi. She'd been so patient with me through my trials. Even when I worried I couldn't get my degree, she was right there by my side. Even when all of my other friends betrayed me, she remained loyal and true.

"I did it!" I yelled when I saw her across the cafeteria. I couldn't wait until we were actually next to each other. Plus, I wanted everyone to know. "I was accepted."

When she turned to face me, I saw her eyes narrow a bit in disbelief. "Really?" she asked as she walked closer to me. "You've already gotten the results?"

"Yes, I'm going to Beijing!"

She was thrilled that I no longer had to go back and teach. "That'll show Joseph and the others," she said. "Success is the ultimate revenge!"

I smiled. Heidi resented my friends' betrayal even more than I did.

But in spite of all that we'd been through, I just hoped our relationship could survive the distance.

12

By the time Heidi and I graduated in 1991, I'd managed to dodge many pitfalls. In spite of the university's efforts to thwart my educational goals, I was accepted into a program to get my bachelor's degree in law. And even after they attempted to silence me about my newfound faith, I'd managed to worship peacefully below their radar. The fears that I wouldn't be able to provide for a spouse and take Heidi as my wife were gone. I was so grateful at how things were working out for us, but I couldn't deny the issues in our relationship.

We fought. A lot. She didn't like the way I walked, she didn't like the way I chewed my food, and it sometimes felt like she just didn't like me. Of course, I sometimes did things to deserve her anger. Once, a group of us took a long-distance bus ride to tour the hometown of Confucius. The girls were taking too long to come down from their dorms, so my group of guy friends went on without them. Heidi was furious when she discovered she'd been left, and she and her friend went on a mission by themselves. Eventually, when she found me, I was eating lunch with an old friend from high school—a female friend—who happened to live in that city. Though there was nothing secret going on between us, Heidi was livid. She didn't say a word, but then again, she didn't have to. Her eyes spoke volumes from across the room and I knew I was in deep trouble.

Other times I didn't do anything to deserve her irritation, but we were cross with each other regardless. One time, it got so bad that I took a bus to the capital city of the province, got a hotel, and stayed there for a few days. As vice president of the student union, I was supposed to oversee the awards ceremony for Chinese Youth Day. Because of our fight and my need for space, I missed it. All was forgiven when I came back to my dorm and found my clothes were washed and neatly folded. I took the stacks of clothes to be an apology. Though the fighting never ceased, we never even considered breaking up.

After college, we reluctantly parted ways. She went back to her hometown to teach English in her local high school—at a salary of less than one dollar a day. I was headed to Beijing, the city I'd dreamed of since I was a kid. On the train to my new city, however, I prayed that the fighting between us would stop. Heidi had a temper, and I felt like I was walking on eggshells most of the time.

* * *

As the country rolled by outside just beyond the glass of my window, I opened up my Bible and smiled. It was a new one, a Chinese translation, which Lao Wu had smuggled in from Hong Kong. Even though I'd been a Christian an entire year, I'd never been able to read God's Word in my own language. This made it harder for me to communicate the gospel to other Chinese people, because it was hard to find the right words to express the Christian ideas easily. Though the Chinese version was not as elegantly translated as the English one, I noticed some of the phrasing was very familiar.

Where have I seen this language? I wondered as I turned the pages in my seat on the train.

I opened up my journal—the one I'd kept since reading the

biography of the Chinese intellectual in the back of the English department—and flipped to the first few pages. I remembered that the biography contained some of the most beautiful sentences I'd ever heard, which I had copied into my little book so I'd never forget.

I put my finger on one of the Scriptures that jumped out at me while I was reading, and flipped the pages in my journal. When I saw the similarity, I almost laughed out loud.

Almost all of those "beautiful sentences" from the biography were actually Scriptures. God's Word had resonated so thoroughly in my heart before I'd even heard His truth!

I shut both my Bible and my journal, gazed out the window, and felt a profound sense of peace. God was in control of my soul, my education, and my relationship with Heidi. When the train pulled into the station, I was about to officially begin life as a post-grad student at the People's University of China, and I couldn't wait.

The first order of business was to meet my roommates. I looked down at the documents the university sent to me upon acceptance. It looked like our dorm was located right in the middle of campus, so I headed in that direction. I hoped we would all get along. Though roommates didn't have to be my best friends, it helped if they were considerate of space and belongings . . . and didn't snore.

"Hello," I said, walking in with a suitcase in each hand. There were five of them, and they were also in the process of moving in. Empty cardboard boxes sat around the room, and they were already dividing up space.

"I'm Xiqiu," I said.

One by one, they introduced each other and gave me the lay of the land. I had three drawers in the chest of drawers—the bottom three—and the top bunk to sleep on. The bathroom and showers, which we shared with the whole floor, were down the hall, to the left. "What about this?" I asked, pointing to a rather small bookcase near the door. "May I have a shelf?"

One of the roommates, named Timothy, looked up from organizing one of his drawers. "That's fine with me. What is that?"

I was holding my Bible, which was not a regular sight for Chinese people. During the Cultural Revolution, the government destroyed any Bibles they could find, and imprisoned, tortured, or even killed the owners. Even after Mao died in 1976, Bibles were hard to find. And that was still true when I was in college and graduate school. Though it was legal to own one, Bibles couldn't be purchased. Most Bibles and religious materials were smuggled over the border in suitcases by courageous Americans and Brits, and then passed secretly to house church leaders, who distributed them sparingly.

"Oh, do you believe in the Jesus religion?" Timothy asked, as I slid the Bible on the shelf.

"Yes, I heard about Him when I was in college," I began. By the end of the story, they'd all heard the gospel message. Immediately, I was dubbed "the missionary," an affectionately derogatory nickname that, truth be told, was pretty accurate. Even though I was a very new Christian, I loved to tell everyone I met about the gospel. My new college campus in Beijing was full of people who hadn't met Christ. Yet. That night, I took a smaller Chinese language Bible and wrote a note to Timothy on the first blank page. "Dear Timothy, I hope this book blesses you. It is the Word of the Lord."

When I handed it to him, he flipped through a few of the pages and then put it in his desk drawer. This quiet roommate, who was intelligent and much taller than I was, instantly became my close friend because he loved to talk about current affairs and international relations. I was always thankful to meet someone who wanted to share their views on issues like elections in foreign countries. Even though he was raised in the countryside, where people generally don't bother too much with international politics, he was a well-informed conversationalist.

Though I appreciated my roommates, I couldn't wait to find other believers on campus. I didn't know who they were or where they were, but I was going to find them. When Sunday came around, I knew many believers across the city would be meeting in either government-sanctioned churches or house churches. I imagined them in their groups, raising their hands to the Lord, singing songs, and listening to the Word.

When my alarm went off, I quietly climbed out of bed, careful not to cause the bunk bed to creak, and dressed. I slipped on my shoes and cautiously turned the doorknob until I heard it click open. After I went out into the hallway, I managed to shut the door without waking anyone, and was thrilled at the fact that I was finally about to find other believers!

I wasn't sure where to go, so I meandered along the sidewalks through a leafy area of campus, past racks full of bicycles waiting for the day. A few early risers jogged around a large sports center and track in the middle of the campus. I walked by an empty basketball court, some flowering trees, and a statue of Confucius. The entire time I walked, I strained to hear singing emanating from any of the buildings. At first, I wanted to find a student group, but I would've settled for finding even a government-sanctioned church after walking for an hour. Though I didn't quite understand how a Christian church could operate under the thumb of the Chinese government, I was hungry enough for the fellowship of believers that I would've tried it. When I got to the wall surrounding the campus, I walked through a gate leading out into the city of Beijing.

Should I turn left or right? I thought, pausing at the intersection. I turned right, walked along the sidewalk, and read all of the signs on the buildings. My mind went back to my first visit to Beijing, when we protested in Tiananmen Square. I shuddered when I thought of the tragedy, of the innocent lives lost, but then shoved it from my mind. I walked for miles, taking in the scenery. Bicyclists wove in and out of traffic with baskets full of groceries. Apartment buildings with laundry hanging out of the windows towered over the city. Supermarkets teemed with people. Though I got to see much of the city, my feet hurt and my heart was heavy by the end of the day. I never saw one church.

"Oh, the missionary is back," my new roommate said as I opened the door and dropped my red backpack on the floor. The other roommates dramatically shushed each other, stopped talking, and then broke out into laughter. "No more talk about women!"

"I don't mind if you talk about girls." I smiled. "As long as you don't mind when I talk about Jesus."

"No, no, no," Timothy said from the top of a bunk, tossing a small pillow at me. "We know our joking offends your 'Christian sensibilities.'" He spoke of my faith like it was a milk allergy. "So we'll keep the coarse joking to a minimum and you keep the Christ stuff to yourself."

I picked up the pillow from the floor and threw it back up at him. "Yeah, that's improbable on both counts."

"A letter came for you," another roommate said, handing me a letter with Heidi's beautiful handwriting on it. I tore it open and began reading it.

"Let me see," Timothy said, trying to grab it.

I yanked the letter away at the last second, pulling it closer to my eyes.

"It must be from someone . . . important," another said, laughing at how I was protecting the letter.

"Dear Xiqiu," I read silently, while my new friends were trying to snatch it. "I really don't think this is working out. The distance is too great for our relationship to overcome."

"What's wrong," Timothy asked. "You look like you've seen a ghost."

Devastated, I grabbed my backpack and headed to the library.

If I was going to employ all of my rhetoric skills to convince Heidi she was my destiny, I was going to need some peace and quiet. "Distance shouldn't affect one's fate," I pleaded once I got settled at a library desk. I poured out my heart to her. The next morning, I went to the post office and prayed she would receive my message with an open heart.

Because this was before the instant communication of email and texts, I would have to wait days or maybe even weeks for her reply. After I dropped my letter into the mail, however, I tried to focus on my academic life. Also, I needed a spiritual family more than ever.

* * *

One day, I came back to my dorm and noticed that I wasn't the only person with relationship drama. Timothy was lying on the bed with his head buried under a pillow.

"Want to go for a walk?" I said, nudging him. "What's wrong? I know you too well for you to pretend that you're okay."

He opened up to me on our walk, explaining that his girlfriend broke up with him even though they had dated since college. He planned on marrying her, but she'd written him and broke the agonizing news that she had another man in her life. When I heard his heartbreak, I started talking to him about the gospel, using a little red book of the four spiritual laws that was in my pocket. Then I shared the good news about God's love.

He immediately broke down into tears, so we sat down on a stone wall in front of the main administration building. He had heard about the gospel before graduate school, but only in his heartbreak did it resonate in his soul.

"Are you ready to make a decision?" I asked.

"You know, I'd read about 'Christian people' before." When he said "Christian people," he used the English words instead of the Chinese words, which indicated that the only way to really find out about Christianity back then was through the missionary materials. "But the first time I really came into contact with any Christians was when I saw you and your college friends. I do find it's very true that you are a peculiar group."

I was crestfallen, believing this was an insult, a way to distance himself from the gospel because of my inadequacies.

"But," he added, "I want to join."

I was thrilled to have a believing friend in my graduate school, and even in my own dorm. However, I still ached for the fellowship of an actual church. "Where do you go to church?" I asked my American teacher after class one day. I assumed most American teachers were Christians and could give me some tips on how to connect with other believers.

"Well, there's a government-sanctioned church just two miles off campus," he said, rolling out a map on his desk. He pointed to a spot that indicated our university. "Look, we're here, and the church is . . . here." He drew a circle around the intersection. There it was, so close to where I had looked before. When I left the campus, I'd simply walked in the wrong direction.

The next Sunday, however, I knew exactly where to go. I walked to the edge of the campus and took a left. When I got to the next intersection, I took Xisinan Street and eventually saw a building that had a cross.

The Hadian Church was part of the "Three Self Patriotic Movement." Because the Communists feared pro-American sentiment growing alongside Christianity, they wanted their churches to have "self-governance, self-support, and self-propagation." This was abbreviated to Three Self Patriotic Movement, but it basically meant the government was keeping track of exactly what happened in the church. Mostly, I assumed, they wanted to prevent any subversive political messages from being taught from the pulpit, and to ensure churches would be loyal to the Communist Party.

When I walked in, I felt like I was home. There were people sitting in the congregation, many of them students, with Bibles opened in their laps, praying. I wanted to walk up to all of them and introduce myself, but I sat in a pew to focus on worship. I almost cried when the music began, and I listened intently to the sermon.

The preacher, Pastor Li, was around seventy years old, and the congregation listened to his every word. It was rare to see older Christians in China, and in the countryside churches believers are considered "elders" when they're in their twenties. But in the government-sanctioned churches, the Communists always selected the most elderly ministers to make sure the churches didn't attract young people. That method apparently didn't work here, because the church had a healthy number of students in the congregation. The following Sunday I traipsed to the service again, and sat near the middle so I could both hear the sermon as well as check out all the people.

That's when I overheard some students around me talking about a Bible study on Thursday night. My ears perked up at the thought of fellowship with other Christian students. All week, I prayed that I would meet some good friends so I wouldn't feel so lonely at grad school. When Thursday finally came, I walked to church, hoping that there'd be a good turnout. How surprised I was to open the door and see a few hundred students gathered together to worship God!

Most of the students were Chinese, with a few international students scattered around. People mingled, introduced themselves, and found their seats as the service was about to begin. A younger preacher named Pastor Feng approached the lectern, and I soon discovered he was an independent preacher the church had designated solely for the college students. He was full of passion, and spoke powerfully about the Scriptures.

Even though the church was government-sanctioned, I could tell that it taught the Bible and was obviously full of faithful believers. I began attending these Bible studies every week and soon was meeting other young people.

"I go to the People's University of China," I overheard some-one say to another.

"Me too!" I interjected, perhaps too quickly. A few others in our circle also attended the same university, so we made in-troductions and began talking about our hometowns and our current areas of study.

"Maybe we should have our own fellowship on campus," I suggested. "We could meet in different dorms, which would be a nice way to stay connected throughout the week."

Everyone readily agreed, and I got the feeling that many of the other students longed for Christian friendships too. Imme-diately, I set up fellowship groups in different dorms. As word got out, our numbers grew. That summer we received training from Campus Crusade to learn how to use the four spiritual laws and to learn how to pray with people if they wanted to believe in Jesus. It might sound rudimentary, but we were very new to Christianity and these tips for evangelism were won-derfully helpful. In fact, in August while I was visiting Heidi's hometown, I led her brother in the prayer to accept Christ to be his Savior and Lord. Then, in September, I shared the spiritual laws with another student who accepted Jesus.

I wrote down everything that happened in a small contact book, as a documentation of my new brothers and sisters in Christ. Though it was somewhat dangerous to record their names, I wanted to make sure I could stay in contact with other believers. And so I wrote in tiny letters and kept the book hid-den in my apartment at all times. By Christmas, my book had many more names in it, and we had a very strong fellowship. We met to pray, sing songs, study the Bible, and discuss how to evangelize the campus.

* * *

"Okay, everyone," I said, early one December evening in our dorm fellowship. "Our fellow students will be interested in Christianity, if only briefly, in a couple of weeks. We should use Christmas as a reason to tell other people about Jesus."

Since Chinese people were interested in foreign and exotic experiences, they sometimes went to Christmas services as a cultural curiosity and to be in a spiritual atmosphere, even if they weren't interested in the faith. Consequently, the government-sanctioned church always planned a very nice Christmas Eve service and invited everyone to come with a sign on the outside that said—in English—"Merry Christmas."

"We should invite everyone we know to the Christmas Eve service," a friend named Andrew said.

"And once they get there, we can hand out pamphlets in case they want to learn more," I added.

"But where can we find religious tracts around here?"

"Let me see if I can work on it." I knew of an elderly Christian couple who lived near campus. Because they had many connections with international students, they were a hub of information, news, and materials that they freely provided. Everyone was excited about the possibilities, and we ended the night with a prayer.

"God," Andrew prayed. "Please help us shine your light on this campus."

The next day, I went to visit the elderly couple, who welcomed me into their home for dinner and served me a delicious, home-cooked meal. While I was there, they told me stories about persecution. The wife had gotten in trouble for following a famous preacher in Beijing who'd refused to join the government church and was imprisoned for eighteen years. Because they'd been in school in America, they had contact with many international Christians. Their house was always full of believers from all over the world, so the couple collected and distributed religious materials. Their house was a virtual library of the underground Chinese church.

"Do you have anything we could hand out at the Christmas Eve service?" I asked.

"I think I've got just the thing," she said. "Let me go check."

The next day, I rushed into our dorm meeting holding a box of tracts. "You won't believe what I have!" I said, putting the box on the coffee table. Andrew rubbed his hands together, carefully unfolded a pamphlet, and began reading as the others sat down in chairs to listen.

"You are created by God," he read. "But you are a sinner, and you need salvation through Jesus Christ. And the good news is that He wants to forgive you."

After reading the entire tract, which was a very simple presentation of the gospel, he said, "At the end, it leaves room for anyone to do follow-up. Should we put our name there?"

"Sure," several people said, nodding.

"Well, we'd need a contact person," he said. Everyone looked at me and smiled. I was the one who'd organized the dorm fellowships as well as the one who'd obtained the tracts. We opened the box, passed out pens, and dumped several hundred tracts on the table. For the entire night, we made sure that every tract had my name, my dorm's phone number, and my address. By the end of the night, our hands were cramped but our hearts were hopeful. We ended like we always did, with a prayer.

"Dear God," I prayed. "Please cause the people who casually attend Christmas Eve service to want to know more about You."

When Christmas Eve finally came, we were smiling from ear to ear. The church building was packed, and the crowd included students we'd seen around campus and friends we'd invited. We divided into four groups and sat strategically near the four corners of the building. The service was beautiful, and the pastor spoke eloquently of Christ's birth. When the last hymn was sung, we activated. Each of our four groups got up, positioned ourselves near the four exits, and handed out the pamphlets.

"If you'd like to know more about Jesus," Andrew said, "here's the rest of the story."

"Join our university dorm fellowship," I said to a student I had invited from the cafeteria at school.

Generally, people smiled as they took the pamphlets and stuck them in their backpacks or purses. After the last person left the building, we gathered outside on the steps.

"How did it go?" I asked.

"We had great success!" Andrew said. "And the people seemed actually interested." People from other groups told stories about how some asked about the dorm fellowship. Others expressed that they wanted to know more. Some, as expected, politely refused.

"Are there any left over?" Because they were so hard to come by, we made sure we collected all of the remaining pamphlets. There were about fifty extras, and I tried to place them in my backpack in such a way that the corners wouldn't be folded or torn.

As we walked back to the campus that evening, we happily chatted about the people we met and the inroads we'd made. It really seemed that God was moving mightily in Beijing, and we were happy to play a small part in His plan.

"Merry Christmas," we wished each other, laughing, as we departed. Chinese people don't grow up participating in foreign holidays, and even though we were Christians, "Merry Christmas" still felt novel rolling off our tongues.

● ● ●

The next day was Christmas, which—of course—meant nothing. When the alarm sounded, we all jumped out of our bunk beds and headed to class. I had trouble paying attention to the professor that day. While I didn't have "visions of sugarplums" dancing in my head, I did daydream about the lives that could've been touched by the little tracts we'd handed out. My academic life was challenging and fun, but I was much more interested in sharing the gospel with my classmates than discussing the

I'm in the front row, to the far right, next to the teacher of the Communist League Committee, Class 2, from Number Eighteen Middle School of Gaomi County. *May 1984*

In high school I dreamed of being Prime Minister. Here my friends and I (right) pose next to the gate of Number Five High School of Gaomi County. *1987*

My elder uncle escaped to Taiwan in 1948 and came back to visit after nearly forty years of separation. Here he poses with me and my sister Qinghua in front of our old house. *1987*

This is my English class in front of the English department building at Liaocheng University. The building still reads, "Long Live Chairman Mao," though they tried to paint over it. *1987*

As classroom monitor, I assigned seats. In an "abuse of power," I always made sure Heidi sat beside me. *1988*

Heidi was one of the writers on my student newspaper, *Ugly Stone*, which we edited together. *1988*

Heidi and I are in the middle of this group of college friends; the American is an English teacher named Dan, who came to my hometown after the Tiananmen Square Massacre. *1990*

I was baptized by house church leader Grandpa Yang in an abandoned factory under a showerhead the workers used. *1992*

In spite of our combative early relationship, Heidi and I knew we were destined for each other.

Pastor Alan Yuan (on the left) and pastor Feng Shi-jun (on the right) after they officiated and preached at our wedding ceremony. *June 1993*

I promised God I would share the gospel with my classmates before graduation. Our wedding was the perfect opportunity. *1993*

This was my teacher's ID for my day job at the Communist Party school. In the evenings I organized illegal house churches, earning me the humorous nickname "God's Double Agent." *1993*

Heidi and I stand in the center of the campus of the Beijing Party School, where I taught from 1993 to 1996.

An Easter celebration of an underground house church in the hills near Beijing.

After we returned from the Easter celebration, we were followed by PSB officers who were gathering information for our eventual arrest.

My sister Qinghua and her children in our Shiziyuan village. Her elder daughter, Denise Zhao, currently attends Texas Tech.

My friend and I sit in the shower room formerly used by Chairman Mao's wife, which Heidi and I made into an apartment. Note the tiled walls! *October 1994*

I stand in front of the building from which I jumped from a second-story window to evade PSB agents.

The friend who snapped this photo of us on the day we were released from prison was later questioned by PSB agents. *July 8, 1996*

Though we feared for our lives, we pretended to be tourists in Thailand and wore those ridiculous pink floral leis. *October 13, 1996*

Heidi had to hide her pregnancy from fellow travelers, so she went to all of the tourist sites—like this Buddhist temple—in spite of her exhaustion. *October 13, 1996*

BANGKOK EMERALD BUDDHA TEMPLE 泰國曼谷玉佛寺留念。

Me in Hong Kong. *May 25, 1997*

To commemorate the anniversary of the Tiananmen Square Massacre, I went to Hong Kong's Victorious Park and distributed the dissident magazine *OPEN*. When I worked in the Party school, I hid this magazine under the bed, but PSB agents found them during our arrest. *June 4, 1997*

Heidi, Daniel, and I were welcomed to the United States by Tom White of Voice of the Martyrs, who pushed for our freedom.

Heidi, Daniel, and I pose for a photo in our Philadelphia house so generously provided at no cost. *1998*

By the time I graduated from Westminster Theological Seminary, Heidi was exhausted from life with two small children. We pose here with Heidi's parents, who stayed with us during this time. *2000*

My nephew Wang Qinyu, his wife, and my father after my nephew helped in my father's daring escape.

My father, Fu Yubo, and me after a six-year separation. *2002*

I kept my father entertained in Thailand by taking him on an elephant ride, which he didn't enjoy a bit.

My father eating dinner with Heidi, Daniel, Tracy, and me on the first day after he was rescued. *June 2002.*

Outside our house, my father plays with his grandson Daniel—the first time they met since Daniel's birth in 1997.

David Aikman, right, and I pray for a dissident who became a Christian during a retreat in January 2002. ChinaAid was birthed out of this retreat.

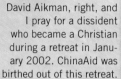

My family stayed in this north Philadelphia house for seven years before moving to Texas. I created ChinaAid in its attic in 2002.

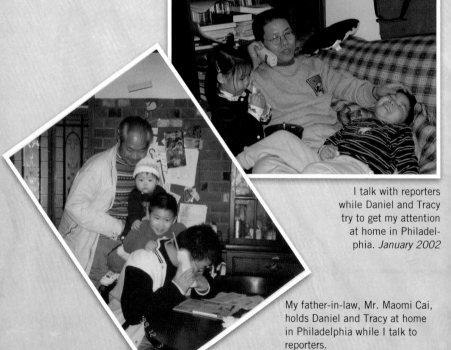

I talk with reporters while Daniel and Tracy try to get my attention at home in Philadelphia. *January 2002*

My father-in-law, Mr. Maomi Cai, holds Daniel and Tracy at home in Philadelphia while I talk to reporters.

Pastor Miao (a house church leader who spent many years in prison), Wayne Graham, Pastor Ron Lewis, me, Trent Franks, "Heavenly Man" Brother Yun, Peter Xu (known as "the Billy Graham of China"), Melody Divine, Kevin York, and Brother Xiao during our historic visit with Trent Franks, head of the Congressional Religious Freedom Caucus. *February 2004*

In front of the West Wing, I pose with Guo Feixiong, who was later arrested and imprisoned for five years. I committed a felony to rescue his wife and two children.

Me, Lord Chan of the British Parliament, former house church prisoner Sarah Liu, and Stuart Windsor, following Sarah's testimony in the UN briefing room about her six years in a labor camp. *2005*

Michael Gerson met first with our delegation in the West Wing before our meeting with President Bush. From left to right: Yujie, Bob Fu, Michael Gerson, David Cheng, Dr. Li Baiguang, Professor Wang Yi, and Guo Feixiong. *May 2006*

Our Midland delegation poses in Geneva. The fourth person to my left is Melissa Rasmussen, who helped set up our ChinaAid office, and the last person is Ann Buwalda, US Director of the Jubilee Campaign. Deborah Fikes, in the middle wearing sunglasses, was instrumental in our move from Philadelphia to Midland, Texas.

President Bush and I met with China freedom fighters on July 29, 2008, just days before he attended the Beijing Summer Olympics.

President Bush receives a Bible that was hand-copied in a Chinese prison. *November 2011*

I spoke at a press conference with Congressmen Wolf, Smith, and Pitts, along with democracy leader Wei Jingsheng and his assistant Ms. Huang Ciping. The Tibetan representatives are behind us. *February 2009*

Dr. Gao Yaojie, with Heidi and me, after I helped rescue her from Chinese house arrest in September 2009. She lived with us for seven months before Secretary of State Hillary Clinton helped her move to NYC as a visiting researcher at Columbia University.

Here I am with the Guo family—Sara, Qing, and Peter—in the Bangkok International airport before we made our daring illegal escape. Peter's wheelchair is part of his disguise. *April 2009*

Li Ying served more than thirteen years in prison and wrote me a very poignant letter after her release.

Pastor Weihan, left, was imprisoned for three years for printing Bibles in Beijing and was set free after Brother Yun (center) and I campaigned for his release. *2011*

Blind dissident Chen Guangcheng testified before Congress from a Beijing hospital via my iPhone. This photo of Congressman Chris Smith (middle), Frank Wolf (left), and me appeared on the front pages of many international newspapers. *May 2012*

I met with Chen Guangcheng in his New York apartment after his amazing escape to America. *May 2012*

During Chen Guangcheng's house arrest, thousands of people posted photos of themselves wearing sunglasses to show their support. This is my photo.

I am holding a copy of the biography of a Chinese intellectual that was instrumental in bringing me to the peace and joy of Christ.

Sadly, my conversion put me on the wrong side of the law. Here, Heidi holds up the address book she successfully—and miraculously— hid from the police when they came to arrest us.

My family has sacrificed so much for my ministry, and I'm so thankful for their support, love, and heart for the gospel.

political intricacies of Thailand. When the class ended, I grabbed my backpack, slung it over my shoulder, and headed out the door. My next class was all the way across campus, so I needed to rush to get there in time. To my surprise, however, a university police guard was standing at the door.

He was wearing a dark uniform, white gloves, and a crisp hat that covered a very short haircut and shaded his eyes. "The Beijing police want to talk to you," he said.

I turned around to make sure there was no one else behind me. "Me?"

Without another word, he grabbed my arm and ushered me off campus. I felt a little ridiculous being shoved through the idyllic campus by a Beijing police officer. More than being embarrassed, however, I was perplexed. What could I have possibly done to merit this?

We walked up the stairs to the station, which had a blue sign on the front of the building marked "Police," and into an interrogation room. It had a bright light hanging over a table with two vinyl chairs shoved up to either side of it. A folding chair sat near another smaller table in the corner. The walls were windowless and stark, except for marks and scuffs from what looked like previous altercations.

"Sit," the officer said to me, which was hardly necessary since he practically shoved me down into one of the chairs. I dropped my red backpack on the floor, but the officer grabbed it and placed it on the corner table. He told me to wait, which I did for what seemed to be a long time. Finally, the door opened and another man, wearing a white button-up short-sleeved shirt and suit trousers, walked in.

"Where is the illegal literature you were handing out?"

"I didn't hand out anything illegal," I protested.

"We have reports that you were handing out these pamphlets at the church." He slammed a copy of the pamphlet down on the table.

"That's against the law?"

"So you're admitting you handed them out?"

"Yes," I said, calmly. I knew I was in trouble, but I didn't want to lie. Not that it could've helped me. I'd handed out at least a hundred, in plain sight. "There was a Christmas Eve service last night, and we handed those out to the people who attended."

"We?"

"I did."

He laughed, mocking me by picking up the paper by a corner like it was poisonous.

"All alone?"

I didn't answer.

"I'll ask you again," he said. "Where is your stash of those pamphlets?"

I forced myself not to look at my red backpack that sat on the table in the corner. After the service, I had gone to my dorm and fallen asleep. When I got up to go to class, I didn't take the time to unpack my bag. The materials the police were looking for were right there in the room, almost under their noses. I didn't breathe and stared right into the interrogator's face. It was pudgy like a baby's, even though he was at least fifty years old. When he talked, any trace of innocence disappeared into crevices created by years of scowling. Right there, while the interrogator stood over me, I said a silent prayer.

Please don't let them find the pamphlets in my backpack, Lord. Just blind his eyes from seeing them.

"What are the names of the people you gave them to?"

"I didn't ask their names," I said.

"No, that's right," he said. "You gave them *your* name on the back of each pamphlet. Very clever."

"It's not 'clever,' it just shows that I had no idea I was doing something wrong."

"I'm not complaining. In fact, you made it easy on my comrades. They already saw you. They were at the church. The only

146

reason they didn't grab you then was because they didn't want to disrupt the worshipers to arrest a criminal."

"I'm no criminal."

"Funny, that's what everyone who sits in that chair says . . . at least at first."

"What crimes have I committed?"

"Oh, do you want me to limit it to last night, or do you want to go all the way back to 1989?" There was a folder on the wooden table between us, which he slowly opened. There were pages and pages of documents, which he carefully turned over one at a time. He lifted up each page with almost delicate hands, pretending to read each one. When he said 1989, of course, he was referring to the Tiananmen Square protests. "Hmm . . ." he said, pretending to familiarize himself with me. "You've been a troublemaker for a long time, haven't you?"

I didn't answer.

"Well, let me give you some time to think about that," he said, carefully shutting the folder, standing up, and sticking it under his arm. He shoved his chair back under the table and left the room.

It was quiet except for the occasional muted conversation as people walked by the door. *Is it locked?* I wondered, but I knew it didn't matter. On the other side of that door was a bustling office of uniformed Communist police officers. There'd be no way to escape.

"Why are you so careless?" I quietly reprimanded myself, putting my head in my hands. "Why do you think the Communist government will let you operate like a free agent? You're indiscreet. It's one thing to get yourself in trouble, but it's another to pull your friends down with you."

I kept talking to myself, to avoid looking at my backpack. I didn't know if I were being watched somehow, so I didn't want to draw attention to it even if I was alone. My stomach growled. My mouth was dry. I needed to go to the bathroom. *When will he come back?*

When the door finally opened again, I jumped and the interrogator smirked. "Am I interrupting something? I can come back later," he said.

I didn't respond. "May I have some water?" I asked, weakly.

"No," he said, unscrewing the top of the water bottle he carried and taking a long drink.

"May I at least go to the bathroom?"

"Guard," he snarled.

The same officer who'd apprehended me earlier appeared at the door and grabbed me by the arm. He led me into a small bathroom, and then followed me inside. "Go," he demanded, pointing to the toilet. It was less than dignified.

When we walked back down the hall, I could see the rest of the station going on with its business. Phones rang. People walked around with coffee mugs. We walked by another interrogation room, this one with a window, which I glanced into as we passed. I stopped in my tracks, causing the officer to tug on me before he followed my gaze. There, sitting behind a big wooden table, were all of my roommates. A large, tall officer stood above them, lecturing them. They didn't notice me gawking at them before the policeman yanked me back to my own room.

"Why are my roommates here?" I asked the interrogator, trying to keep the panic from my voice. He looked at me sternly.

"You refused to tell us where you were keeping your illegal materials," he said. "So we decided to go look for ourselves. You might want to start keeping your room a little more tidy."

"What do you mean?"

"When we got there, the beds were turned over and all of your drawers were dumped out. It looked like you'd been robbed or something." I swallowed hard and tried not to cry. Oddly, I felt more violated about them going through my belongings and talking to my friends than I did about being detained in the police station. "But we are having a nice chat with your roommates. They said they didn't know where you kept your illegal Christian material, but that you keep a backpack with you all the time."

At the word backpack, a chill ran all over my body. It was sitting not ten feet from me, and it was bright red. Had he turned around and opened it, he would've found the whole stash. Those tracts had been smuggled in from Hong Kong. Plus, if they found the tracts, they might charge me with possession and keep me for days.

"Where's your backpack with your illegal literature?"

While I was being interrogated, the urge to lie was so strong that I had to force my mouth to remain shut while I considered my options. I didn't want to be put into prison, but I also knew God could protect me without me having to use deception. In the Bible, He broke Peter out of jail. I shrugged my shoulders, and decided to be honest.

"I use that bag." I pointed over to the small table, where my backpack had been sitting the entire day. I made sure not to say, "This is the bag holding the illegal literature." Instead, I just shrugged my shoulders and pretended like it was nothing.

The interrogator turned around, saw the backpack, and smiled.

13

"Do you think I'm stupid?" the interrogator said, holding my backpack up in the air. My blood ran cold, because he was holding the illegal literature he'd been looking for all day. "*This* is not the bag."

Though I was completely baffled, I put on the most disinterested face I could muster and shrugged.

"We have talked to your roommates, your buddies from church, and even your friends from class," he said. "And they all told us you carried a yellow backpack." He dropped my bag on the table, then came and sat back down in the chair across from me. "Does that bag look yellow to you?"

"No, sir."

"Care to tell me where the *yellow* bag is?"

"I couldn't tell you." By this time, I had to stifle a laugh. I had been in that room for hours—I couldn't tell how many—without food or water. Though I was scared, I asked God to keep the police from finding the stash in my backpack. Somehow, all of my friends forgot its color, even though they saw it every day. Immediately, my heart was filled with relief over the pamphlets and dread over the fact that other fellowship members might've been apprehended too.

"We separated your pals into different groups," he went on,

pacing around the room. "We questioned them intensely and asked them to show us your backpack. So far, no one could find it."

I guess they didn't think to look in the police station, I thought.

"But we will," he said, placing his hands on the table and leaning toward me. "Don't worry, we won't stop looking. In the meantime, write down the names of your Christian friends on this piece of paper." He took paper from the folder, slid it across the table, and dropped a pen on top. "Also, write down where you got this illegal material."

I didn't want to lie, but I didn't want to get anyone else in trouble. The older couple near campus had already suffered enough persecution for their faith. Instead, I sat in silence, hoping the interrogator would give up. Of course, as the hours rolled by, it looked less and less likely. I grew thirstier under that ridiculously bright lightbulb.

"Where did the pamphlets come from?" he demanded. By this time, because of fear and lack of food, I was feeling sick and a bit woozy.

"I don't want to tell you!"

"You could save yourself some of this agony."

"Okay," I said, regretting every syllable that was about to come out of my mouth. "I got them from a tall man in the church! He didn't give me his name."

He ran out of the room to tell the officer, and I instantly felt sorry for all of the tall guys at my church. A few minutes later, he came back in and said, "Now, how hard was that? You should've told me, so you could've left sooner." He walked up to the table, and I could see a small vein protruding from his temple. "You know what, Xiqiu? I want to arrest you right here on the spot! You show so much disrespect to the rule of law by handing out inflammatory messages."

"Our pamphlets had no political messages!" I said, but I

knew the Communist government believed Chinese Christians were too sympathetic to America. "We were merely sharing the gospel. Look, every word came from the Bible."

"That doesn't make it legal."

"If it were illegal, would I have made it so obvious? I wasn't passing them out on the street corner, I was passing them out at a church . . . a church sanctioned by the government, no less."

The scowl on his face grew ever so slightly smaller, and he seemed to be listening to what I was saying.

"At church, you do church things," I continued. "It's simple."

"You were doing illegal religious activities and are in violation of Chinese law," he said, opening the door for me. "Go. But don't worry. We'll be watching you."

Honestly, I believed him, and I felt like I might need to vomit. I walked out of the police station and looked up at the sky. The sun was just going down, and I realized I'd been in the interrogation room for more than eight hours. But I wasn't thinking about food or water. Instead, I was eager to find my Christian fellowship friends to see if any others had been apprehended. I went back on campus, got my bicycle, and began riding around the university area in a very circuitous route. I kept looking back over my shoulder, scanning the pathway to see if anyone was following me. After I felt confident no one was following me, I finally went back to others in my group. They were having a Christian fellowship meeting, so I walked into the dorm room and shut the door firmly behind me.

The scene touched my heart. My friends were kneeling on the floor, their hands raised to God petitioning for my safety. When they saw me, they ran to embrace me.

"Are you okay?"

I looked around the room and did a mental checklist. All of my friends were there. I exhaled deeply and collapsed into a chair. It had been a long day. "You won't believe what happened!" They listened silently, eyes wide with fear, as I detailed every moment from the time the officer blocked my entrance into class. A palpable sense of fear filled the room.

"Did they get to any of you?" I asked. Everyone shook their heads no, silently confirming that the government must not have known our fellowship existed.

Andrew spoke up, breaking the silence. "Hasn't the Lord prepared us for this moment? We've been nurtured by those older Christians, who've already experienced so much suffering. They've testified that God is faithful even during their persecution."

"Their testimony had always encouraged us," a concerned female student said. "But I didn't want the opportunity to walk through our own trials."

"Well, this is our moment," I said. "Apparently, the government doesn't know our fellowship group exists. We need to keep it that way."

For the next hour, we discussed how to "go dark" and become an underground group. Of course, I'd been through this at college, so I mapped out some techniques we'd implemented there. We developed code language and made plans to be more discreet.

"Just assume there's someone always watching you," I said.

"Even at church?"

"Especially at church."

"So, when we meet students from different universities," someone asked, "should we invite them to our group or introduce them to other students from their colleges?"

"Yes, but we need to be cautious," Andrew explained. "From now on, consider yourselves secret agents."

On the way home from my fellowship meeting, I looked at everyone I passed on the sidewalk. They all looked suspicious.

Even though I'd been released from interrogation, I knew the police could dramatically affect my life and future. They'd already told me they were following me and expected me to return to check in. They could easily make an example of me. Not only could they put me in jail, they could also kick me out of school. That would mean my utter and complete financial ruin.

• • •

When I finally got back to my dorm room and opened the door, I gasped. The bunk beds were turned over, the drawers were out of the chests, and clothes were strewn all over the floor. All of the books were tossed around, lying on their spines, pages folded and torn. Our desk was toppled, and homework papers were everywhere. My roommates were on their hands and knees, trying to put the room back together. When they saw me walk in, they looked up at me in anger and confusion.

"What did you do?" a roommate asked. "And why did they come here looking for illegal religious materials?"

That night as I laid my very tired head down on my pillow, it felt lumpy. Under my pillow was the Bible that my roommate Timothy had given back to me. He apparently no longer wanted to take the risk of possessing it. I opened it up and read the inscription it seemed that I had written so long ago.

"Dear Timothy, I hope this book blesses you," I read, choking back tears. "It is the Word of the Lord."

14

Confucian ethics teach that marriage is a social duty more than a way to satisfy one's individual desires. Therefore, dating in China was laden with expectations from the start. Both women and men expected a dating relationship would lead to marriage, so people didn't "shop around" to find their so-called soul mate. Relationships were undertaken with the utmost sobriety, and I had no doubt: Heidi would be my wife.

Of course, her parents weren't so sure. Especially her father. When Heidi first disclosed our relationship to him, he didn't believe I could provide for her, and consequently for her parents, like another man possibly could. Because of his wrongful imprisonment during the Cultural Revolution, he was more dependent on her future than he otherwise would've been—a fact that motivated me to study late into the night during college. Once I got to Beijing, however, Heidi's father was satisfied with my occupational trajectory, though I was hardly a safe bet. After all, he was well aware of my involvement in the student protests, and he knew firsthand how harsh the government could be.

With his tentative blessing, Heidi and I also seemed to overcome the natural problems associated with long-distance relationships. Most of our arguments came from her testing me to make sure my intentions were true. After all, I was earning my education in the capital city, which seemed so glamorous compared to her life back in her province. She was earning next to nothing, while I was preparing for a lucrative job. Though I assured her otherwise, she couldn't help but wonder if I'd stick with her. When I realized the source of her insecurity, I began to understand the underlying cause of our fighting. I wrote her a letter almost every day assuring her of my love, and I eagerly anticipated her replies.

Of course, we needed a bit more than romantic letters. For the three years I was in graduate school, we made sure to see each other at least once or twice a semester. Most of the time, I took trains to visit her. However, when I went to see my family, she would take the bus to my hometown to see me there. I also visited her during the summer and winter breaks.

Even though we were not Christians when we began dating, we both now had God in our lives. He gently showed us where we were selfish and childish. Through the work of the Holy Spirit, we changed. Over time, our relationship began to be more peaceful, and I was thankful to have a strong, feisty woman like Heidi. This would come in handy many times throughout our lives.

● ● ●

There was never a moment when I asked Heidi to marry me. Marriage, however, was always a part of the backdrop of our relationship. We talked about our wedding and where we might live, but there was no dramatic proposal, tears of joy, or gigantic ring. Though it might not sound romantic to Western ears, our life together was not proffered as some sort of possibility that could either be accepted or denied. Our relationship was set in stone, established, and secured from the beginning. It might not be the kind of romance Hollywood would make a movie about, but there's something wonderfully intoxicating about surrendering to one's romantic destiny.

In other words, we knew we were going to get married. The only question was when.

Graduate school had not been the easiest road. Though my spiritual walk grew every day, I feared the authorities would swoop in and arrest me. For what? That didn't matter. I knew they could, and possibly would. Though my roommates were initially terrified at being questioned by the police, they soon loosened up. My roommates' conversations around the dorm may have centered on women, dirty jokes, and sex instead of God, but I was still thankful to have a pleasant living arrangement. I made sure I was more discreet in sharing my faith. This meant more peace of mind for me, but it also meant I wasn't able to tell as many people as I wanted about Christ. Because of this tension, I made a pledge to God.

"Before graduation," I prayed, "I want every one of my seventeen classmates in my program to hear the gospel."

After two years, I'd not been able to pull off this endeavor. I needed an opportunity to have all of my friends in one place. What better way than to have a wedding? Frequently, people plan their weddings around the seasons, or meaningful dates, or commencement ceremonies. What about having a wedding ceremony that could not only marry us but also introduce the guests to their Savior? Heidi and I could make sure our wedding ceremony would include a clear presentation of the good news of Jesus Christ. Of course, we'd have to forgo the traditional Chinese ceremony for a more Westernized version, but if we sent out invitations to all of our classmates, they'd feel bound by politeness to attend.

Heidi was all for it, even though it meant that she'd travel to Beijing for the wedding, then immediately return home to finish out the school year. We'd be separated while she wrapped up her teaching job, but then we would be reunited in Beijing. Even though it was less than perfect timing, she also had a strong desire to spread the gospel. Plus, I like to think she was ready to become my wife! There was one problem. Technically, the wedding would be illegal because students weren't allowed to get married while still in school. We applied for the license anyway, but the school denied my request. It was a real setback, because graduation was drawing near.

"I have an idea," Heidi wrote me when she heard the bad news. "I have relatives who work in the government here. Come to my hometown and we can apply here. I think we can manage to get permission through a back door."

It worked, and we excitedly started trying to find a date. We originally hoped to get married on June 6, but it was too close to June 4, the anniversary of the Tiananmen Square massacre. Every year, that anniversary brought new political tension and unrest, which could've posed problems for our guests coming from America, Australia, New Zealand, and Hong Kong. Consequently, we settled on June 19, just a few days before graduation.

We didn't have a great deal of extra money set aside for a wedding. Even before we were married, I got several tutoring jobs while in Beijing to send extra cash to Heidi. Because her family was so dependent on her, she was living on less than five yuan per month (a little less than an American dollar). The rest of the salary she made as a full-time teacher she gave to her parents.

After graduation, I kept telling myself, *I'll finally be able to make real, substantial money*. At the time, all university students had to work for the government after graduation in some capacity. The Communists believed it was a way for students to give back to the government as well as a way to foster loyalty to the state. But even with that restriction, graduates from my university program had their pick of jobs. Someone who could speak English fluently could easily find a job in a major corporation or a state-owned international export/import company. Since I knew English and was familiar with international trade relations, I could work for a corporation, the government, the Communist Party, or any of several other organizations.

Finally, after so many years of hard work, I'd completed what I'd told my mother I'd do so many years ago. I'd waded past the low-paying teachers' jobs, was accepted into a prestigious post-graduate program, and could cash in on my success as soon as I graduated.

As I was going through my options with James, an American professor in my Bible study group, one idea kept coming up.

"I want to work in ministry," I said.

"There's no such thing as 'full-time ministry' in China unless you're working in the government-sanctioned church," he replied.

"Well, that might be the case, but I want to find a job that allows me to dedicate the largest portion of my time to ministry and the smallest portion of my time to the Communist Party," I told him. "In fact, as I was praying about my future the other day, that's what I promised to God."

"Then He'll work it out," James said, "according to His purpose."

Since Heidi and I were getting married before I graduated, and consequently before I got a good-paying job, we had to cut corners on the ceremony. Thankfully, one of our fellowship couples represented a big company in Beijing and lived in a big apartment building that had the entire first floor dedicated to the Chinese military. The General's Widow Building was a hotel reserved for wives of generals who'd passed away during the Chinese Communist Revolution, as a demonstration of the government's gratitude and provision. The hotel was beautiful, expensive, and luxurious, and our Christian fellowship friends pulled some strings so that our wedding could occur there. In fact, since Heidi was still residing in her hometown, our friends planned our entire wedding. They got all kinds of free trinkets, picked out a charming skirt for Heidi, and created a beautiful floral arrangement for her bouquet. They also arranged for an older Christian lady to play the piano and got some talented musicians from a music school to accompany her. Because of their resourcefulness, I only spent $120 on the wedding. (I should never have told Heidi how little I spent, because to this day she says I still owe her!)

When the big day came, I watched from an adjacent room as one by one, my classmates filed in and took their places on the neatly arranged chairs. *One, two, three*, I counted. Not only was I about to join my love in matrimony, I was also about to fulfill my promise to God. *Fourteen, fifteen, sixteen . . . seventeen!* When every one of my classmates was present and accounted for, I was ready to get the ceremony started. Though neither Heidi's parents nor my dad could attend due to the great distance, we had about thirty or so foreign guests. This brought our audience up to around eighty people, some of whom were unknowingly about to hear about Jesus.

We were married by Yuan Xiangchen (better known as Alan Yuan in the West), who was one of the most famous Christian dissidents in China. I could tell that my guests were excited when Yuan Xiangchen walked in. He had risen to notoriety after being arrested one April night in 1958 for refusing to join the Three Self Patriotic Movement.

• • •

Yuan had refused to join for three basic reasons. First, he believed Jesus and not a political group should be the head of the church. Second, his church had always been independent from foreign control. And third, he didn't like the theological modernism that characterized the leaders of the Three Self Movement. Because of his refusal to join, he was charged with "counterrevolutionary" crimes and sentenced to life imprisonment. He was sent near the Russian border to a labor camp where the temperature routinely dropped to thirty degrees below zero. He was in prison for twenty-one years and eight months, most of which were spent in a freezing cold cell. He encouraged himself by singing "The Old Rugged Cross" while the other prisoners had their smoking breaks. Miraculously, he survived the ordeal without abandoning God, but he paid a hefty price for his faith and didn't see his wife and six children for almost twenty-two years.

When he was released from prison, he went right back to having a house church, which he refused to register with the Three Self Patriotic Movement. He and his wife never compromised their faith and never stopped ministering the gospel in their home. He'd gained notoriety in China because he received much media attention from foreign correspondents. Billy Graham had even visited him and his house church.

Heidi and I had met him through an older Christian lady, Ms. Jing Huifu, who knew Pastor Yuan in Beijing. He and his wife invited us to their modest home. Their living room had a photograph of Billy Graham hanging on one wall. As we sat in that little room where so many people had come to know the Lord, they encouraged us.

"If you want to be a faithful minister and follower of Jesus in China," he said, "you should learn prison theology."

I nodded, though I wasn't quite sure what he meant. "In prison," he explained, "you find out more about God and His faithfulness than anywhere else. Jail is where God prepares His church in China."

A chill ran over me. We'd talked to many persecuted faithful believers in China, like Pastor Yuan, Watchman Nee, Wang Mingdao, and others. We saw how people who stayed true to the Bible eventually ended up in jail. I looked at Heidi, who smiled weakly at me. I knew without even speaking to her what she was thinking. Our faith was not yet strong enough to endure that "prison theology" test, but I tucked Yuan Xiangchen's words in my heart.

I admired his hardline stance against the government-sanctioned church, yet we attended a government-sanctioned church every Sunday. I could tell that it was filled with many Bible-believing Christians and had a pastor who was passionate about the true gospel. In fact, Pastor Yang Yudong even told young people about Jesus, even though the law prohibited the conversion of minors.

Before we left their home, Pastor Yuan and his wife told us to stay true to the gospel, and to preach it in season and out of season. We could see from their tranquil, smiling faces that they were joyful and without bitterness. Their attitudes and perseverance had a deep impact on us, and we were so blessed when he agreed to conduct our wedding ceremony.

● ● ●

I also invited an elder preacher who used to be in our Thursday Bible study to deliver the sermon during the wedding. Since Chinese weddings are long, somber affairs, I decided to pack it full of the gospel. The preacher got up and delivered a simple presentation of the gospel, very solemnly. By the time he sat down, I'd fulfilled my pledge to God. All of my classmates had now heard about Jesus.

After the sermon was delivered, I needed to make my pledge to Heidi. Yuan Xiangchen approached the lectern to conduct the official business of making us man and wife. Sadly, the government had spread rumors about Christianity, saying pastors had forced people into marriage. Because the Scriptures warn against being "unequally yoked," the Communists said Christianity included the practice of "forced marriage." In fact, many pastors were imprisoned under this false charge of forcing people into wedlock.

Communism, the government assured its citizens, gave people "freedom of marriage." Just to make sure everyone realized our wedding was both government-approved and purely volitional, he held up the government-issued wedding certificate and read it aloud.

"According to the People's Republic of China's wedding law," he read, "you are certified as a married couple."

Afterward, we served refreshments in a beautiful area of the hotel. Normally, this is a time when the guests give gifts and give blessings to the bride and groom. And, make no mistake, people mingled, wished us well, and gave us wonderful presents. But as people ate cake and sipped punch, we also had a powerful time of evangelism.

Many of our friends had never heard the truth about Christianity, and they were processing all they had heard in the wedding ceremony.

"Have you ever heard of this 'good news'?"

"Do you believe what they said about this Jesus?"

"How could God forgive sins?"

Right there, in a hotel dedicated to a communist military, we talked about Jesus, shared about His transformational power, and told many about how to become His followers.

As we walked out of the hotel, I grabbed Heidi's hand . . . my wife's hand.

"Do you have any idea what you've just gotten into?" I asked, playfully.

"Not really," she responded.

Thankfully, neither of us did.

15

One morning, I got up, put on my nicest clothing, and breezed down the sidewalk to a job interview. Now that I had a wife and two university degrees, it was time to get a good-paying job. At a young age, I had realized money could help solve many of life's problems. In fact, I had thought it could even bring about equality and justice. As a Christian, however, I now knew money was not the cure-all solution I'd concocted in my youthful imagination. But I did know it could make life easier. If I had a high-paying job, I could support the ever-growing list of people now dependent on me.

The waiting area was packed with similarly dressed job applicants, so I found a seat and looked at my shoes. When my name was called, I walked into the meeting with as much confidence as I could muster.

"I'm Xiqiu Fu," I said when I entered the room. "And I'm here to interview for the translator position." The interviewer was Chinese, smartly dressed, and had penetrating eyes. Even though I was a little nervous, I believed my answers were short, pertinent, and appropriate. If I got the job, I would work as a translator for China's general company for road and bridge construction, our nation's largest state-owned company. After about an hour of intense interviewing, he stuck out his hand. "You have the job! And you will receive double salary. One part will be paid in American currency and the other paid in Chinese currency. Our company has a new job in Kenya, so that might be your first assignment."

"Thank you," I said, trying not to calculate how much money I'd now have per month. "I accept."

I walked home singing a tune. After so many trials and so much trouble, I'd finally overcome my humble beginnings. But when I got back to the silence of my home, I didn't have the peace I figured would come with this new job. That's when the Lord reminded me of my pledge.

I tried to shove it out of my mind. After all, I'd scrimped by on almost nothing my entire life. Now that I had a wife, couldn't I simply make a little extra? Or even a great deal extra?

"I think I might be going to Kenya," I told James during the next men's prayer meeting.

"To Kenya? Won't that complicate your plan to spread the gospel in China?"

I knew God wasn't going to let me get away from His will for my life. I broke down and told James all about my occupational decisions and struggles. I wanted to make money, but I'd pledged to God I'd take a job that would allow me to do ministry as well. While I discussed my options with my friend, it became undeniably clear.

"I should be about the kingdom's work," I said at last. "The Lord will honor my commitment and show me what job is best for my circumstances."

There was one job option that would give me flexibility during the evenings and enough money to make ends meet . . . barely. Neither of us said the word *teacher*, because we both knew I'd been rebelling against that job my entire life, but that was the only option that would allow me to keep my promise.

"Yes," my friend said. "There's got to be some sort of job." His voice trailed off ambiguously. "God will make it clear."

I wasn't the only one who didn't want to be a teacher. Many educated Chinese graduates also shunned the job. The Communist Party School was the training ground for those on their way to becoming high-ranking Communist leaders. Since party members had elite educational backgrounds, they turned down such low-paying jobs in favor of more prestigious ones. Consequently, the Communist Party School couldn't find enough English teachers within the party to teach their budding officials. The school began hiring non-communist members.

"We still need one more teacher," a woman who'd graduated from the same university program told me. She'd taught English at the Communist Party School for a few years and seemed quite content.

"Sorry," I said. "I'm not a communist."

"I was the first non-communist they hired," she said. "Believe me, they'd prefer I were a member, but it came down to a teacher shortage. They needed me. If you're interested in a job, I think you'd be perfect."

The next morning, I shuffled into the heavily guarded, unmarked campus far from Tiananmen Square. This time, when I met my interviewer, I was neither nervous nor excited. If I got the job, I knew it was because God wanted me there. So, right away I told him, "I'm not a party member."

"That's not a disqualification," he assured me.

I didn't disclose my Christianity, however, which would've been a deal breaker. An hour later, I walked out of that school with a job offer and a smile.

"You won't believe what job I just got," I told James after the interview. "God let me keep my promise to Him by giving me a job training high-ranking Communist officials."

The irony of it all made us both break into laughter.

●　●　●

Heidi was living in her province, finishing her school year and studying to pass the graduate entrance exam to the People's University of Beijing. She realized teaching was too much work for too little pay, so she hoped she could get into a program to study aesthetics and philosophy. In the meantime, I moved into the Communist Party School compound, where I was assigned a dorm with another married man whose wife was also living in another city.

When Heidi passed the exam, she wrote me excitedly. Not only was her future opening up, she could move to Beijing and we could finally live together as man and wife.

"The only problem is that tuition costs 24,000 yuen," she wrote. At that time, that amount was about three thousand American dollars. It was such an unobtainable amount of money there was no way she'd be able to attend without divine intervention. Thankfully, as Christians, we believed in miracles. Every day for weeks, I prayed for her education. Then, during one of my prayer meetings, I shared my financial need with the other men. As the deadline for the money drew close, I was already mentally composing Heidi's family a letter explaining why their daughter would not be able to pursue her dreams. But on the day before the deadline, James came up to me and shoved a small bag into my hands.

"What is this?" I asked, peeking into the bag and shutting it immediately once I saw it was full of money.

"Don't get too excited." He smiled. "It's not for you; it's for Heidi."

I glanced at my watch, and noticed it was almost time for the financial office of the university to close. I thanked James profusely and practically ran through the campus, holding the bag of money like I'd robbed a bank. When I finally got to the office, I walked in and dumped all of the cash onto the counter.

"This is the tuition for my wife," I said proudly. The clerk's jaw dropped.

As she hurriedly put the money into stacks, I realized exactly how generous James had been. It was enough for an entire year of graduate studies.

Finally, after many months of separation, Heidi moved to Beijing that summer. As my living situation with the other married man certainly didn't fit our needs, we began searching for another place to live. Soon, I found there was a huge shower room in the administration building near my office that was not being used. A "shower room" had both a shower and a toilet, a luxury usually reserved for the highest-ranking officials. While most people lived in dorms with a common bath down the hall, only a select few had their own private baths.

"What do you think?" I said to Heidi, opening the door with a borrowed key. "Would you like to live here?"

"In the bathroom?" she asked. It was actually a pretty big room, with high ceilings and tile floors. It was separated into two areas, with one side dominated by a gigantic monstrosity of a bathtub and the other with a smaller, more reasonable sink.

"This shower room was used by Chairman Mao's wife, Jiang Qing," I said. "She stayed in this building after China was liberated. This was her private bath."

Heidi laughed as she walked around the dusty bathtub, which hadn't been used for years. "Is that supposed to be a selling point?"

I knocked on the gigantic tub, causing a cloud of dust to rise up and encircle me. "This was imported from the Soviet Union," I said, coughing. "They just don't make them like this anymore."

"Wow," Heidi winked at me. "I think God prepared a newlywed bedroom for us. Let's clean it up and make it our bedroom—our home."

The next day, our friends from the student fellowship came to help us transform the shower room into our first residence. The young men spent a whole day tearing out the bathtub and helped us move in a bed donated by an older Christian man. By the time we were finished, we had a lovely place to call home.

* * *

Heidi was a very hospitable woman, but one day when I told her about an upcoming guest, she was less than enthused.

"*Who's* coming here?" she asked.

"Heidi," I said, trying to calm her down. "Joseph was a good friend of mine."

"Right, he *was* a good friend, until he turned on you," she snapped.

"That's not exactly true."

"Well, what would you call it when he wrote in the newspaper that student protestors like you should be killed?"

"Maybe he's changed."

"Also, he took your job as the class monitor and made sure no one talked to you for months. In fact, he's the main person who drove you into a depression, which almost drove you to suicide. Why is he coming here?"

"He said he was in the area," I said. "I don't know."

"Well, I've said this ever since he betrayed you. He's an opportunist, a bad guy, and I hope I never see him again!"

"Well, you won't. He's coming by in the evening. Perhaps it would be best if you were gone."

A few days later, we were sitting in our little room when someone knocked on the door. It was midday, right before I was to leave for class, so we were a little surprised.

"Xiqiu!" I heard when I opened the door. There, four hours early, stood Joseph.

"Welcome," I said, ushering him into our room. "Heidi," I said, very slowly, hoping to give her a little time to collect herself. "Remember Joseph?"

"How could I forget?" she said.

"I'm so sorry, Joseph, I was expecting you later," I said, glancing at my watch. "I was just leaving to teach my class."

"It's okay," he said. "I can wait. In the meantime, I can just talk to Heidi."

I looked at my wife—my lovely, beautiful wife—who simply smiled and said, "That would be great. It will give us a chance to relive our old college days."

Even though I knew she was furious, I had no choice but to teach my class. When I closed the door behind me, I wondered what kind of scene I would find when I'd return a couple hours later. I couldn't focus on the class as my mind wandered to what could be happening back at my home. When the class was over, I scurried over to our place, hoping that they hadn't eviscerated each other.

When I opened the door, I was astonished at what I found. Heidi and Joseph were sitting at our tiny table with a Bible between them. Both of them were grinning from ear to ear.

"What's going on here?" I asked.

Joseph jumped up from his chair and exclaimed words I never thought I'd hear him say.

"Xiqiu," he exclaimed. "Your wife led me to Christ!"

16

One Sunday morning, Heidi and I walked into the courtyard of our church. For the past several months, we had been going to the Gangwashi Church, a congregation closer to my work. But on that day we stopped just beyond the gate. Something was wrong.

Signs were posted everywhere, and my friends from the youth group were gathered in a circle, holding hands in the middle of the courtyard, heads bowed. As I walked toward them, I read the signs. "Pastor Yang Yudong is no longer fit to preach the gospel, and has retired as of today."

Dread filled my heart. Pastor Yudong, the seventy-year-old patriarch of the church, was a man of truth. He loved God and even covertly baptized people of any age who wanted to be Christians. Under his leadership, our church grew so quickly it went from one service, to two, to three. Eventually, we had multiple services per day—even a Korean language service. Perhaps it grew too quickly, because the government definitely noticed.

"What happened?" I asked. "Is the pastor okay?"

"Last night, the Communists went to his house and forced him to retire," an obviously bereft congregant explained. "They've kicked him out."

"Is he speaking today to say goodbye?" I asked. I'd grown quite attached to him.

"No," she responded in a whisper. "Supposedly, they told him he was done. They put a guard outside his house and forbade him from showing up today."

I'd attended the Gangwashi Church every Sunday and could tell that it was filled with many Bible-believing Christians, but I wasn't sure how true a church could be under the authority of an atheist organization. Heidi and I joined hands with our friends outside the church building and cried out to the Lord.

"God, is this Your church?" we prayed. "Is this a real sancti-fied church? Are You the head of it?"

When it was time for the service to begin, we went inside the sanctuary, where there were hundreds of people I'd never seen before. Instead of our loving pastor sitting on stage as he'd done for years, a line of religious affairs bureau officials stood on the stage. They were wearing dark suits and somber faces. It was odd, even a little funny, to see those proud atheists up on stage at the church.

"At this time, we'd like to invite the president of the Beijing Three Self Patriotic Movement to deliver a word to us," one official spoke into a microphone.

The man, who himself was around eighty years old, made his way to the microphone.

Heads turned as we looked at him and wondered if this was the new government-selected pastor. Pastor Yudong's wife sat in the congregation alone, her head bowed in prayer. The eighty-year-old pastor who was the head of all the Three Self Patriotic Churches in Beijing walked slowly up the stairs, and everyone wondered what he'd say on such a day.

"America," he began, "is a capitalist empire, which has op-pressed the people of China for a hundred years."

We listened in disbelief as he delivered a scathing sermon against American imperialism without even mentioning the odd circumstance of the day. For that matter, he didn't even mention Jesus. At the end of the diatribe against the United States, he explained that he was going to be the new pastor of the church. It was like an afterthought, similar to an announcement for a potluck. He even explained that Pastor Yudong had been asked to resign because he was too elderly to lead a church of our size.

"But Pastor Yudong is ten years younger than this guy," I whispered to Heidi.

The entire congregation began murmuring, and the elder pastor held up his hand to quiet us. "Pastor Yudong is not fit to serve here," he went on. "He is—"

Just then, a door opened on the stage and Pastor Yudong jumped out from a secret hallway. "I'm still here!"

Apparently, he'd snuck out of his home under the cover of darkness, broken into the church, and hidden in a secret corridor that connected the hallway to the stage. All night, he'd crouched there waiting for his opportunity to tell the church what really happened. And this was his moment.

At the sight of the brave pastor, the congregation collectively gasped. A few people screamed in surprise, some stood to their feet, some applauded, others began yelling, and still others prayed aloud right there in their seats. The seventy-year-old walked to the microphone right in front of the Communist officials and began explaining what happened.

"I wasn't even allowed to say goodbye to you, my beloved congregation of so many years," he said.

As the pastor was pouring his heart out, one official jumped up, grabbed his microphone, and pushed him aside. The front five rows of the church that were filled with people I'd never seen before were actually undercover police officers, sent to keep order in case of a riot. They stood and began protecting the stage from congregants who were rushing to the defense of the aged pastor.

His wife, sitting in the congregation, stepped up to defend her husband but was pushed down. She grabbed at her heart as she fell. Right in the middle of the church service, she began having a heart attack. Several congregants tried to make their way to her, but the officers blocked any rescue attempts. Finally, a few people got through and tried to take her to the hospital. They didn't get very far. The officials yelled out to the police, "Arrest anyone who tries to save her!"

The officers immediately apprehended the people rushing to get to her, threw them into police cars, and arrested them. The congregation was ordered to remain in the building, while the pastor's wife was dying in front of our eyes. A man in the congregation had gotten out a video camera, and the police tackled him and began beating him.

My friend sitting next to me looked at me and said, "Let's find a phone." I led him to the back of the church and watched for officials as he picked up the phone and called the emergency line. When the operator answered, he said, "Please send an ambulance. A woman is having a heart attack!"

"What is your location?"

"We're at Gangwashi Church on Xidan Street."

My friend pressed down the receiver over and over. "It went dead!" he told me.

He slammed the phone down, then quickly dialed again.

"Why did you hang up?" he yelled. "A woman's dying!"

"Sorry, we were told not to service that area today."

The phone went dead again. Not only had the government forcibly retired our pastor, they had also prepared for a bloody riot and wanted to be able to deny us all assistance.

My friend's face grew red in fury and he banged the phone against the wall. He ran out into the street and flagged down a taxi. When the cab stopped, he leaned into the open window and said, "I need you to take a woman to the nearest hospital!" However, just as he got the words out of his mouth, the police ran up to the car and commanded it away.

"Wait!" he yelled, but it was no use. The police had set up a perimeter around the church and cabs weren't allowed to enter.

He knew the pastor's wife didn't have much time, so he ran out beyond the perimeter, saw a taxi, and literally jumped on its hood. "I need you to take this woman to the hospital," he yelled from the hood.

"We aren't supposed to stop here today," the driver protested.

"Well, you just did!"

After forcing the cab to the gate of the church, the congregants who hadn't been arrested managed to carry the pastor's wife to the car and gave the driver a handful of cash. "Take her," they yelled, and he sped off just as the police reached the scene. My friend, after successfully getting her into the cab, was thrown to the ground and arrested.

In 1989 I'd gone to Tiananmen Square because my hope was still in government reform. Only when the tanks started crawling over people did I lose hope in the government's ability to transform. That Sunday was my "spiritual Tiananmen Square." As we stood there with our mouths hanging open in shock, we saw atheists barking commands to the police, silencing a man of God, and leaving an elderly woman to die.

Our petition to God was answered. No matter how beautiful the services, the ultimate lord of the Three Self Patriotic Church was communism and God had no place in it.

17

Before that terrible Sunday, I believed I might be able to work within the government-approved framework and spread the gospel. But after the crackdown at Gangwashi Church, I knew it wasn't possible. I also learned that Pastor Fong, who conducted the youth Bible study at Hadian Church, had been dismissed because he preached from all of the Scriptures instead of just the sanctioned ones. After the Communist Party ousted him, he continued to teach Christians in secret. One day, when he was walking home from ministering to a house church in a suburb of Beijing, he was stabbed in the chest. A police car drove by as he was bleeding on the sidewalk, and he waved his arms, trying to get assistance. The policeman looked at Pastor Fong and kept on driving. Thankfully, another person offered assistance and he survived.

The Communist Party wouldn't tolerate my beliefs. The incident at Gangwashi Church clarified that for me. Pastor Yudong's wife did make it to the hospital and survived her heart attack. The man who dared to try to videotape the riot was tailed for months and beaten for his efforts. Many congregants were like me and simply decided that government-sanctioned churches were not really headed by Christ. After that service, prison felt inevitable, like a shadow constantly following and threatening to overtake me.

I felt it in my bones. I was going to go to jail.

On a particularly anxious day, I went to visit my friend and mentor Jonathan Chao, who was visiting Beijing, and told him how I was feeling.

Though Jonathan was born in northeastern China, his parents were Presbyterian missionaries who escaped before the Communist Party took power. He was raised in Japan until his teens, when his father, Dr. Charles Chao, moved them to California in 1958. There, his dad was a pioneer in translating reformed Christian literature into Chinese, which he then smuggled back into his home country. Jonathan, in the meantime, was educated in America, receiving a degree from Geneva College, a Master of Divinity degree from Westminster Theological Seminary, and a PhD from the University of Pennsylvania. He knew he wanted to be a missionary to China for most of his life, and after the Cultural Revolution he quietly began to train Christian leaders in China despite the fear of government reprisals. He founded an organization called China Ministries International (CMI), which is how our paths crossed.

Under Jonathan's direction, CMI sent a few missionaries to explore ministries on university campuses and among Chinese intellectuals. Since I was in Beijing ministering to students, I met with his group and later met with Jonathan himself.

Although he was very accomplished academically and spiritually, he was incredibly modest, a true missionary, a servant, and a scholar. The outside world didn't know his name, but the Chinese government considered him public enemy number one. Not only did they dislike him because he was helping spread Christian teachings and doctrines, they hated how he drew attention to social and political issues as a scholar. He had a ready smile for everyone he encountered, but his innocent appearance concealed his very subversive trade of evangelizing China.

"If you're ever arrested," he said, "just blame it on me."

"I don't want to throw you to the wolves," I protested. "If I blamed you, they'd come after you."

"I have more protection than you. Plus, if you give them information about me, perhaps they will treat you less harshly." He took off his glasses, which normally perched steadily on his round, full face, and rubbed his eyes. His eyes were red, but—then again—he always looked like he could use more sleep. When he put his glasses back securely on his nose, he said, in perfectly accented Mandarin Chinese, "I'll be all right. I'm an American citizen."

I knew what he said was true. He was the most influential overseas Chinese Christian in the development of the Chinese house church. The term "house church" was actually first introduced to the West by Jonathan, who started his research and mission to China even before they formally opened its door after the Cultural Revolution in 1976.

● ● ●

Later that evening, I talked to my new bride. "The Lord promised He won't give us suffering our faith can't endure," I said. "But I don't want to go to jail."

"I don't either," Heidi said.

I told her about my conversation with Jonathan, who so far had also evaded prison.

"Let's pray," she suggested. "Let's ask God to give us a certain amount of time before we're arrested."

"How long?"

"Long enough to mature us," she said. "We've only just begun to understand the gospel. I don't know if I could survive prison!"

And so, we got down on our knees and prayed, "Dear Lord, please grant us three years to do Your work and to begin to understand the richness of the gospel."

"Well, if the Lord gives us enough time before we go to jail," we said, "we can do many things for the kingdom." In a way, we bartered with God. As long as we had freedom, we were going to advance the gospel.

And so, we set to work.

During the day, I taught at the Communist Party School. My classroom was located in the same building as our apartment, and I soon felt pretty comfortable in my new position. My class had about five rows of desks facing the blackboard, and my desk was off to the side at the front of the classroom. If my students knew I was not a Party member, they didn't seem to care. These future Communist leaders were nice and generally polite, but I could tell some of them weren't incredibly interested in the subject.

Two young men in particular, Dingbang and Feng, sat in the back and were always goofing off or laying their heads on their desks. At first, I tried creative ways to engage them. When that didn't work, I tried to be stern. Finally, after they didn't do their homework on several occasions, I figured they were the sons of some heavy hitters in the government and would be okay whether or not they could speak English. Most students, however, realized English was another tool to help them rise through the ranks of the Communist Party and were diligent in the classroom. It didn't take much preparation for me to teach them English, so I quickly settled into a routine that didn't require much outside work. This, of course, was my plan all along. With such an undemanding day job, I had more energy to spread the gospel.

In the evenings, Jonathan, Heidi, and I were involved in all sorts of illegal religious activity. As the church spread, Jonathan wanted to make sure that everyone was both a missionary and a scholar. He was from a Presbyterian family and consequently was very serious about not only spreading the gospel but also teaching people the correct theology. One summer, he organized clandestine training in modern Chinese church history in my reconstructed restroom-apartment. Right there at the Communist Party School, he taught new Christians about the history of the People's Republic of China, how political changes affected religious policy, and how house churches could be a powerful response to those policies.

Jonathan and I also organized secret training for our campus ministry co-workers in a small restaurant near a university campus in Beijing. Jonathan and his father smuggled in many books and videos from well-known Chinese evangelist Dr. Stephen Tong, which they used to teach about a Christian reformed worldview.

"We need more copies of these videos," the ministers said after receiving their training. I didn't have the technology to copy videos at the time, so I went to the Communist Party School's video publication center, the China Youth Video Publishing House. It was Beijing's main publisher for Communist Youth League's propaganda video materials, so we had to be discreet.

We befriended two young men who worked there and convinced them to copy hundreds of evangelistic videos during the night. They agreed to work for free, not because they were Christian sympathizers but because they were thrilled to see illegal videos. However, while they made copies of the films, night after night, the message took hold of their hearts. There, in the Communist propaganda department, they were secretly converted.

● ● ●

One night, I was talking with Heidi about our new life together. During the day, I taught future Communist leaders. During the night, I trained the illegal house church.

"I'm a double agent," I said, and laughed.

"It's quite possible the people you teach during the day will one day arrest you and those you teach during the evenings," she said.

We didn't have too much time to think about how dangerously we perched on the edge. We knew China was inhospitable to the truth of the gospel, and every spare moment and every spare yuan went to helping the underground church while we could. This caused many problems within our family. There were certain expectations that came with living in Beijing.

"Why did your son get all of that education just to be an English tutor?" my dad's friends asked. Though my family supported my decisions about ministry, I feared they might resent the fact that we weren't sending them more money. My salary at the Communist school was so small it hardly mattered, and everything else went to the church. It was difficult for both Heidi's family and mine, and it pained me very much to know that they were struggling financially because of our choices.

We pressed on with our work. I accompanied Jonathan to academic conferences in universities in Beijing. I went with him to the very poor areas in the Chinese countryside to train house church leaders. We noticed the urban university students had a lot of Bible knowledge, but not a lot of passion. In the countryside, the believers were full of fire—willing to die for the Lord—but lacked basic biblical knowledge.

That summer, we created "Fire Taking Time," a program designed to get the university students into the Chinese countryside. The students stayed with the house church leaders, who, though they had nothing, were lavishly hospitable. Even though they were poor, they prepared the nicest meals they could for us and tried to pamper us. Every morning when we woke up, for example, we'd find that our coats had been washed. Their pure faith and love for Christ were so evident that it deeply affected the university students. Miracles and signs followed the house church leaders. We heard so many stories that Heidi and another Christian sister from a university tape-recorded many testimonies to preserve them. We heard stories of healings and miraculous provision. One man told a story about how he fell off a tractor and was run over by it. However, he was unharmed.

That summer in the countryside, Heidi and I visited one house church network comprised of over six hundred churches.

"What a great network you have," I said to one of the leaders. "How many preachers do you have?"

"Well," he said sheepishly. "We only have two teachers for six hundred congregations."

I looked at his face, which was full of the joy of the Lord, and I thought of the passage in Hosea that says, "My people are destroyed for lack of knowledge" (Hos. 4:6).

Instantly, I knew I was supposed to help educate more people about Christianity, but I was a brand-new Christian too. Over the past few years, my main source of theological information came from dog-eared books smuggled into the country in strangers' suitcases. Though I'd devoured all the Christian material I could find, my knowledge was incredibly limited and I felt ill-equipped to meet the ever-widening need. I spoke to his little house church, but within a few short minutes I'd used up all of my big theological words. I told them about "general revelation," "special revelation," and "common grace," and then I was done. That exhausted my knowledge of theological terms.

I went to Jonathan Chao and an American evangelist named Ronny Lewis, who'd founded King's Park International Church in Durham, North Carolina. "Those house churches in the countryside really need training," I said, and explained the situation.

They listened intently and were in complete agreement. "We'll do all we can to support you," they said. We decided to establish a Christian training center for the underground church. First, however, we had to train our co-workers. Pastor Ronny and a missionary from Taiwan volunteered to teach a Bible training session on the tenth floor of a tall Beijing apartment building owned by a Christian. To avoid arousing the suspicion of the residents, we climbed the stairs instead of using the elevator. Most of us wouldn't go out for the week during the training. Heidi, however, was tasked with going out to shop for groceries and run errands. That meant she had to climb up and down the ten stories almost daily. It wore her out. (Even to this day, she takes the elevator or escalator if she has the option.) But we appreciated her sacrifice, because it allowed us all to stay holed up in the apartment and learn about God.

"Therefore let us move beyond the elementary teachings about Christ and be taken forward to maturity," Pastor Ronny read from Hebrews (6:1 NIV). He decided to conduct a topical exegesis on that chapter, which included the basic foundations of faith. I was thankful to be with people like Pastor Ronny and Jonathan, who always encouraged biblical scholarship. I felt suspicious of some of the more emotional experiences I'd heard about in China and wasn't a big fan of the charismatic movement. As we moved forward in ministry, I wanted to make sure our students were trained to think logically and clearly about the Holy Scriptures.

When Pastor Ronny began talking about baptism, we realized several of our co-workers hadn't been baptized. "What's stopping us from being baptized now?" someone asked. Without a baptistery handy, we did the next best thing. The apartment had two bedrooms with attached bathrooms. The women went into one of the bedrooms, while the men went into the other. One by one, we had baptism ceremonies right there in the showers. Afterward, we went back into our training session, full of joy. As we all settled back into our seats, Pastor Ronny continued to read where he had left off. "We have this hope as an anchor for the soul, firm and secure" (v. 19 NIV).

Just as the words were coming out of his mouth, I felt a breeze on my face, looked up, and was surprised that no windows had been opened. My co-workers looked up from their notes as well. Suddenly a very strong wind, like you might feel while standing by an ocean, filled that Beijing apartment.

I knew from my reading of Scripture that God sometimes performed miraculous works with wind. When God parted the Red Sea for Moses and the Israelites to elude Pharaoh's army, for example, He did it by causing an east wind to blow. Later, on the day of Pentecost, a noise like a strong, blowing wind filled the whole house where the apostles had gathered. Though I'd read about the Spirit of God in the Bible, I'd never felt it—literally and physically—as I did on that day.

As the wind whipped around us, we began praying aloud and crying out to God. People began speaking in what sounded like other languages, which was very much at odds with my solid Presbyterian training. As I called out to God, however, the Holy Spirit came upon me and I too spoke in tongues. A peace and comfort surrounded me, and I was filled with unspeakable joy.

After the training, we were filled with boldness and courage. We worshiped the same God as the ancient Israelites, the apostle Paul, Wang Mingdau, and Billy Graham. And this same, unchanging, eternal God equipped us to spread the gospel throughout China. *I Amen*

• • •

With Jonathan's and Ronny's support, Heidi and I moved forward on our secret training center for house church leaders. We found an old, deserted factory in the Fangshan District of Beijing.

"This is perfect!" I said as I stood in the wide-open space, imagining it teeming with young Christians.

"What are you going to do?" Heidi asked. "Just hang out a sign that reads 'Theological Training'?"

"Actually, I was hoping to camouflage it a bit," I said. "We need to establish a fake business to give us cover."

"What kind of business?"

"I don't know, but we need to be creative," I urged. "Let's say we're a school for technological training. Do you know anyone who has any computers?" After asking around, we came up with one old, outdated 386 computer, which we set up right in the middle of the large factory.

Heidi walked around the single computer on the lone desk,

every step echoing in the massive room. "Do you think one computer is convincing?" she asked. "Where will all the students sit?"

"I think I have an idea," I said. The next day when I went to work, I asked about a large stash of old chairs with attached desks. When I found out the Communist Party School was willing to sell them at a reasonable price, I purchased them. That's how our new Christian ministry training center was stocked with red desks decorated with Communist Party logos.

We set up the center, arranged for foreign teachers to present lectures, and found full-time teachers to live in the center. We spread the word among different house church groups that we were ready to offer ministerial training. We didn't want to have too many people in the building at once, because we couldn't risk drawing attention from the authorities.

"How will we select our students from all of these?" Heidi said, holding up several hundred applications. That night, we waded through the applications and selected thirty students for our first ministerial training center. Students in our first class would be coming from as far west as Tibet and as far north as the provinces near Russia. Because we'd conduct classes under the most dangerous circumstances, we had to be almost militaristic about the operation.

When we alerted the students, we told them what would be expected of them. They had to come for three solid months, meaning they weren't allowed to leave the four walls of the building the entire time they were in training. Our full-time teachers would organize the living quarters, provide food for the students, and leave the school for discreet errands. Every day, those thirty students grew in biblical knowledge and were being trained to go into China after graduation to teach the good news of the gospel.

Not only was I one of the leaders of my house church in Beijing and a teacher at the Communist Party School, I was suddenly the cofounder of this theological training center, as well as an instructor there. Every week, I took a two-hour bus ride to the center, where I taught and ministered. Frequently, I'd design and grade tests for my Communist Party students on the way.

The work just grew and grew. Every week, Heidi and I had to go to the airport to pick up guest teachers on their way to the training center. We also had to find hotels for them and give them basic instructions on how to not tip off the police. We also received many Bibles smuggled in from all over the world and had to find appropriate places to distribute and store them.

All religious literature in China was strictly controlled, which meant that there was always a Bible shortage. The Bible was the only religious book among all religions that was not allowed in any Chinese bookstores. To purchase a Bible, a believer had to travel to a Three Self Church and buy it at the church bookstore.

In China, only one press was authorized to print Bibles, which meant it was only available in limited numbers that could not meet the rapid growth of the church. Many believers couldn't travel the long distance to the church to acquire one. Some people ordered Bibles from the church, got traced, and were promptly arrested. We didn't want to deliberately violate the law, but we also knew it was very important for the church to have access to the Holy Scriptures.

Since some of our church members were skilled printers who worked in the government-owned printing press, we decided to use their skills to print hundreds of thousands of Bibles. Printing was much safer and more economical than smuggling. Usually a foreign mission organization or a church funded our efforts, but one day a woman we didn't know appeared with an order.

"I'm a friend of Craig's," she said, referring to an Australian missionary who was a dear believer in Christ. "Can you help us print three thousand copies of the *Moody Bible Handbook*?"

"Did you say three *thousand*?" I asked, shocked to receive such a large order from an individual.

"I have cash." She reached into her purse and handed over

three thousand American dollars. "I think that will cover the deposit. When you're ready, I'll send more." I accepted the order and gave the money to my co-worker Zhuohua, who was in charge of the illegal printing.

This was life: meeting with believers, taking chances, and breaking laws.

• • •

Back in Beijing, our house church grew exponentially. Pretty soon, it had multiple fellowships in different locations. Heidi, who was a full-time student, studied long hours in the evenings and helped me as much as she could during the day.

One night, I fell asleep grading papers, and Heidi gently woke me to guide me to bed. When I looked at her, her brow furrowed and she bit her lip.

"You look pale," she said. "Do you feel okay?" She placed her hand on my forehead and immediately recoiled. "You're boiling!"

She called a cab and took me to the emergency room. The doctors took one look at me and hospitalized me, giving me several different medications to lower my temperature.

None of them worked.

I couldn't open my eyes, but I could feel Heidi dabbing alcohol on me to cool me down. Later, Heidi told me I was murmuring and saying things that didn't make sense.

"He could die if we can't get this fever under control," the doctors told her.

Heidi prayed, the doctors worked, and eventually the fever released its grip on me. Immediately, I went right back to work, training Communists during the day and conducting illegal house churches at night. The clock was ticking and I'd made a promise to God I fully intended to keep.

Our secret training center's first class was an amazing success. After three months of intense training, we commissioned them to go into China and preach the gospel. The day after graduation, however, we got unwelcome visitors.

"We're in danger!" Dragonfly, one of my co-workers, yelled into a phone. I was home in Beijing, grading my students' tests, when I got the call. Apparently, some men from the local business bureau showed up at the secret ministry center to "collect taxes." Except for a few strays, the students had already gone home after graduation, and the teachers were preparing for the next class to arrive. The building was still relatively empty, with our lone computer surrounded by thirty Communist desks.

Of course, the center hadn't paid any taxes because the center wasn't actually a business. But the business bureau officials weren't really there to collect taxes—they wanted bribes. At the end of the year, it was customary for companies to bribe officials. The business bureau would create trouble for any company that didn't abide by these unwritten rules. Usually, they'd look around the businesses, searching for any possible violations to report to hold over the business's head. Most of the time, the corrupt officials concocted false charges to use as leverage to receive even larger bribes.

"What did they say?" I asked, with a growing feeling of dread.

"They asked, 'How is your business going?'" Dragonfly replied. "And then they asked, 'Want to renew your license?'"

Of course, our entire organization was a violation of law. Dragonfly watched the officials as they walked through our building with puzzled faces. One of them stopped at the computer, looked at him, and said, "Your 'high tech center' is not so high tech."

Almost nothing happens in China without bribery, I thought as I heard the details of the story. *Should we have thought to send bribes to the officials so we could preach the gospel?* The whole thing seemed odd and wrong, but not as wrong as having officers walking through our top-secret evangelism school.

The officers had found a Chinese church history book that

had been hastily hidden under a pillow. It was written by a man whose name would pique the interest of any law enforcement officer.

Jonathan Chao.

"So they gathered up all of the evidence against us—armloads of biblical literature—and walked out the door," Dragonfly told me.

As the gravity of the situation dawned on me, I called all of my friends over to our home for prayer.

We'd been compromised.

18

I snapped a pencil in half, set the two pieces on my desk, and asked my students, "What's wrong with it?"

My lesson for the day was to make sure my students were able to describe items with proper English adjectives and past participles. I looked into their eyes, waiting to see if anyone could come up with the word *broken*.

"Dingbang?" I said to one of the two students who were perpetually asleep in the back of the class. He barely lifted his head and shrugged his shoulders.

"Feng?"

His friend looked up from doodling on the margins of his paper and said, in perfect Mandarin, "You broke it."

"That would be great if I were trying to teach you Chinese," I said, as both students continued to ignore me.

Then I called on another student sitting closer to the front.

"What's wrong with the pencil?" I asked again. The student shuffled in her seat. It was May 9, 1996, and I couldn't keep my mind on class either. While my students flipped through their books, I repeatedly glanced back at the door. It had already been one day since our training center was discovered, and I knew I was living on borrowed time.

After class, I went back to our apartment and found Heidi

preparing lunch. Her brother was visiting us after his college graduation and was out sightseeing. She expected him home soon.

"I made it back," I said with a smile, sitting down at the table and accepting Heidi's offer of tea.

"This time," she said quietly. Silence filled the room. When the phone rang, both of us jumped. We looked at the phone and then at each other.

On the third ring, I reached for it.

"This is the Party School police station," said the man on the other end of the line. "The Beijing police are here and want to speak with you."

It had been three years since we first prayed God would give us time before we were arrested. Suddenly, I regretted selecting a specific, arbitrary number. Why did I ask God for three years and not, say, fifteen? However, we knew God was in control of all that was happening to us. In fact, God had been preparing us for this day in many ways. Even our personal Bible study had recently led us to 1 Peter.

"I'll meet them at the office," I said, before placing the phone back on its base.

"I think it's time for prison theology," I said to Heidi, and smiled. Before I left, we got down on our knees with our Bible, and I read aloud the passages we'd been studying that week:

"Beloved, think it not strange concerning the fiery trial which is to try you, as though some strange thing happened unto you. But rejoice, inasmuch as ye are partakers of Christ's sufferings; that, when his glory shall be revealed, ye may be glad also with exceeding joy" (1 Pet. 4:12–13).

Heidi folded her hands over her chest to stop them from shaking, and I continued reading. "If ye be reproached for the name of Christ, happy are ye; for the spirit of glory and of God resteth upon you: on their part he is evil spoken of, but on your part he is glorified. But let none of you suffer as a murderer, or as a thief, or as an evildoer, or as a busybody in other men's matters" (vv. 14–15).

A tear from my eye fell on the Bible, and Heidi joined me as I read the last sentence.

"Yet if any man suffer as a Christian," we read together, "let him not be ashamed; but let him glorify God on this behalf" (v. 16).

Then we held hands and prayed.

"There's one more thing," I said, getting up, walking to the corner, and returning with the tiny little book in which I'd recorded all the contact information of the brothers and sisters who had become Christians over the past few years. I'd kept the little address book since 1992, when we were ministering at the university. I'd kept meticulous records because it was the only way to keep in touch. Plus, I wanted to document the growth of the underground church, in spite of what the official government numbers showed.

"Please," I said to her, pressing the book into her hand. "Don't let this fall into the wrong hands."

I walked down the stairs on my way to the school office with my head swirling. What would become of Heidi? Would I ever see her again? How long would I be in prison? Would they torture me? But my reverie was cut short as a group of special agents cornered me just as I walked out of my building.

"Xiqiu Fu," I heard as I turned the corner. The police, probably believing I would flee, had wanted the element of surprise. And they definitely had it. "You are under arrest for illegal religious activities. But before we take you to the station, let's take a little trip back up to your apartment."

My heart almost stopped. Only seconds ago, I'd placed the address book in Heidi's hand. She had no way of knowing the police were on their way to her, so she wouldn't have time to hide it. Plus, if they were going to search our apartment, no place would be safe. The officers ushered me up the stairs, their video cameras recording every moment of the encounter.

Knock, knock, knock.

When Heidi opened the door, her face was completely solemn. She didn't look surprised or upset. She simply stepped aside and let them in. Her hand was down to her side, and she casually stood so that her arm hung on the other side of her body. I couldn't tell if Heidi had the address book. However, I knew the officers were looking at me intently and could easily follow my gaze, so I hung my head.

"Search everything," the head officer barked as he walked over to our television set. "Don't leave any centimeter of this place untouch—"

He stopped, chuckled, and held up a stack of American dollars. "What do we have here, right out in the open?" He flipped through the stack like a casino operator in Vegas. "There must be a thousand dollars here."

"That isn't ours," I said. Recently, a flood had devastated a nearby town, and a Taiwanese missionary sent money for disaster relief. We'd left the cash sitting out because we were just about to pass it along. "That's money for the flood victims."

"You really should keep your money more secure." He laughed. "You know, for the sake of the flood victims."

Heidi and I watched silently as officers opened our desk drawer and dumped its contents on the floor. They ran their hands through the papers, over a stapler, and through a small box of paperclips. I scanned the contents for the address book but didn't see it. The officers stuffed anything that looked important into a satchel—our wedding videos, photographs, bank statements, posters we'd gotten during the Tiananmen Square protest—and I tried not to think of all of the memories they were stealing. The address book was compact, almost small enough to be hidden by Heidi's hand. As the other officers were busy dumping out our belongings, I looked at Heidi, whose eyes were as hard as steel. She didn't smile or blink. The only motion she made was to ever-so-slightly rotate her arm so I could see the edge of the book in her left hand.

I forced myself to look back down at the floor. I was thankful that she had it. They certainly would've come across it during the ransacking. But how long would it take before they noticed she was holding something?

An officer went over and flipped our bed, causing our pillows and blankets to fall into a heap on the floor. Within fifteen minutes, every nook had been searched and every item of interest had been stuffed into satchels.

"Okay," the head officer said, gathering up their loot. "I guess we're done here." I breathed a sigh of relief. Had the officers found the address book, they would've had a blueprint for the underground church in that area, complete with names, phone numbers, and addresses. I looked at Heidi and was overwhelmed with love for her. After all, what other woman would be so brave and fearless as uniformed officers destroyed so many of her personal belongings before hauling her husband off to prison? However, God had prepared our hearts.

"Who's got the money?" the head officer asked, just as they were gathering up our things. They looked in their satchels and found nothing. Somehow, in all of the ransacking, they'd lost the thousand dollars.

"You!" one of the officers yelled. He rushed to my side and grabbed my arm. "Where did you put it?"

"I haven't moved from this spot," I said, holding my hands up in the air with my palms out. The relief I'd felt was replaced by an acute dread as they searched me for the money.

"Empty your pockets," he said, pointing to my pants. I slowly put my hands into my pockets, grabbed the inside cloth, and pulled it out so the officers could see that I hadn't stolen the money. I wish I had. Heidi was standing right there among the officers, her hand behind her back. I moved as slowly as I could, hoping to give her more time to think and prepare. After seeing my empty pockets, however, they whipped around to Heidi.

Oh God, I prayed. *Give her presence of mind.*

"So it must've been you," the officer said, getting to within two inches of Heidi's face, studying it for traces of guilt. "You look like you're hiding something."

"Sir," she said in a remarkably even tone of voice. "I wouldn't steal money that wasn't mine. Haven't you noticed I haven't moved from this spot either?"

"Empty your pockets!"

The entire world seemed to slow down as she took her left hand and slipped it into her pocket. In the distance, I heard a plane flying overhead. A clock on the wall ticked. The officers' eyes were fixed on Heidi's pocket, which now contained her hand and the book she was hiding.

After she yanked out her pockets, she pulled her hands away. From across the room, I could see the corner of the address book right there in her hand. However, the officers' eyes were fixed on her pockets, which they'd anticipated would contain the money. When the pockets hung out of her pants, some lint fell out and onto the floor. The officers were so surprised her pockets didn't contain money, they stood there transfixed, staring at the cloth lining. They didn't even notice the book in her hand.

The head officer's face grew red and splotchy. "Well, if you think you're so clever that you would steal money from police officers, maybe we should arrest both of you."

I'd never considered that Heidi would possibly be put in jail as well, and I wanted to cry out to her. Just then, one of the officers shouted because he'd found the money under a stack of counterrevolutionary magazines.

"Take him away," the head officer said to another officer, who shoved me out the door. "I'll take care of his wife."

19

"How did you organize the underground church training center?" the interrogator asked. The room had a desk, a few stools, and no windows. It had been days since the police had taken me away from our apartment and dragged me to a car waiting on campus. For hours, I had watched from the backseat as they carried boxes of our belongings into a truck. I noticed a wedding photo fall on the ground into a puddle. An officer stepped on it and stuck it back in the box.

I looked away. I knew the contents of those boxes were merely "things," cheap mementos of past events, and it was the events themselves that were important—but the photos, love letters, and posters were tokens that caused us to pause, remember, and smile. As I sat there watching those items taken, combed over for evidence, and destroyed, it felt so personally insulting, like they were denigrating enormous portions of our life together.

When I arrived at the prison, I resolved not to give them the names of my other Christian friends.

"Who was involved?" he asked, leaning across the table. He waited for only a second before he yelled, "Who provided the teachers?"

I sat up straight on my stool, jarred by the volume of his questioning and the spittle that landed on my face. My head pounded. *What did they do with Heidi? Did they find the little address book? Are my friends being detained because of me?*

Suddenly, a thud on the side of my head caused me to wince.

"Who are your foreign connections?" he snarled. "Now do you hear me?"

"You have to obey the law," I said, with as much authority in my voice as I could fake. "I have a law degree from the People's University, and I know there are laws that govern how prisoners are treated."

The guard who'd whacked me massaged his knuckles, and another pulled him aside. "Don't hit him. He's a lecturer at the Communist Party School, an intellectual. And put that away." He pointed to the electric shock baton the guard was holding, a commonly used torture device that had a voltage as high as 300,000 volts. "He knows the law. If he gets out of here, he might know some important people who can discipline us. Plus, it looks like he's been preparing for this moment for a long time."

Secretly, I was gratified I was holding up well under the questioning. I felt God's presence surround me in the interrogation room, and I found some degree of peace.

"Oh, the law?" My interrogator threw his head back and laughed. "If you cared about the law so much, why did you create an illegal Christian training center?"

"Doesn't the constitution say Chinese citizens have freedom of religious belief in Article 36?" I said. "I'm a Chinese citizen!"

"You need to read the Constitution carefully," the interrogator said. "It doesn't say 'religious freedom,' as you claim. It says 'freedom of religious belief.' If you'd simply believed and kept those beliefs to yourself, you'd be home with your wife today."

"But doesn't the universal declaration of human rights in Article 18 give me protection?" I asked, realizing there was no use seeking to iron out our different interpretations of the Chinese constitution.

"You're employed by the Communist Party School," he

scolded. "You know you aren't an ordinary citizen and should conduct yourself more properly. Why do you insist on talking about this Jesus?"

"The Lord died for me and saved me from despair," I said simply. "I wanted the others to know about God too, so I—"

The interrogator slammed his fist onto the table. "Nobody will utter the word 'God' in this room!"

As I sat there, deprived of sleep and water, the temptation for sarcasm was too great. After all, I was already in prison. So I said, in a very serious tone, "Oh no. You just now mentioned the forbidden word!"

All of the guards whipped around to look at my interrogator. They apparently weren't used to jokes, because my flippant answer incensed him.

"Enough!" he yelled, baring his teeth. "Do you think you're impressing us with your stubbornness?" He walked around the table and sat down beside me on a stool. His mouth got so close to the side of my face that I felt his breath in my ear. It was hot, a strange sensation because the room was so cold. "Well, your wife is *much* more stubborn than you. She hasn't said a word . . . yet."

I swallowed hard. My fears had been confirmed. Heidi had been arrested. *She'll be okay*, I thought. *After all, she's prepared.* In fact, both of us had been trained on how to survive an interrogation. Jonathan Chao had taught us from a handbook based on interviews with hundreds of tortured Christians. Heidi and I knew how best to resist coercive techniques: we needed to come to terms with our imprisonment, to appear submissive, and to remain silent. But I could tell my refusal to answer questions was wearing thin.

"We need the names of your accomplices," he said. "Do you know Jonathan Chao?"

"No."

"Answer us honestly!"

"I only obey God."

"You don't obey the Bible?"

I paused, and then answered hesitantly. "I try."

"All of it? Even Romans 13?" I nodded, a little shocked that this man could name a book of the Bible. "Because there's one verse in there which might apply to this case. It says, 'Let everyone be subject to the governing authorities, for there is no authority except that which God has established.'"

I didn't move.

"Are you deaf? We're God's servants, according to your own Scriptures," he said. "We're hired by God."

He got up from his stool and began to pace back and forth in the small room. "So according to the Holy Bible, we have authority over you, so you need to obey us."

He paused a moment, then swung back to face me. "So now tell us who helped you set up the school. Was it Jonathan Chao?"

Is he telling me the truth, God? Should I obey him? I prayed. Though I knew it wasn't the Lord's will that I endanger His church, I also knew He didn't approve of deception. Should I make up stories, or would that cause more harm to my fellow believers? Had Heidi been able to keep the book safe, or were my Christian friends already on their way to the station?

"No," I lied. I'd been interrogated for days and—at the time—it felt like the best course of action.

"You apparently don't realize that we've been following you for quite some time," the interrogator interrupted. "I know you aren't telling the truth."

My shoulders slumped and I put my head in my hands. He was right about my deception, and I felt so guilty that I wanted to hide my face. However, once I was in that slight position of repose, I felt I could shut my eyes and rest forever. The palm of my hand was as comfortable as any feather pillow, and the arms of sleep wrapped around me like a blanket. The harsh light of the room dimmed and I felt a tingly sensation all over my body. Suddenly I felt warmth, joy even, then—

Thwack!

My interrogator stood before me and I felt a stinging sensation on the side of my face.

"Wake up!" he said. "Bad Christians like you don't deserve to nap. You think because we've been in here for three days that I'll tire of questioning you. But that's where you're wrong. I get to leave this room and rest in my big, comfortable bed, and another person is ready to question you. We could do this all week. I'm going to ask you this again. Do you know Jonathan Chao?"

"I do not!" I exclaimed.

My interrogator—with a rather unnecessary dramatic flourish—then placed a single photo on the table in front of me. It was of me, Jonathan Chao, and the illegal Bible printer, Zhuohua Cai.

"Don't you?"

When I realized an agent had been following me with a camera, I relented. They knew. I knew.

"Okay," I said. "I do know Jonathan."

It almost hurt my mouth to say my mentor's name. I respected him more than anyone, and had benefitted so much from our fellowship. However, as an American citizen, he'd offered himself up as a possible way to get out of interrogation. I recalled his suggestion, when I had shared my fears about prison with him, that I use him as a way to deflect attention.

The interrogator's eyes lit up as he slid a piece of paper and a pen across the table. "Tell me what you know about the notorious Mister Chao."

My hands were shaking with guilt when I took the pen. However, I simply turned this confession into a mission statement. I explained Jonathan's vision for China, which included the "evangelization" of China, the "Christianization" of Chinese culture, and "kingdomization" of the Chinese church. In English these all end in "ization," but in Chinese they ended in "hua." Using several pages, I elaborated on what Jonathan called the "three huas."

"Basically, Jonathan's plan is to share the gospel to as many as possible in China and to shape the Chinese culture into Christ-like culture," I wrote. It was hard to write coherently when the lines on the paper kept moving. Sleep deprivation was supposed to make me more suggestible and less resistant to questioning, but it also made my vision blurry. My speech was slurred. My head was pounding. At first, I tried to remember everything about Jonathan's ministry without compromising the secret details of operations. Plus, I wanted to defend his name. "Jonathan loves China more than anyone else. He's not anti-China. He's an American citizen. Why does he come here to sacrifice so much? Every time I met with him he was tired. He wore himself out trying to help China." By the end of the tenth page, I had trouble keeping my pen on the paper.

When the interrogator came back into my room, he looked like a dog anticipating a meaty treat. But when he was finished reading the papers, he slammed them on the desk and yelled, "This is what you give me? The three huas? Jonathan Chao is not a friend of China. You're trying to lure me with this so-called gospel. But you can't spread that venom here."

He knocked on the door and a guard appeared. "Take him away!"

Finally, my interrogation stopped after three days and nights.

* * *

It felt good to stretch my legs and to actually be moving, even if I was moving toward prison. Had I said the correct things? Had I compromised Jonathan? Were they torturing Heidi? The guard escorted me from the interrogation center, a building adjacent to the prison, to the first gate of the compound, and tossed clothes at me. Apparently, the interrogators tried to get you to talk, whereas the guards made sure you didn't. In fact, no one was allowed to talk in the prison compound, so I silently unfolded the uniform—a long-sleeved blue shirt and black trousers, with no belt. After I put on the clothes, the guard walked over to me and pointed to my face. I didn't understand until he reached up and yanked my glasses off. *Suicide prevention*, I thought. No one was allowed to have anything that could be used to kill oneself. I tried not to panic as my eyes adjusted to the room without the aid of my glasses. Severely nearsighted, I could only see things that were close to me, whereas distant objects were blurry.

Without a word, he moved me from the room and down the dark corridor. I'd never been more fatigued, and every motion was an act of will. *Left foot, right foot, left, right.*

Suddenly, I felt a sharp kick to my back, and I fell to the floor. For the next few minutes, the guard beat me because he'd apparently motioned for me to move over to another room to get fingerprinted. Since I couldn't see his gestures, he used his feet to "speak" to me. He grabbed me by my shirt to lift me off the ground, and then kicked me all the way down the hall until I made it to the correct location to get my fingerprints taken. I limped into the room as quickly as I could.

After I was fingerprinted, we walked down the corridor and stopped at the west prison cell, in section one, room four. From that moment forward, I was no longer Xiqiu Fu. My new name was Xi Yao Si, which meant "west side, section 1, room 4." The iron door slammed shut behind me. My new home was about two hundred square feet and had a toilet and a sink in the corner of the cell, behind a glass wall. I instantly shuddered at the thought of going to the bathroom in plain sight. There was a long limestone bench along one of the walls. Some of the men there stood, others sat on the floor. But one—and only one—was reclined on the bench. When I walked in, they all turned to stare.

"What have you done to land here?" the guy on the bench said, after getting up and walking slowly over to me. He had a thick neck and dark hair. His bushy eyebrows covered dark, tiny eyes with glances as lethal as bullets. Everyone had beards of varying lengths, and I could tell how long someone had been in the prison by the length of their facial hair. I began to open my mouth, but the man covered it with his hand. It was wet and smelled of mildew.

"Not so fast," he said. "You're not allowed to talk." After a moment, he removed his hand from my face and I realized I'd been holding my breath. He walked around the men sitting on the floor like a king walking among his peasants—if that king was missing some pretty prominent teeth and had forearms the size of tree trunks.

"They call me Da Ge," he said, which is Chinese for "big brother," or "head of the cell." "Since there are only a privileged few who can talk around here, I'll tell you what you must be wondering. They charged me with corruption, but I am innocent."

Actually, Da Ge was wrong. I was wondering if he was going to beat me. I nodded, and no one else said a word—not to me and not to each other. I noticed the bench was Big Brother's domain, so I tried to find a small patch of space on the wet floor. After three days without sleep, I figured I could doze even if I had to stand. Near the back of the room, close to the toilet, was about three feet of space. I crouched down, and just as I was about to lay my head on the wet tile floor, Big Brother motioned to the concrete bed, and said, "Sleep here."

It's hard to imagine a concrete bed was a place of honor, but everything is relative. In prison, the concrete bed—I later learned—was the most coveted position. Though I wasn't sure why I was being treated so nicely, I didn't have time to figure out the social strata of the cell. Instead, I laid down and finally—mercifully—succumbed to sleep.

I'm not sure how long I was out. It couldn't have been very long, but my slumber was deep and troubled. I dreamt of Heidi, of prison, and of a man screaming in horror. It seemed distant and tortured and I wanted nothing more than to awaken myself from it. However, when I opened my eyes I realized it was no dream.

A drug dealer named Little Tiger was holding a new inmate on the floor by his throat. "Hey boys, want to see if our new friend uses drugs?" The other prisoners cheered like they were at a sporting event. The inmate was scrawny, no match for Little Tiger, who knew kung fu. He immobilized him by holding his head to the floor while other men tore his clothes off him. Another prisoner emerged with a bucket of freezing cold water—and then another, and another. It was winter in Beijing, and the water from the sink was intolerably cold. As the naked man writhed in pain, apparently from drug withdrawal, they proceeded to pour bucket after bucket of water over him.

The other men laughed hysterically as he shrieked.

"Are you okay?" I asked, leaning down to him. *Why would freezing water cause so much agony?* I wondered. Though cold water over one's naked body would be terrible, unpleasant, and humiliating, he was screaming like he was being tortured. "How do you feel?"

"Please just kill me!"

"We've got another druggie," Little Tiger exclaimed. The jail erupted into cheers. I soon learned certain drugs, like heroin, make users much more sensitive to cold and pain. Big Brother could tell by their eyes whether new prisoners were users. If he suspected it, he'd have them stripped and pour freezing water over their naked bodies. This wasn't because Big Brother was offended by drug use, but because the freezing water—plus the withdrawal symptoms—provided some entertainment.

"Why don't you tell us a story," he asked, kicking him in the side to get his attention. "The new guys are supposed to entertain us."

"What kind of stories?" he moaned, gasping for air. "I don't know any."

"I was hoping you'd say that," he said as he drew back his

foot and kicked him in his ribs. He kicked him again and again, until the man, now listless from the pain, relented. "I'll do what you want!" In his agony, he was forced to tell a pornographic story, while the other prisoners sat around and whooped and yelled. I don't know if the man actually had a girlfriend or if it was all made up for the sake of the other prisoners. But even in his pain, he was able to tell some disgusting details about his sexual escapades.

After the drug addict had listlessly regaled everyone with stories, another prisoner jumped on him and began beating him mercilessly. I watched in horror as the others jumped in, making an uneven fight almost homicidal. By the time it was over, the new prisoner was left bleeding in a heap. Later, after he could collect himself, he dragged himself through the cell with a broken arm and possibly even a broken leg.

I couldn't believe it. I'd only been in prison a few more hours than this guy. Why did they almost kill him, but not lay a finger on me? Was I imagining it, or did the other prisoners move away from me and almost seem afraid?

The second night of my imprisonment, I was on "suicide watch" with another prisoner. Our job was to stay awake all night to make sure no one woke up and tried to kill themselves. During my shift, I turned to the other prisoner and whispered.

"Why does no one talk to me?"

Before answering, he looked around the cell to make sure no one saw us. "No one talks except Big Brother," he whispered.

"But people don't even look at me."

"You didn't come here to make friends, did you?" he hissed, turning his back to me.

Though he wasn't very forthcoming, I knew I wasn't imagining it. As I sat there in the darkness, I was overcome with sorrow and grief. I couldn't imagine what Heidi was going through. Had she suffered a worse fate than I had so far? Did the other women inmates attack her? Did the guards use the electric shock baton on her? I knew from other imprisoned Christians that sometimes the guards used the baton on the women in ways that made it impossible for them to have children. Had Heidi been raped?

How long would I live in this place? Ten years? Twenty? They'd charged me with "illegal religious activities," and they only knew a fraction of it. In addition to the illegal training center, we'd also printed thousands of Bibles without permission, had an entire underground training network, and had facilitated the smuggling of religious materials. If they connected the dots, I could be locked away forever. I sighed heavily, my mind in turmoil.

My thoughts were interrupted when I felt a hand on my arm.

"I'll tell you the truth," the other prisoner said, in the smallest voice possible. "Before you arrived, the guards warned us about you."

I almost laughed. I was an intellectual, a bookworm who couldn't see without my glasses. "Why would corrupted officials, drug dealers, and murderers stay away from me?"

"They said you carried some sort of poisonous message that could harm us if we spoke to you," he said.

"Oh . . ." I said. "Yes, I'm a Christian."

"A what?"

"You know, a follower of Jesus."

"Well, I've never heard of that," he said. "But we were warned not to talk to you."

"Do you want me to explain?" I asked, motioning to the sleeping prisoners. "We've got nothing but time."

"No," he snapped. That was the last word he said for the rest of the night. However, as I sat there in the darkness, I was filled with gratitude. God had prevented me from receiving the "new prisoner treatment," and I'd survived the first two days of my prison theology class.

Though I knew God was with me, my prison life took on a dreary pattern as the days passed. In the mornings, the guards brought us two meals. Breakfast was one long piece of corn-bread. The first time I bit into my piece, worms were burrowed into the bread. I immediately spit it out in disgust, but tried to put a spiritual spin on it.

"I'm fasting," I explained. But Big Brother, who was a strange combination of cop, dad, and room monitor, reported me to a guard.

"Xi Yao Si, there is no God here," the guard said through the iron door. "If you don't eat, you'll be fed through tubes in your nose." Force-feeding, I learned, was a torture method the guards used on prisoners who staged hunger strikes to protest their imprisonment.

And so, I took the wormy cornbread and pretended to eat the parts I couldn't choke down. Every day after breakfast, we were told to sit on the floor in rows. We had to keep our necks, backs, and legs completely straight. We couldn't look to the left or the right, and had to stare straight ahead without moving at all. We sat like statues every day for ten hours. After sitting there for so long, we got blisters on our thighs and buttocks. The pain of sitting there was unbearable, especially after the blisters burst. The skin around my bottom festered with sores and my skin constantly fell off. If anyone moved, the guards beat us.

We sat motionless every day on the perpetually wet floor. (It was wet because the only way to take a shower was to dump a bucket of freezing water over one's head.) The prison cell had no windows, but there was a very tiny hole in the high ceiling. That was the only "clock" I could use to calculate the time of day, as a tiny beam of sunshine moved through the dark cell. It first appeared at noon, and the pinhole of light would creep across the wall for hours until it was time for our second meal of the day. Those were the longest hours.

The second meal was comprised of rancid steamed bread, which was raw cornbread with moldy vegetables swimming in hot water. Once in a while, there'd be fat floating on the top.

Once, when I first saw that substance, I hungrily went for it in my bowl. It at least resembled nutrition.

"Stop!" another prisoner said, in a rare word to me. "That fatty material has been floating in the kitchen for months. Plus, that part goes to Big Brother." Apparently he had dibs on all the "good" parts of the meals.

One day, a guard came into our cell and said to me, "Someone deposited money on your behalf."

I was absolutely shocked. Apparently, a friend had been searching for us ever since we were taken away, going from prison to prison. His name was David Li, and he was a convert who had grown up in Beijing and was therefore familiar with all of the places where we could've been held. When he finally found our prison, David deposited money into an account designated for me. This allowed me to buy overpriced items from the guards. I bought a cup of Ramen noodles, which I made with the freezing water from the sink. Though the hard noodles barely softened in the water, it was the most scrumptious meal I'd ever consumed. Of course, I only ate what was left after sharing with Big Brother, who was always allowed to eat whatever he wanted first.

● ● ●

I tried to keep track of the days. One day I realized that it was the anniversary of my wedding to Heidi.

"Little Tiger," I whispered to one of the more notorious inmates. He was a drug dealer able to bribe the prosecutor and police officers to smuggle in goodies. "My wife's in prison on the women's side and today's our anniversary. Could you help me get a present for her?" Though it sounded improbable, I wanted to try to pass a gift along. Maybe I could convince a guard to hand it off to her, or perhaps a fellow prisoner could help me smuggle it to her cell.

"What do you want?" he asked. "Cocaine? Cigarettes? Heroin?"

"Can you get candy?" I asked, feeling a little ridiculous. Then, thinking "candy" might be some sort of euphemism for an illegal substance, I added, "Like the sugary kind?"

By midmorning I had two hard, heart-shaped pieces of candy, which I hid in my hand the whole day. I pressed my face to the bars at the top of the door, hoping a prisoner or guard would pass by so I could ask him to pass it to Heidi. I waited and waited, straining to hear any footsteps in the corridor, but no one came. Much to my dismay, the last hours of my anniversary elapsed, and I reluctantly laid down for sleep.

"If you see anyone walk by," I told the suicide watch team, "grab them for me." But the next morning I woke up with the candy melted to the palm of my hand.

One day, a bribed guard brought Little Tiger a pair of shoes. A few minutes later, I saw the notorious drug dealer, who made the cell miserable for so many people, weeping in the corner. His wife apparently had hidden a loving note in the shoe. Very discreetly, I went over to him, and he actually cried on my shoulder. In fact, all of the inmates gradually softened toward me. Sometimes I was assigned the duty of cleaning the toilet with another prisoner, which was a welcome break from the monotony of prison life. We only had paper to use to clean the toilet, which meant the commode was never clean. Little Tiger sometimes made prisoners clean the toilet with their bare hands. He also sometimes stuck their faces in the toilet and made them drink the water.

The toilet, for me, was a way to share the gospel. One by one, I made some very close confidants in the cell. Some poured out their hearts to me, confessing mistresses, misdeeds, and any number of crimes, and I—in turn—told them about the saving grace of Jesus. Eventually, I'd earned the trust and respect of everyone in the cell, and I became somewhat of a "counselor" to everyone.

"Xi Yao Si!" The shout yanked me from sleep. A hand grabbed me by the collar and jerked me up. Was it finally happening?

Was I finally going to receive the beating I'd feared? When I opened my eyes, however, it wasn't a fellow prisoner. Instead it was the prison guard, dragging me out of the cell and into the chief security guard office.

"You're sharing superstitious messages with the prisoners!" an interrogator shouted at me. "You're not only destabilizing this prison, you're destabilizing our Chinese culture!"

"No." I held up my hands to explain. "Christians actually help society by stabilizing individuals and families. In fact, we have a saying, 'One more Christian, one less criminal. One more church, one less prison.'"

"If you're so against prison, why do you spend so much time here?" he snarled.

"If anything," I added, "we're true patriots."

At this, the head security agent stood up, furious, "*You* are a true patriot? Communists are true patriots. And this prison is the holy ground of the Communist Party," he growled. "You cannot speak of the gospel here!"

When I went back to the cell, I knew someone had ratted me out. I wasn't eating much food, I couldn't see very well, and my head throbbed from my blurry vision. I slept very little, I lived in fear of getting beat up, and I witnessed terrible acts of cruelty and torture.

However, there was one aspect of prison that was somewhat appealing: I had absolutely nothing to do. Before I was arrested, my life had become so busy—so amazingly busy—that I used to joke that the only way I'd get a chance to rest was to get arrested. One day, I was looking at the dot of the sunbeam. It was on the twenty-seventh stone to the left of the door, which meant, by my calculations, it was three o'clock. We were sitting in silence, and my lower back was throbbing. In spite of the pain, I felt so thankful to God that I wanted to sing. I cleared my throat and began singing a song from my underground house church days.

"Give thanks with a grateful heart," I mumbled, causing everyone to—at least momentarily—break form and look at me. Nothing ever happened out of the ordinary during those ten-hour stretches. The most excitement we ever saw was when someone readjusted, or scratched their nose, or sneezed, and got severely beaten if the guard happened to be walking by. However, the guard didn't seem to be near, and so I added the next few lines. "Give thanks to the Holy One, give thanks, because He's given Jesus Christ, His Son."

Though everyone immediately went back into form, I could tell the atmosphere was electrified by my defiance. I don't remember anyone ever speaking during those torturously long ten-hour sessions, and I certainly never heard anyone sing. Since the guard didn't come, however, I kept singing.

"And now let the weak say, 'I am strong,' let the poor say 'I am rich,' because of what the Lord has done for us . . . give thanks."

When I finished my song, I looked at the gigantic iron gate and waited for a guard to come swooping in with his electric baton. I'm not sure if he was on a break or just not at his station, but since I hadn't been punished yet, I started my song again.

"Give thanks . . ." To my surprise, another voice joined in with me. I couldn't see who it was, but the sound emanated at first from a few rows behind me. Then, another voice started singing from my left. We sang "Give Thanks" two or three times. It was an amazing thing because when we started the fourth repetition, every man in the entire cell was singing. Much to our delight, one of the drug dealers knew how to harmonize! I was amazed when we heard the cells on both sides of us also singing to God. I had to believe some of the inmates were sincerely thanking God, while others were singing as an act of rebellion. In fact, most had never even heard of the God to whom they sang. Whatever the motivation, the prison that day was turned into one huge worship center, and it split me wide open.

"Xi Yao Si!" I heard the next morning, then felt the now-familiar sensation of being jerked from sleep and dragged to the chief security guard office.

"What did we tell you about sharing the gospel?" the irate head security guard yelled.

"You said not to speak a word of it," I said.

"And yet you led the whole prison in your superstitious songs?"

"Well, I didn't speak a word of it," I said. "I sang it!"

After another stern warning, they tossed me back into the cell. This time, I was more like a conquering hero instead of a reprimanded prisoner. Everyone seemed to respect me. That day, when we were made to sit like statues in our uncomfortable positions, I knew I'd get beaten if I sang out again. Instead, I simply hummed the tune to "Give Thanks." Once again, the other men joined in with my humming. Pretty soon, the prison was a gigantic beehive of praise.

With every passing day, I grew closer to my fellow inmates. Little Tiger, Big Brother, and another drug dealer all came to me for advice, and I shared with them the meaning of the song we were singing. There was something transformative about befriending these particular men. In the past, as a student and an intellectual, I had never considered the plight of the prisoner. But being with the same thirty people, in the same two hundred square feet, did something to me.

● ● ●

One day, as our evening slop was being delivered, a guard came to the gate, pointed at me, and said, "It's time to go."

I'd been praying that if I were going to be in prison for my entire life, I'd be transferred to a "reeducation through labor" camp. In China, these camps produced any of a number of products, including steel pipes, shoes, toys, chemicals, and clothing for export. Prisoners mined minerals, grew cotton, made tea, and farmed—sometimes twenty hours a day. Many people died from the exhausting labor, but I thought it would be preferable to only a pinprick of sun for the rest of my life.

When they came to get me that day, I thought I was headed to do some sort of repetitive labor, like packaging ten thousand chopsticks per day. However, the guard looked at me, and said, "Come on. You're being released."

I'd been in prison for two months.

The other inmates, some who'd been in jail for years, looked at me and smiled. It felt wrong to leave them, but I couldn't wait to go outside and breathe air that didn't smell of thirty dirty men, eat food without worms, and lay down on—I quivered at the thought of it—a pillow.

"Wait," Big Brother said in a softer voice than I'd ever heard him use. "Let me give you the phone number of my family so you can tell them hello for me." Little Tiger added, "Yes, and please call my family. They'll visit you or treat you to a meal."

I took their information and promised to follow up, but smiled at the thought of welcoming my fellow prisoners' families to my home. I wondered if they'd bring cocaine with them if they visited and what Heidi would say.

Heidi.

Would she be okay? Had she been tortured? Would she have scars? Did she survive?

Then, I said goodbye to my fellow prisoners—my friends—and walked out of my prison cell, fighting the temptation to run.

20

"We're finally getting rid of you," the Communist official said, as he flipped through my release papers. He gave me a small bag with my belongings from two months ago, and I immediately rustled through it for my glasses. When I put them on, I could see everything clearly.

"Will I still be able to teach?" I asked.

"Yes. We want you to stay at the Communist Party School," he said. "Now that you owe us, you can help make sure others are loyal to the party. But don't get too excited. We'll be watching you too. We've assigned you two special agents who will be right there with you, every step of the way. In fact, here they are now."

I followed the direction of his gaze as two officers walked through the door. I was completely shocked when I saw their faces.

"Dingbang?" I said. "Feng?"

I knew them as the two lazy students who sat in my English class at the Communist Party School, day after day, refusing to lift their heads off their desks or learn even the most basic English phrases.

"What are you doing here?" I asked.

"Remember how we told you we'd been watching you for a long time?" the official asked. Suddenly, it all became so clear.

No wonder they were such terrible students. They were spies. They were everywhere. Always watching. Ready to pounce. My jaw hung open, but no words came out. I thought about all the times I'd tried to teach them the basic construction of English sentences, adjectives, and even easy conversational phrases. Had I known they were spies, it would've saved me a great deal of time.

"These will be your special agents," he continued. "They already know everything about you, so don't try to pull anything over on them."

"And quit trying to teach us English," one sneered.

I gathered my things and began to walk out the door, overwhelmed by my situation. Even though I was free from jail, one was never truly free in China. As I turned the corner, I looked down the long, brightly lit corridor and saw a solitary figure walking toward me.

Heidi. She was pale, thin, and—when our eyes met—she smiled. That's when I knew everything was going to be okay, and so many emotions rushed through me. I wanted to run to her, sweep her up into my arms, and kiss her. Of course, I didn't. After all, public affection is not the Chinese way, so we didn't even touch when we met in the hall. However, when we got to the privacy of our little ransacked apartment, I was able to properly show her how I felt. I took her hand, stepped over the overturned lamps, passed the flipped furniture, and led her to the bed. The Beijing police had dumped the mattress on the floor, but I promptly put it back onto the frame, looked at her, and said, "Want to commit a tremendous act of rebellion?"

The Communist Party was so controlling and heavy handed it reached into every aspect of life. China's notorious one-child policy meant couples had to obtain permits for pregnancy or else the government would force an abortion or even sterilization. Every time Heidi and I were intimate, this threat loomed heavily on our minds. Consequently, we had used contraception without fail during our entire three-year marriage. In fact, birth control was given out free of charge by the Communist Party School.

"Without *anything*?" Heidi asked. The question hung between us as we considered the prospect. They'd kept us apart for two months, and we wanted to be together without their influence. Plus, our time in prison had created in us a severe disdain for the Communist Party. Heidi smiled, opened her mouth, and said—at the same time as I—"*Beng guan tamen*," which meant, "Who cares about them?"

Seeing defiance in her eyes, I grabbed Heidi and we practiced our first act of "civil disobedience in the bedroom."

Noncompliance never felt so right.

21

"I have a surprise," Heidi said, putting down her trash bag and disappearing into our closet. We were knee-deep in the clutter the police had made of our home, but were slowly putting everything back into its place. There were huge empty spaces on our bookshelves and in our drawers—voids left by the police department. Thankfully, they left the refrigerator, television, and washing machine we had finally been able to afford just before we landed in prison. When Heidi emerged from the closet, she had a tiny book in her hand.

"My address book?" I jumped over a gigantic box of trash and embraced her. "How did you do it?"

"Before they took me to jail, I told them I needed to grab my sweater from the closet. Since they'd already ransacked that area, I knew they wouldn't return to it. I had the book in my hand like this," she adjusted it down into her palm with her thumb securing it, "and when I reached for my sweater, I threw it into the corner of the closet."

I flipped through all of the names of our fellow believers and friends, and was so proud of my clever wife. For weeks, we regaled each other with tales from prison. I was very relieved to hear Heidi hadn't been tortured, though she was kept with hardened criminals and forced to clean latrines. They called her "Graduate Student," because she was apparently the most educated prisoner they'd ever met. She shared the gospel in the cell, very discreetly, and even got to be good friends with someone in prison for financial crimes. I told her about Little Tiger and Big Brother . . . and warned her that we might be getting some visits from their families. I told her about those two heart candies that melted in my hand on our anniversary. But even as we got used to life outside of prison, the government was still looming over our lives.

One morning, the Communist School personnel official called me. "The Beijing Communist Party committee is asking you to leave the school, because you're not qualified to teach here anymore."

"I was qualified to teach two months ago," I protested. "In fact, I'm overqualified. Agent Li said I was supposed to teach. We had an agreement."

"No," he said. "We've talked to the relevant parties and the decision was made."

Of course, they weren't content to merely take away my livelihood. When we were arrested, Heidi was just one week from her final exams at the People's University. After three years of graduate school, she had already made plans for her life after graduation. However, right after I learned I would lose my job, Heidi received some bad news of her own. First, her graduate school decided not to give her a diploma or degree and kicked her completely out of school. To add insult to injury, the work unit with whom she'd contracted refused to employ her, citing political reasons.

It felt like a noose was tightening around our necks. Little by little, our freedom was being squeezed from us. Our friends began getting harassed. Dragonfly, part of our Christian fellowship, came home one day to find his apartment had been sealed, making him homeless. He took off, fearing arrest. Two church friends were summoned to testify against us, and we were even threatened. We were told we had to report every phone call, letter, or guest. And just in case we didn't accurately report this information, they stationed guards at the entrance of our apartment building. Our rather large building was shaped like an "E" and had three exits. Much to the chagrin of the other residents, the police shut down all of the doors except the main entrance in the front. The guards on the first floor checked anyone entering the building who looked suspicious. Whenever Heidi and I left the premises, security sent an alert to our special agents, who would follow us around the city. They wanted to shut down our ministry and turn our neighbors against us.

They were successful.

• • •

One afternoon, Heidi emerged through the door holding a bag of groceries and looking completely flustered.

"Are you okay?" I asked.

"You'd think if the agents were following me anyway, they'd offer to help carry my groceries," she sighed. "I'm so tired."

"It's probably just the post-prison exhaustion," I assured her. "You've been through a lot."

"Yes, and my back hurts, and I just feel so uncomfortable."

Our eyes met, and neither of us said a word. I took the bag of groceries and set it on the table. We sat down on the couch and held hands. I was the first to speak what both of us were thinking. "So, you're fatigued and have a general feeling of discomfort?"

"Yes," she said, very slowly.

"Do you think you could be—"

"After just once?"

We both felt children made a marriage complete. During our busy ministry time, however, we didn't have time to think about anything more than smuggling Bibles and conducting our illegal religious training. Nevertheless, we wanted at least one child; China's onerous one child policy didn't give us the luxury of dreaming of a large family. In China, the government heavily regulated pregnancies. To begin a family, couples were required to get a pregnancy permission card—a yellow card—before the woman could legally conceive. If a pregnancy occurred without the yellow card, the woman was likely to be arrested and forced to have an abortion. Tens of millions of babies were aborted per year, sometimes just days before they would've been born. And not only did family planning officials show up to do random searches for secret pregnancies, other citizens were expected to report women who looked pregnant.

We'd seen this firsthand. When my older brother's wife got pregnant with her second child, for example, she left to live in a secret location to have the baby. When the family planning officials realized she'd mysteriously disappeared, they broke into their home, grabbed my brother, and put him in a prison in the village. There, the Communist Party had hired a few strong men to beat him up, trying to get him to disclose where my sister-in-law was hiding. So, while we were filled with joy over Heidi's pregnancy, we were also filled with trepidation.

"Let's don't think about 'what if,'" Heidi said. My wife believed in knowing all the facts before making decisions. However, I had a feeling our bedroom civil disobedience had been a roaring success. "Let's find out for sure."

We went to a local hospital, where Heidi had a pregnancy test. As we waited for the results, I imagined holding a tiny person in my arms. Tiny feet, little hands. An infant seemed so innocent, so precious. After a couple of minutes, the nurse came back out and said, "It's positive!"

Heidi and I left the hospital immediately. Authorities didn't care if you were pregnant. Women had abortions all the time. In fact, a friend of Heidi's had eight abortions during grad school. If a woman tried to keep the baby, however, terrible things could happen. When we got back to our building, we passed the guards at the door and went up to our apartment. "I wonder if it will be a boy or a girl?" Heidi asked, excitedly. "Where will we put a crib?" she said, looking around the little apartment. "Do you think the baby will look like me or you?"

Heidi, as she talked about the baby, seemed suddenly different to me. For the first time in our relationship, I was looking at the mother of my child instead of just my wife. I'd always been attracted to her intelligence, her kindness, and her dedication. But during that moment, I realized the same attributes that made her a great wife would also make her a great mother.

"But wait," she suddenly said, yanked from her thoughts of diapers and baby bottles by the reality of the family planning laws. "I don't have a yellow card! They'll arrest me and kill our child!" she said.

"He'll be fine," I said. "Or, if it's a girl, *she'll* be fine. The Lord will provide a pathway." I kept my voice calm. I regretted the dark shadow of the family planning system that hovered over the excitement of our good news, so I tried to figure out the best way to proceed. Since I wasn't from Beijing, I talked to David Li, the friend who'd deposited money for me while I was in prison, and secretly told him of my predicament.

"Oh, you're in big trouble," he said. "You'll both be arrested for noncompliance, and they'll force Heidi to abort."

"Isn't there anything I can do? I'd like to see an actual doctor, to make sure the baby's healthy."

"You'll land back in jail if you show up to a doctor without your yellow card," he said. As I saw our options dwindle, I was filled with despair. I wanted to protect Heidi and our unborn child so much I couldn't think clearly. Plus, even if we could figure out a way to have the baby safely, I couldn't support a family.

"There's got to be a back door solution," I said.

"I know a doctor who might be able to help," he said. "She's a believer at a nearby hospital, so maybe she could do a check-up off the books. But it's a risk."

"How so?"

"She's supposed to call the police if anyone shows up without their yellow card."

"Do you trust her?"

"I do."

I had no choice, so I trusted her too.

• • •

I placed my hand on the small of Heidi's back and ushered her into the brightly lit doctor's office. The walls were a pale but cheery yellow, but nothing could calm my nerves. On the way up to the third floor of the hospital, I'd taken note of all the emergency exits in case we needed to make a quick escape.

Dear God, I prayed, *please don't let it come to that.*

"What have we gotten ourselves into?" Heidi whispered as we waited to see the doctor.

When the doctor finally came in, she was holding a clipboard reviewing our medical information.

"It's nice to meet you," she said. "However, we're missing some information." I shifted in my seat and tightened my grip on Heidi's hand. "Do you have your yellow card?"

"Well, I need to talk to you about that," I said, lowering my voice. "We are friends of David Li, and he said you might be able to help us. Heidi got pregnant without a permit, and we were hoping you could check to make sure the baby is healthy."

She immediately stood up, and put her hand on the doorknob like she was about to leave the room.

"You shouldn't have come here," she said. "Do you realize how dangerous this is? I'm obligated to call the police." I looked at Heidi and it looked like all of the blood had run out of her face.

"I understand that," I said, trying to keep the emotion out of my voice. "But David thought maybe you could do something for us."

"If I 'did something for you,' I'd be arrested, would lose my medical license, and be thrown in prison," she whispered.

"Do you at least have any advice for us?" I pled. "We won't be able to keep this a secret forever. They'll arrest us for sure as her belly grows."

The doctor's eyes softened when she looked at Heidi, who hadn't said a word. I could see she had compassion, but was restricted by her very reasonable desire not to land in prison for two people she'd never seen before. She put the clipboard down and walked toward us. Her voice was so quiet that we had to lean in to hear her. "You are in grave danger. Even if you could hide the pregnancy in public, the family planning officers will stop by your house to check on you. If you're already on their radar, there's no way you can escape their reach."

I listened intently, hoping to hear some sort of hope. I thought maybe she could direct us to another doctor, or a more rural province, or give us some direction at evading arrest and avoiding the forced abortion.

"What should we do?" I asked, desperation creeping into my voice.

"The only advice I have for you," she whispered, "is to run."

22

"How was the train ride?" I said, welcoming my dad into our little apartment. I took his suitcase from him and placed it alongside the wall. We had no guestroom, but we'd set up a nice place for him to sleep during his visit. Heidi poured him a cup of water. I swallowed hard as I saw him sitting there in our place, completely oblivious to our turmoil. We wanted to protect him from our illegal religious activities as much as possible, so he didn't even know we had spent time in jail. We figured the less he knew, the better. If the police detected he knew any information, they might torture him to extract it. Instead of telling him we'd gotten into trouble, we acted as if nothing was wrong. It was our way of keeping him safe, and we were thankful not to burden him with our predicament. His visit would hopefully cause the police to let their guard down. An extended visit from my disabled father made us seem less mobile, less apt to try to escape. Mainly, though, I wanted to see him at least one more time. He sat at our table, sipped water, and told us about his trip on the train. I remembered the first time I'd ever seen a train. When I was a young boy, I had secretly stowed away on the same bus my father was on for a business trip. He discovered me, but only after we were too far away for him to send me back home. Instead of being angry, my dad let me enjoy the rare trip outside our village. We stayed at a hotel, and he even let me see a train up close. I remember running my hand along the iron track, and wondering how far they could take me.

Everything was simpler then, but life had never been easy. I blinked back tears. Occasionally, during our visit, I excused myself to the restroom so I could collect myself. Even though the police had told us not to leave Beijing, that's exactly what we needed to do. Just like the doctor had advised, we were going to run.

We enjoyed several weeks with my dad, carefully concealing Heidi's pregnancy and just trying to act normal. Still, we jumped at every loud noise and were startled by every visitor. When the phone rang one afternoon while my father rested, we looked at each other with trepidation.

"You're in danger," a friend said, causing Heidi to immediately sit down at the table with me and lower the phone so I could listen in. On the other end of the line was a friend whose wife worked in the Public Security Bureau, or PSB, and he had inside information about the sarcastically titled "Old Friends Day." In Beijing, the Communist Party had an annual tradition of rounding up former prisoners and putting them back into jail on October 1, Chinese National Day. This was simply a way for the government to flex its muscle and intimidate its citizens. Some prisoners would stay in jail for just weeks, and others would die there. The arbitrary nature of the Chinese legal system meant they did to you what they wanted. Heidi passed the phone to me.

"What's going on?" I asked.

"My wife saw a list of the former prisoners the police plan to round up," he said into his receiver. "I'm sorry to tell you that your names are on it." I let a few moments pass as a shudder ran through me. I didn't want to go back to jail, especially now that I was about to become a father.

"Are you still there?"

"Sorry," I mumbled. "When's the round-up?"

Since it was already August, we weren't sure when police would start rounding up people. Consequently, we decided it was time for my father to go back to his village. We had honored him the best we could with our hospitality; however, we had enormously heavy hearts as we helped him get back on the train.

"Goodbye, Father," I said, choking on the word. I looked down at my shoes so he wouldn't detect my emotion. My dad looked up at me, smiled, and said, "I'll see you at the Spring Festival, won't I?"

I could only nod, knowing my voice would certainly betray me. Then I watched as the train disappeared down the tracks. Once we got back into our apartment, however, I steeled my emotions and discussed our escape plan.

"I need to jump," I said.

"From our window?" Heidi gasped.

"No," I assured her. "I'll go down as many floors as possible, and jump into that bushy area of the landscaping. Those shrubs might break my fall."

"You're betting your life on a lazy gardener?"

Our goal was to get out of Beijing without being detected by the police, which meant we needed to split up. After much deliberation, we decided Heidi could disguise herself and simply walk out of the building late one night. We got a scarf, a hat, and a different style of clothing. Heidi worked on walking with a different gait. It was definitely a risk. But we hoped they wouldn't necessarily notice a single woman going out for a late stroll. After all, they normally saw us together.

At midnight, she walked into the room with her floppy hat and different clothes. "It's time." We said a quick prayer together before she walked out of the apartment. The only items she carried were the little address book and a collection of business cards we'd collected from our Christian friends and acquaintances, tucked into her pocket. A suitcase or bag would arouse the officers' suspicions. When the door shut behind her, I didn't have much time. If her disguise didn't work, the officers would apprehend her and then come to the sixth floor to arrest me.

But I wouldn't be on the sixth floor. Heidi had the idea of leaving our apartment lights on, so the security watching from the street would think we were having a late night before bed. I made it to the second-floor restroom windowsill and jumped.

I'm not sure how long I was out, but I was surprised when I woke up in a mound of vegetation next to my apartment building. My face tingled and my body ached, but I seemed to be all in one piece. When I opened my eyes, however, everything was blurry, like a Van Gogh painting. I momentarily thought the fall had damaged my eyesight until I realized my glasses must've fallen off during the drop.

It is so hard to be a political dissident with bad vision, I thought as I painfully lifted myself out of the shrubbery and crawled around on my hands and knees, feeling for my glasses. *First I get beat up in prison because I can't see the guards, and now this?* I looked back up to the window from which I had jumped, and calculated that the glasses had to be within a certain radius of where I fell. However, the grass was so tall it hit me in the face as I crawled through it, feeling around, hoping my fingers would land on something . . . Aha!

I almost broke into tears when I realized I'd found the proverbial needle in the haystack. Then I got up, put on my glasses, dusted myself off, and headed out to meet Heidi and face the rest of my life on the run.

• • •

"Two tickets, please," I said, sliding some of our last bit of money through the slot. Heidi and I had met at a prearranged rendezvous point on the street, hailed a cab, and headed to the train station.

"We did it," I said to Heidi, as we boarded the train.

Though we didn't speak much on that train ride, the motion of the car on the tracks was pleasantly lulling to our troubled souls. Heidi closed her eyes and drifted off to sleep, but I was wide awake. I kept thinking about my dad, our little apartment, and—believe it or not—our television, washer, and refrigerator we'd left, which had taken us so long to purchase. But mainly, I wondered what the police would do to my family once they realized we were gone. With every stop, I watched the doors open and close. No agents jumped on to apprehend us. Rather, the train lazily meandered from location to location until we stopped at our destination.

We emerged from the train and inhaled the fresh air of the country. It was both liberating and unnerving to step out of the car without any bags or money.

"Do you think anyone followed us?" Heidi asked.

"If they had, we wouldn't have made it this far," I assured her, as I looked around to figure out how to get to our next destination. Our plan, for lack of a better one, was to stay in the home of a high-ranking police officer who had secretly become a Christian. We'd never met him. "Ready to go?"

She looked at me with exhausted eyes. "What if he turns us in?"

"What choice do we have?"

I'm a bit like my father in that I put my trust in people easily. However, I really believed I could rely on the officer not to turn us in, because he was a believer. Whenever I came across another Christian, I felt an inexplicably deep connection and loyalty. After all, we belonged to the same family! In China, if someone professed Jesus, he was doing so at great cost. Though I couldn't be totally sure of this officer's sincerity, we really had no other choice. We showed up at the family's back door and were quickly ushered in. And with that simple gesture of hospitality, they were guilty of the crime of harboring fugitives.

"You can stay here," the wife motioned to a nice bed they'd

set up for us in the corner of their home. They also gave us food and even helped arrange a medical check-up for Heidi. Otherwise, we stayed indoors, slept a great deal, and tried to figure out what to do next.

"I have an idea how you can have a normal life and make a living here," our host said to me one day.

"I'm listening."

"McDonald's," he said.

"You want me to work at a McDonald's?"

"No, I want you to operate one!" The largest McDonald's in the world opened near Tiananmen Square in 1992. With seven hundred seats, it had served forty thousand customers on opening day and captured the imaginations of Chinese citizens as a symbol of American entrepreneurship. With their limited menu, spotless restaurants, and equal seating, the restaurant chain even emanated a spirit of democracy. Everyone, regardless of social status, was served there. "Let's open a McDonald's here. I could own it and you could run it, since you know English so well. You and Heidi could make a nice life for yourselves here, far from the eyes of the Beijing police."

He didn't know it, but I'd always wanted to open a restaurant. When I was in college, I read Lee Iacocca's biography late into the night, dreaming of starting a restaurant that incorporated his ideas of customer service. "That's a wild idea," I said. "But I'd love it!"

Within minutes, we dialed the number of the headquarters of McDonald's in Hong Kong.

"I'd like information on starting a McDonald's in my area."

"Where are you located?" She put me on hold as she looked up our area, then came back and said, "I'm sorry. Your city is not big enough to be a lucrative location for our franchise. All of the large Chinese cities are in queue for our restaurants, and it'll be another ten years before your location can sustain one."

I hung up the phone. We thought all we had to do was to

receive permission to start a restaurant and hang up a home-made sign with the golden arches. We didn't know we'd have to put down at least a hundred thousand dollars to rent the building from the corporation, or purchase the food through their headquarters. Ironically, I didn't even have enough money to buy a Big Mac.

The next day, we said goodbye to our lovely new friends who'd risked their lives for us. We'd stayed there two weeks, and it was time to move to the next location. From then on, we moved every three days, relying on the kindness of members of the underground church to sustain us. Occasionally, we were able to get chilling reports from our friends back home. The Beijing police were combing the city looking for us. They called our friends and said, "Have you seen Bob and Heidi? We want to help them and give them amnesty for their crimes, but we can't find them."

My friends always responded as we'd planned. "Oh, they're just visiting family."

That deflection meant the Beijing police were in constant contact with the local police in the villages of my dad and Heidi's parents. We got reports they'd gotten pretty rough with our parents, but had relented when they realized our parents really didn't have any information.

"I just want to live a normal life," Heidi said in exaspera-tion. We'd moved every three days for weeks. "I want a place where our child can be free to play in the yard and go to school. Somewhere we won't have to constantly watch our backs." My heart ached for my family's situation. As long as we lived in China, we'd live in fear. But there was no way to cross the bor-der without passports and there was no way to get passports without getting rearrested.

"Wait a minute," she said. "Do you remember when we met Craig at church, and he asked us to reach out to that new Chris-tian man to disciple him, the one who worked in a travel firm?"

Craig was the Australian missionary who'd tried to connect us with others to make sure new Christians received good teaching, theology, and support. "I think he handed us the man's business card," I said, sheepishly remembering that I had never followed up on his request. I retrieved the stash of cards we'd carried all the way from Beijing and began to flip through them. I found one with the man's name in foil lettering.

"Maybe we should call him and get advice about getting passports and leaving the country."

"Do you think he'd remember that Craig told him about us?"

"I doubt it," I said. "But if I could get him on the phone, perhaps I could discreetly jog his memory." I flipped the card back over to its front and dialed his number.

"Hello, is this Zhang Shaoping?" In China, people don't ask for people by name unless they're very good friends. However, I wanted to give the impression of familiarity.

"No," a man answered. "This is his assistant. Do you know our director? Mr. Zhang's out of the office right now, but what can I do for you?"

Suddenly, I realized the man we'd met in Beijing was the head of the entire agency.

"Yes," I said slowly, trying to figure out the best way to handle this new information. "My wife and I want to travel overseas. Can you help us?"

"Of course, sir," he responded. "That, after all, is our business. All you have to do is send me your identification and your passports and I can get you wherever you need to go."

"We don't actually have passports yet," I responded. I couldn't explain my situation, which is why I'd hoped to speak to Mr. Zhang directly.

"No problem," he said, very happily. "All you have to do is apply through your work unit."

"Well, there's a complication," I said, thinking of a plausible story, while twirling the cord of the phone between my fingers.

"I'm a teacher at the Communist Party School, so I can't leave the country without permission from my school. But if I ask for permission, my co-workers at school will be jealous we're traveling abroad."

The assistant chuckled a bit. For one moment, there was an awkward silence, and I knew I was overreaching. I was just about to make up an excuse to get off the phone, when the assistant said something that would change the course of our lives.

"Well, since you know my boss, I can do you a favor," he said. "Let me help you apply for a passport. Can you send over photos of you and your wife? Also, would you like to take a tour? We have a nice one here that will take you to Bangkok and then Hong Kong."

"That sounds lovely," I said, trying to maintain a steady voice. If we could get to Hong Kong, then under British rule, we could apply for asylum in the United States as religious refugees.

The assistant paused and said, "The total cost will be 24,000 yuan."

He might as well have asked me to jump on a rocket to collect moon dust, but I assured him I'd send the money. The only person I knew with access to cash was Zhuohua Cai, since he printed so many Bibles illegally. For days, I tried to track him down.

"Cai," I said, when I finally got in touch with him. "Where have you been?"

"Me? Where have *you* been?" Apparently, he'd been walking to our apartment back in July but arrived just in time to see me being pushed into a car by the police. "I took off and have been running ever since!"

"Any chance you have any money you could send me?" I asked.

"Would three thousand American dollars help?" he asked. "Remember that lady who showed up out of the blue asking us to print thousands of Bible handbooks? She said she was a friend of Craig's? Well, we began her printing job, but she never came back to pay the rest of the deposit. I've been keeping her three thousand American dollars ever since."

At that time, the conversion rate between the US dollar to the Chinese yuan was one to eight, which meant we had 24,000 yuan . . . precisely how much I owed the travel agency.

We were getting closer, but the agency still had to verify my employment to get my passport, a strictly enforced regulation. When we got a call from our travel agent, however, he said, "Everything's set up. You should be getting your passports in the mail. Have a great vacation!"

"So," I asked, very hesitantly, "you had no trouble getting the passports?"

"The Sitong Corporation verified your employment, and you're ready to go."

I mumbled out a few pleasantries in my confusion, and hung up the phone. The Sitong Corporation was a privately owned computer company in Beijing known for helping with the 1989 student protests at Tiananmen Square. In fact, after the government crackdown, the People's Liberation Army occupied their headquarters to investigate their involvement in the protests. Their leader fled China to live in the United States.

"You're not going to believe this," I said to Heidi, who had been listening to my side of the conversation. "We got our passports." I explained how the assistant broke several laws to help us secure them, even though he didn't know us. In fact, we hadn't even met his boss.

When the passports came, we were astonished to see a letter of employment, verified by the Communist Party committee associated with the Sitong Corporation, giving us permission to take an overseas vacation.

"After all the punishment they've undoubtedly endured, why would they be willing to take such a risk?" I asked. "Without us asking? Without even knowing us?"

"These are the types of questions we'll sit around in heaven and ask," Heidi said. "In the meantime, let's just be thankful for God's provision and get out of here."

"Okay," I said, pushing the questions out of my mind to deal with the more pressing issues. "We're going to be going with a travel group to Bangkok and then to Hong Kong."

"Great," she said. "This might work after all!"

"There's just one problem," I added, in the softest voice I could muster. "The travel group is leaving from Beijing."

23

"Quit smiling so much," Heidi suggested. "It draws attention."

We were in the Beijing airport, even though we'd risked our lives to escape that city. I put on my most casual expression as I carried a small suitcase past security cameras, police officers, and customs agents. We found our travel group gathered around a grinning guide holding a Chinese flag, chatting excitedly about their vacation. I didn't engage in any real conversation, so if the police later had to question them about us we wouldn't have made an impression. My main goal was to blend into the group, make it through customs without arrest, and get safely in the air.

"Welcome, everyone," the guide said. "I hope everyone is excited about your trip, which will begin in exotic Bangkok."

He collected everyone's customs declarations and passports as everyone got to know each other. Our group consisted of about eighteen people, and included a doctor, a lawyer, some retired educators, and some engineers. Cameras hung from every neck.

"Xiqiu Fu," the man from the tour group said while clumsily handing me an armload of materials. "I'd like to appoint you the head of our group. Here's your flag, your itinerary, and everyone's custom clearance information," he said.

"I've never even flown before!" I figured he wasn't accompanying us simply to save money.

"I can tell you're a natural-born leader." He smiled, before adding, "Plus, you can speak English." After thanking everyone for using their tour group, he left me standing there among the group of tourists, holding a red Chinese flag above my head. Heidi stood off to the side and gave me an exasperated look. In one glance, I knew what she was thinking. *And we're trying not to draw attention to ourselves?*

I grabbed her hand once we got into the airplane for the domestic leg of the trip. "Are you afraid of flying?"

"I'm afraid of staying," she said as she gazed out the window and watched as Beijing shrank from view.

We touched down at Shenzhen airport, and I had to assist our entire group through customs. *Of all people, he selected the one who might actually be arrested to be their tour guide?* I wasn't sure how sophisticated the national customs and border control computer systems were, so I just said a prayer and willed myself to approach the counter. Our passports were wildly inaccurate, but our names were real. If I didn't make it through, Heidi was supposed to make a run for it.

"Passport?" the lady at the counter asked, taking it from my hand. She looked at my passport, then back up at me. Even though the photos certainly matched, I found I was unable to breathe. Thankfully, a couple traveling with an unruly small child was at the counter to my left, which provided a nice distraction. The baby repeatedly threw her pacifier on the floor and wailed. I pasted a look of impatience on my face and looked annoyed at how long the process was taking. The airport official flipped through my passport as if she was trying to make sure it wasn't counterfeit. Was this taking longer than normal? I wiped the beads of perspiration from my upper lip as I bent over to pick up the pacifier the baby had mercifully flung at my feet.

"Thank you, sir," she said, handing me my customs form, my passport, my visa, and my boarding pass. "Now the others?" I handed her the forms, which she glanced through. When she handed me back all of the passports, I forced myself not to run away from the counter, casually strolling with my group to the security line. I was so nervous that I almost forgot how to walk normally. Miraculously, we managed to get through security without any problems. When the door shut and the plane lifted off the ground, I looked at my wife and smiled.

Suddenly, we were tourists. As far as anyone knew, Heidi wasn't pregnant, we'd never been in jail, and we were not Christians on the run. In fact, I was a tour director who took my job seriously. I made sure everyone safely made it onto the bus in Bangkok and wore a pink floral lei to start the vacation right. I helped check our group into the hotel, informed everyone of our dining options, and passed out itineraries packed with tours of Buddhist temples, shopping, and elephant shows. Much to my dismay, I noticed one of our stops was to Bangkok's cabaret shows featuring transvestites and transgendered performers. We'd heard that the shows exploit their performers, who were frequently treated as sexual slaves.

"Should we go?" I asked Heidi.

"What choice do we have?" she replied. "We're supposed to be normal tourists, not Christians on the run. After all, *you're* the tour guide."

We sat in the audience watching the performers, some of whom were merely young girls, sing, dance, don sequined costumes, and sport gravity-defying hair. *Is this what religious dissidents should be watching?* Afterward, we overheard a member of our tour group trying to "rent" one of the young girls for the night. Both Heidi and I felt sick to our stomachs.

Bangkok was a city that specialized in sensory overload, which made it difficult for Heidi to secretly fight the symptoms of pregnancy. In spite of her extreme exhaustion, she joined in all of the group's activities. After one of our long days, we got on the elevator with our group and so many shopping bags I doubted the doors would shut.

"Did everyone have a great time today?" I asked. Though I had so many other issues on my mind, I felt it was necessary to keep up the ruse. I pushed the button for the fourteenth floor and took a deep breath. The air was hot and thick with humidity, and our clothes hung on us heavily.

"We got good deals on crystal elephants," a man celebrating his wedding anniversary responded. Just then, as we reached the eleventh floor, I felt Heidi slump against my shoulder. I turned to her, thinking she was resting her head, but I soon discovered she'd passed out.

"Help!" I said, causing all of my fellow tourists to drop their bags and try to lower Heidi gently on the floor when the elevator stopped. She'd bitten her tongue and blood was trickling out of her mouth.

"Lord, help her!" I yelled out in spite of myself. So much for trying to keep our faith under wraps. A Thai medical practitioner from the hotel passed some strong smelling substance under her nose, and she woke up with a start.

"You scared me!" I said later, when she was safely in our room. I dabbed her forehead with a wet cloth.

"I think I'm just exhausted," she said. "Plus, God might be punishing us for sitting through that show last night."

By the time we finally left Bangkok, we'd sampled Thai food, seen elephants do tricks, and had come to believe "forced tourist shopping" should be prohibited by the Geneva Convention. Hong Kong was our next destination.

"After you check into your hotel rooms we'll meet downstairs for dinner in two hours," I said to my group in my last instruction as their tour guide. I'd actually grown quite fond of some of them.

We had no intention of going to dinner. After we made a show of going to our room, we slipped out a back door and met Dragonfly, my co-worker who ran the university student ministry in Beijing and who had been on the run since our arrest.

"I wish I could see the faces of our tour group when they realize we totally disappeared!" I laughed.

Dragonfly took us to the apartment of Jonathan Chao, whose wife was mercifully letting us stay at their apartment even though Jonathan was out of town. Their generosity was a confirmation that they didn't begrudge my forced confessions against them when I was in prison. Because we had no money, the free apartment was an amazing sign of God's provision. Also, we met a missionary named Tim who had graduated from Westminster and was sent by CMI to work with Jonathan Chao's organization. Tim was moved by our story and helped spread awareness of our situation. One Christian businessman from Philadelphia, named Charlie, vowed to send our family $100 per month for each family member. Not only did we not have to worry about lodging, we no longer had to worry about food! This was important to Heidi, of course, who needed sustenance for the baby. Every day, I bought fresh fish or chicken at the same market, watching my back as I went. Even though we'd never met the man from Philadelphia, the money arrived every month. It was a sign of God's merciful provision.

And speaking of provision, the lady who'd left the three-thousand-dollar deposit for a large printing job was from Hong Kong, so we tried to find her while we were there. Sadly, we never could track her down.

"Let's just ask Craig when we see him," Heidi offered, referring to our Australian missionary friend. When she'd hired us to print the booklets, she had told us Craig had referred her to us for the job.

• • •

When we reached Hong Kong it was October 1996, and Hong Kong was nearing "the handover," when the British would hand back the nation to become a Special Administrative Region of China. Many feared how the modern city of six million with its free economy and press would fare under the heavy hand of the Chinese government. If we were there on "handover day," we'd be right back where we started. Thankfully, the Hong Kong government created a special team to handle the cases of political dissidents. They warned us to stay indoors to avoid kidnapping.

Jonathan introduced us to a Christian reporter named Ron, who reported about Chinese house churches. Since he was familiar with our story and with the US Consulate, he was nice enough to write our story and submit an official request for refugee status. Though we thought we'd be accepted quickly for protection from the Chinese takeover, the United States gave precedence to political dissidents over religious dissidents.

"We need to get out of here or we'll be thrown into prison," I told the reporter.

"Sorry," he said to me. "They don't even understand what an underground house church is!"

I was astonished that the American government was unaware of the ever-growing underground church movement in China. Using Jonathan's research, we tried to educate them about the movement, but they were not interested. It was as if they considered political refugees as courageous and religious refugees as zealots. From that moment on, our case was caught in a bureaucracy morass. Repeatedly, our case was tossed out: the US Consulate didn't recognize religious refugees, didn't understand house churches, and only accepted famous political refugees. As we filed and re-filed our case, and time passed, Heidi grew more impatient and frustrated.

"Look at it this way," I said, trying to cheer her up. "We're pioneers! We have the honor of being the first Chinese house church refugees."

"But where will our baby be born?"

It was a question I'd never researched, since I assumed our child would be born in the land of freedom—America! After I checked into hospitals in Hong Kong, I discovered that public hospitals offered labor and delivery for free if one of the parents was a resident. If not, they charged the equivalent of $20,000. Suddenly, we had another reason to get out of Hong Kong, and fast! We spread the word amongst our friends—some who were in America, some in China, some in the countryside churches—and asked for prayer.

As word of our situation spread, people showed great concern and tried to find ways to expedite our case with the United States. In fact, we got the attention of Dr. Carol Hamrin, a senior career China analyst with the US State Department who was also a Christian. Thankfully, she had heard of our plight from some Christian friends in Beijing and worked tirelessly on our behalf. Also, an American legislative assistant working for the Chairman of the House Government Oversight Committee and a member of the State Department flew to Hong Kong to put pressure on them to process our case.

We were blessed to receive all of this attention. However, it didn't seem to be helping.

"Bad news," the legislative assistant said after she walked out of the US Consulate in Hong Kong. I had been waiting for her outside the compound, because I was not allowed to go in. "The United States will not take the Fu family, period. Apparently, they're very concerned about offending China during this transition."

Sweden and Switzerland, I soon learned, felt the same way.

"Sorry, we can't help you," representatives of both countries responded.

Our tenuous circumstances made it quite difficult for Heidi, whose belly was growing larger every week. Weeks passed, then months, and our case was not one inch closer to resolution.

"What will happen if I go into labor?" she asked.

"I have to believe God hasn't taken us this far only to abandon us here."

The ring of the phone interrupted our conversation. "This is the Hong Kong immigration office," a man said. "We need to see you and your wife in our office tomorrow morning."

Because we'd stayed in Hong Kong longer than expected, we had to get a temporary permit to live there. Every three months, we trudged to that office, filled out a form, and came home. "Will you tell me what this is about?" I asked. As far as I knew, we were current on our paperwork, so I hated to drag Heidi through the streets of Hong Kong as close as she was to delivering the baby.

"You must come in."

Reluctantly, we went to the office, once again, watching our backs the whole way. When we got there, the clerk at the immigration office said, "The Hong Kong government has agreed to give you a temporary residence card."

"What do you mean?" I asked.

"This will entitle you to the benefits of a Hong Kong resident until you are able to leave." He said it very matter-of-factly, but I wanted to reach over and hug him. "Please stand here to be photographed for your identification."

As we left the office, Heidi and I were practically skipping. "Did we apply to be Hong Kong residents?"

"I didn't!" I said. "It's not possible."

Though Moses parting the Red Sea was probably a more dramatic miracle, Heidi and I must've praised God just as earnestly as the children of Israel. Only recently did I discover that a Hong Kong pastor who had helped a few hundred Chinese students escape after the Tiananmen Square massacre had arranged this for us. To this day, I've never met with him or been able to properly thank him.

Now, as Hong Kong residents, we could deliver the baby for free. Which is exactly what happened one week later, on April 4, 1997. Heidi went into labor and was admitted to Prince of Wales public hospital at absolutely no charge.

• • •

I was told I couldn't stay with Heidi during her labor, and we soon found out why. Heidi was in a room of thirty other laboring women. Every few minutes, a baby arrived and the nurses would move on to the next screaming woman. Though it was customary for men to wait at home, I waited in an area outside the elevator, one floor down from the labor and delivery floor. Nurses constantly rolled babies by me on their way to checkups, and I'd look at every one. *I wonder if that one's mine,* I'd think, peering into the mobile bassinettes to determine if any resembled Heidi or me. The next day, I wandered over to a room where babies were lined up like Chinese dumplings, peered through the glass, and saw Heidi's name next to a tiny, beautiful baby wrapped tightly in a mobile cart.

"He arrived last night," a nurse said.

He.

His Chinese name would be Boen, which means "abundant grace." But in English, he would be called Daniel, because he was born while we were still in the lion's den.

"I like that," said Heidi, who was recovering from her delivery in a room of fifty women. "He was born as an exile. He has no motherland. No country will recognize him."

"Yes," I said, tracing my finger through his wispy hair. "But his citizenship is in heaven."

Day by day, every television channel, radio station, and newspaper had a countdown of the days remaining until the handover. On June 4, Prince Charles and Hong Kong Governor Christopher Patten held a joint commemoration of the historic occasion. I attended a large gathering of over a hundred thousand people at Victoria's Park, because it was the anniversary of the 1989 massacre. In the crowd was a palpable fear that Hong Kong was about to be taken over by a nation capable of such violence against its own citizens. Looking out into the crowd, I was touched that people were intent on remembering what had happened in Tiananmen Square. Then, out of the corner of my eye, I saw a light. A political dissident who'd been unable to attain refugee status had lit himself on fire. People began to scream as he sat there. A human torch. The Hong Kong police ran over and promptly put out the fire that was ravishing his body. However, his actions showed the desperation we dissidents felt.

As we fought off despair, many people advocated on our behalf. Danny Smith, founder of the Jubilee Campaign, heard about our case. The Jubilee Campaign is an organization committed to ending slavery, childhood prostitution, and other injustices, so he flew to Hong Kong to advocate for our freedom. He gave a personal letter from Lord David Alton, a British upper parliament member, to Governor Patten. However, the American consulate doubled down. "We can assure you that the US will not accept the Fu family," they responded. "Find somewhere else."

We were already exhausted from staying up all night with our new baby, who screamed unless he was in constant motion. This news was almost too much to take.

"If America will not accept you," Danny said when he saw our crestfallen faces, "Great Britain will."

"Oh, are we going to ride on the same plane as the prince?" I asked, but no one was in the mood to laugh.

We exhausted every avenue, even applying to a Baptist seminary in the hope that student visas could give us some time to figure out our immigration status. To my surprise, I received a terse response. "Unless you are members of a Baptist church, you cannot get into our school." Though I had no idea what a "Baptist" believed, I looked in the phone book, found a Hong Kong Baptist seminary, got a copy of the Baptist confession, memorized it, and tried to look for a Baptist church to join. However, when we contacted the school with questions, they responded, "You won't be considered a member unless you've been at that church for three years."

In other words, we were a family without a home—spiritually or nationally.

One day, I went to a McDonald's in Hong Kong, where I was eating and reading a newspaper with a headline that screamed, "Seventeen Days Until the Handover." Though I sometimes wanted to forget my plight, I couldn't look anywhere without a reminder that the handover—and my family's certain demise—was 17 . . . 16 . . . 15 . . . days away. *Time is running out*, I thought, as I took a bite of my hamburger. Just then, I noticed a little excitement as a film crew came through the doors of the restaurant. One guy had a camera on his shoulder, and another was holding a microphone labeled "ABC."

"Hello, I'm doing a segment about the handover for *ABC News with Peter Jennings*," the man said to me at my little table. "Would you like to tell us your views on it?"

I looked around at the other people in the restaurant. I was supposed to be keeping a low profile, as the Chinese police were apparently trying to kidnap dissidents seeking asylum. However, I couldn't turn down this opportunity to plead my case on national television in America. Reluctantly, I agreed.

"We're speaking to Bob Fu here in a McDonald's in Hong Kong," the reporter said, sticking the microphone in my face. "Bob, are you apprehensive about the handover?"

"Actually, I'm a religious dissident from China, and my family will certainly be arrested—again—for our Christian religious beliefs unless the United States government will act on our behalf," I said. *How's that for keeping a low profile?* "The countdown to the handover is a countdown to our imprisonment. Please, America, stand up for religious freedom."

Everyone around me in the restaurant got silent as I pled my case to the American people. Though I feared for my immediate safety, it was my last chance. Diplomacy, after all, hadn't worked.

"Reporting from Hong Kong," the reporter said. "This is ABC."

With this one small interview, awareness of our situation spread throughout the United States. Though we didn't know it at the time, several prominent people worked on our behalf behind the scenes. The Voice of the Martyrs organization published a letter signed by dozens of US senators requesting the United States accept our family. Robert Schuller, of the famed Crystal Cathedral, wrote a letter to President Bill Clinton requesting he personally intervene on our behalf. Senator Jessie Helms, chairman of the powerful Senate Foreign Relations Committee, faxed a letter to the Hong Kong US Consulate asking that they speed up the process of our release.

And lastly, the president of the National Evangelical Association, Don Argue, phoned President Clinton. At the time, Don was a member of President Clinton's Committee to Review Violations of International Religious Freedom and Persecution, so he reported on religious persecution around the world. When the president picked up the phone that afternoon, Don encouraged him to pay attention to my small family across the world. "I think you should intervene in this case," he said. "Getting the Fu family out of China would give a great boost to your leadership in promoting international religious freedom."

One week before Hong Kong was handed over to China, Danny got a phone call in the middle of the night from the US Consulate. It was the White House National Security Council with a strong and decisive message from the president: Let the Fu family go.

Bill Clinton saved us!

All refugees are required to have an official sponsor in America, and my church sponsor was King's Park International Church, the home church of Pastor Ronny Lewis, and my government-appointed sponsor was World Relief. When the consulate discovered he'd been overruled, he suddenly sent word of a requirement that any refugee needed to have an American bank account with $10,000. This was the first time we'd ever heard of such an onerous requirement. How could a refugee set up an American account? How could they get such a large amount of money?

Desperately, we contacted Pastor Ronny and asked for a very big favor.

"Can you set up a bank account and give us $10,000?"

Ron had a decision to make; everyone else at the church had already gone home and the clock was ticking. Without even asking permission from King's Park, he transferred the money into an account with my name on it. (He didn't even know my Chinese name, so it was created for "Bob Fu.") I was astonished at the trust he put in me, and that money was our last roadblock to overcome before heading to America.

On June 27, we were called by the United States with the official word of our travel—one hour before our flight was to take off. We were taken to the Hong Kong airport and used a special back entrance to board the plane so the Chinese PSB agents wouldn't seize us. In God's perfect timing, it was the last working day of the old Hong Kong government.

Finally, we were free.

24

We arrived in America with nothing but a diaper bag and a long list of people to thank. First, we landed in Dulles International Airport, where a World Vision official helped process our refugee paperwork at customs. We also met two friends, Dr. Carol Hamrin, who had worked at the State Department as a senior China analyst for decades, and Mr. Greg Chen, assistant to the mayor of Washington, DC, who'd worked tirelessly behind the scenes on our behalf. Then I went to Raleigh, North Carolina, where I thanked Pastor Ronny and promptly transferred the church's ten thousand dollars back into its account.

I also thanked King's Park International Church for being my sponsor, and one of its congregants for letting us stay in his family's home for the first couple of weeks of our residency. I went to Washington, DC, where I thanked Assistant Secretary of State John Shattuck, who'd also worked so diligently for our freedom.

And we still weren't done thanking people by the time we arrived in Philadelphia, where I would attend Westminster Theological Seminary. There, the first thing I did was find Charlie, the businessman who gave us food money every month while we waited for freedom. He and his wife were so kind, and it was wonderful to finally meet them.

"Where are you staying?" Charlie's wife asked, after I explained how much their money had helped us. "Do you already have food?"

"With a friend and—honestly—where do you buy food around here?"

"Let's go." She laughed. "The first week's supermarket bill is on us."

"What's a supermarket?" Heidi asked as we pulled into the parking lot. The store had gleaming white aisles and was stuffed with beautiful, fresh tropical produce, even though we were in the middle of a northeastern city.

"How do you decide?" I asked, gawking at the green grapes, red grapes, purple grapes, and seedless grapes. This was the first time I realized a free society had its own kind of torture: the agony of unending choices. We filled our cart with foods we'd never seen before, without paying attention to the price. When we got to the cash register, I was embarrassed we'd racked up a two-hundred-dollar food bill.

However, they paid for our groceries happily and, over the course of the next few weeks, showed their generosity in ever-increasing ways.

"This is yours," Charlie said, tossing me the keys to a brown Ford station wagon.

"I've never even driven before!" I protested.

"Why do you think it's fully insured?"

Tim Conkling, the American missionary responsible for introducing me to Charlie while we were in Hong Kong, was in Philadelphia that summer. I made sure to thank him for the introduction.

"It's made a huge difference in our lives," I said. "He even gave us this car!" I pointed to the station wagon.

"Do you know how to drive it?"

"I don't even know how to pump gas," I admitted. Tim kindly took me to a station and conducted a short tutorial on how to get fuel from the pump to the tank.

A few months later, Charlie bought us a two-bedroom house in north Philadelphia that was near the grocery store, near Westminster's campus, and within walking distance of an elementary school.

"As long as you are staying at Westminster and doing China ministry, this is yours. No insurances, no taxes," he said.

We were overjoyed.

However, there was one more person integral to our escape whom we couldn't find to thank. She'd come to our illegal printing press on the referral of our mutual friend Craig. After placing an order, she never came to collect the books. Since she hadn't even left her name, we couldn't track her down. When it came down to the wire, we had ended up using her deposit money to flee China.

"Please give us her address so we can write a letter to thank her," I said to Craig, after he came in from Australia to visit with us. We had been so eager to tell him that story, and he listened with rapt attention.

"My mind's been racing," he said, "but I never told a woman about you."

A hushed silence fell over us. To this day, we've never heard from this woman or discovered her identity. Billy Graham referred to angels as "God's secret agents." Had God employed one of his divine secret agents to help us escape communist China?

All of these blessings intimidated us.

"You know the Scripture that says, 'To whom much is given, much is required'?" Heidi asked. "Do you think this is all some sort of test?"

Very recently, I had eaten wormy cornbread and slept on a concrete slab. Now I attended seminary and had a beautiful son, a house in Philadelphia, and a vehicle with a tank full of gas. We couldn't help but wonder what God was about to ask us to do and, more importantly, if we could meet the challenge.

● ● ●

Life was hard without even considering ministry. Westminster was a new world of opportunities and challenges. Hebrew, a more oriental language, seemed beautiful and rhythmic, but Greek perplexed me. Plus, I struggled with English. Though Heidi and I both had learned the language in China—and even taught it—the classroom was much different than north Philly.

In the meantime, Heidi was thrown fully into the world of domesticity. Daniel, who wasn't an easy baby, grew into an energetic toddler. When Heidi got pregnant again, we discovered her mom and dad were coming to live with us because her mother needed open-heart surgery. This was good, since we missed our friends and family in China. In fact, I'd had no direct contact with my family for so long. About one month after we arrived in Philadelphia, I was finally able to make calls without being monitored. In fact, I didn't understand AT&T's various calling plans, so my international calls drove my first phone bill up to six hundred dollars! In spite of the cost, however, I was thankful to be able to connect with some of my friends from school.

"Please tell my father we arrived safely in the United States," I said to one friend from my family's village.

"Xiqiu," my friend whispered. "I'm glad you finally called. The PSB officers have been here. They treated your father very harshly."

I hung up the phone with a heavy heart, wondering how my disabled father fared under their abuse. Another family member told me the details. Two Public Security Bureau officers interrogated my father after we left Beijing in September, demanding he tell them how I fled China and who helped me escape. In August, a few weeks after we had left Hong Kong, they came back for more interrogation.

My ministry friends had more dire news. "Sister Wang got arrested and was tortured," one friend told me. "Brother Li was sent to labor camp," another one said. With every conversation, I learned more about my old friends who were tortured or suffering for the sake of the gospel. As I sat in my comfortable house, memorizing Greek and Hebrew vocabularies, China was on the other side of the world. But I carried it—and its people—in my heart.

● ● ●

Heidi went into labor with our second child, and we were so thankful to be living in America. This time, I could accompany her into the labor and delivery room. But we had one complication. Heidi's parents had just arrived from China and offered to babysit, but they weren't familiar with our toddler. Since we didn't feel comfortable leaving him, I ended up toting Daniel to the hospital and taking care of him in the delivery room while Heidi labored. Even though it was a less than ideal situation, Heidi gave birth to a beautiful baby girl whom we named Yaning, or "elegant peace." Her English name was Tracy. Of course, she made our lives much more interesting. But even as Heidi recovered from her pregnancy and struggled to adapt to the rigors of having a second child, I began receiving speaking requests from church groups and organizations.

"Should you really go speak again this weekend?" Heidi asked, holding a baby in one arm and a toddler in the other. While my life had gotten so much larger, hers centered on diapers, acid reflux, laundry, and potty training.

"We're in America," I said, motioning around the house. "The least we should do is speak out on behalf of our brothers and sisters." Heidi nodded, but her bloodshot eyes indicated she wasn't ready to accept the heavy burden that came with freedom. I wasn't either. At night, I lay in bed and stared at the ceiling, and my mind raced with terrible scenarios. If I brought too much attention to China's treatment of Christians, the PSB would retaliate. "Do I stand up for truth to protect the millions of people in the Chinese church?" I asked God as I wrestled with my dilemma. "Or do I remain silent to protect my dad and siblings?"

Of course, I really had no choice. So when God gave me speaking opportunities, I took them. I made a speech at the National Presbyterian Church, where I met with John Shattuck. Afterward, he asked me for a list of people I knew being persecuted for their beliefs, which he promised to pass along to President Clinton before his visit to China. Also, I testified before Congress in several hearings, including one hosted by Senator Arlen Specter and Congressman Bill Goodling. I also testified in Los Angeles in front of the US Commission on International Religious Freedom, and spoke in Atlanta for the International Day of Prayer for the Persecuted.

Though I was sleep-deprived, stressed out about seminary, and distressing Heidi by my frequent trips, I told anyone who'd listen about the situation in China. Very few people understood that the underground Catholic and Protestant churches vastly outnumbered the government-sanctioned churches, and that millions of Christians would rather gather illegally than submit to the theological manipulation and retaliation of the Three Self Patriotic churches. Some didn't even know persecution was still going on in these modern days. And so I told them story after story of how the communists used Maoist-style propaganda, Cultural Revolution–levels of surveillance, and torture techniques that led to death. Even though I'd seen it with my own eyes, it was hard for me to prove these things happened. If I spoke out too aggressively, I might further endanger the victims of brutality. Plus, without documentation, how could I really prove that China—which had long boasted of religious freedom—was crushing the church?

The ache in my heart for my family back in China grew unbearable. In 2001, when I found out my sister Qinghua had installed a phone in her home, I could no longer resist the temptation to call.

"Qinghua?" I said. I strained to hear the familiar sounds of my old peasant village, but a fire truck barreled down the street outside my window. "This is Xiqiu! How are you?"

"We are fine," she said, in a very serious tone. I waited for more details, or for her voice to soften toward me. But, after a silence, she said, "There are many new bridge construction projects around here, and the economy is doing very well."

I wasn't sure how to respond. Her stilted conversation was at odds with the loving sister I remembered. "Okay," I said. "May I speak to Father?" My heart was so full of expectation and longing for home that I could barely get the words out. When I heard his voice, it took me a second to collect myself.

"Hello, Dad!" I said. "How are you?"

"I am fine," he said.

I decided not to mention any of my public activity in America, but I did tell him about my studies at Westminster and my ever-growing family. When I hung up the phone, I felt worse than before. Something seemed wrong. Later, I learned the PSB was monitoring their calls and had forced them to brag about the government construction programs. They wanted me, and the whole world, to believe China was a land of freedom and prosperity. And without any real documentation, who was I to say otherwise?

That year, however, China overplayed their hand. Underground Christianity was becoming increasingly popular. For example, the South China Church, a loose network of illegal house churches, had over fifty thousand members. To clamp down on its growth, the Communist Party labeled it an "evil cult" and arrested hundreds of church leaders, confiscated more than five hundred homes and properties, and fined, beat, and harassed thousands of the members. In a secret trial, five pastors—founding and senior Pastor Gong Shengliang, Xu Fuming, Hu Yong, Gong Bangkun, and Li Ying—were sentenced to death for "using an evil cult to undermine the enforcement of the law." Gong Shengliang was also convicted of rape and twelve others were also convicted of "using an evil cult to undermine enforcement of the law."

● ● ●

On New Year's Day 2002, Xiong Yan and I held a retreat. Xiong had been labeled one of the "twenty-one most wanted national student leaders" during the 1989 student movement. He went into hiding, but he was caught and served several years in prison. After his release, a house church Christian gave him a book called *Streams in the Desert*, and he became a believer before escaping to the United States. He and his wife both joined the United States Army and served two tours in Iraq. He even became a high-ranking Army chaplain. In 2000, after being transferred to Westminster, he asked me to be the executive director of the God Bless China Foundation, which was co-founded by Jonathan Chao. I immediately said yes, and through this organization hosted a retreat at the US Congressional retreat center in Maryland. It was called, a "Symposium on Christian Culture and the Future of China." Many Chinese pro-democracy leaders attended, including Dr. Wang Bingzhang and Peng Ming, as well as many American leaders from academia, churches, and the media, like Os Guinness, who let us use the retreat center at a discounted rate. Former Congressman Beau Boulter, whom I knew through his son Matt, a classmate at Westminster, spoke at our retreat.

During our time at the center, however, we received the very disturbing information about the five South China Church leaders' death sentences, which had been pronounced just a few days prior on Christmas Day. We also received multiple pages of smuggled-out testimonies of torture from those arrested in the South China Church.

"Let's just pause," I said, "and ask God what we should do in response to this information."

Our hearts were heavy for our brothers and sisters being persecuted for their faith, and we cried out to God on their behalf.

"Actually," Beau said after we had prayed, "I'm going to lead a delegation with two current congressmen to visit China in a week or so. We'll be the first United States congressional delegation to visit there since the attacks on 9/11." In January 2002, he was assigned to talk about religious freedom issues with the Chinese president, and we were thankful to have that direct line of communication with such a world leader.

At the retreat, we discussed various ways to help the South China Church, and decided to help to provide a good legal defense. We hired a Christian attorney in Beijing to help coordinate a legal team of fifty-three lawyers, and decided to ask believers in all of our various networks to help cover the costs.

"I know we can get Christians to donate money," I said. This draconian use of force to obliterate the church and the trumped-up charges disturbed people throughout the world. "But who'll collect it?"

"We could have an organization sponsor it," someone offered. "They could accept the donations and then designate the money for legal assistance."

However, one Christian organization after another turned us down. No one was willing to accept the funds because they feared retaliation by the Chinese government. Without a nonprofit organization to sponsor us, the donations would not be tax deductible. Though I didn't feel like I had the energy or the inclination to start my own nonprofit organization, I decided I had no choice. I had to help the South China Church.

When I got back home to Philadelphia, I sat in my attic where I set up an "office," meaning a chair and a tiny desk next to boxes of Christmas ornaments and summer clothes.

"Justice for China," I wrote, as I brainstormed names for my new organization. I crossed it out because it seemed too clinical.

"Just China," I wrote down, but that sounded too selfish.

"ChinaAid," I wrote. I wasn't sure if it was catchy, but it did give me some room as I figured out the mission of the organization. "Aid" could encompass a great deal of activities, after all, from flood relief to legal help.

• • •

In 2002, one man's guilty conscience sent political shockwaves all over the world. An official in China's Ministry of State Security felt terrible about how he'd been treating the various religious groups. He'd been told evangelical Christians, Falun Gong, Tibetan Buddhists, Uighur Muslims, and Roman Catholic bishops were all "cult members," and was given very harsh protocols to deal with them. The official decided he could no longer execute the protocols, so he left his position, turned over top secret government documents to a man in New York named Shixiong Li, and went into hiding. Other officials in China's PSB provided documents as well, which were smuggled out of the country by a network of Christians.

When Shixiong Li, president of the Committee for the Investigation on Persecution of Religion in China, or CIPRC, contacted me and spread the documents out on a table, I knew we had a treasure trove.

"Only twenty-eight copies of these were made," Shixiong told me. He'd grown up in a Chinese gulag, after the PSB had put his parents in prison. "And here's one of them."

"What are you going to do with it?" I asked.

"You mean what are *we* going to do with it?" Shixiong said, smiling. "Will you be the executive director of CIPRC?" he asked. Though I was already stretched so thin in my life, I wanted to be a good steward of the material so many people had risked their lives to smuggle out of China.

When I went home and told Heidi of the new developments, her face fell. She'd spent the whole day running tedious errands in one of the largest cities in America, though she had just received her driver's license and had trouble communicating in English.

"What should I do?" I asked her late that night after everyone else had gone to sleep. Heidi's eyes were bloodshot, her hair was mussed, and her shirt was covered in baby spit.

"How much does the position pay?" Heidi asked, trying to find at least some silver lining.

"Zero dollars." At the time, I made videos of Chinese Christian testimonies for Voice of the Martyrs, which paid five hundred dollars per month. We were able to live on that, since we didn't have to pay for our car or lodging. I knew I had a responsibility to Daniel and Tracy, but as we looked at them, tucked so sweetly into bed, our consciences were quickened.

"There are so many 'Daniels' and 'Tracys' in China who are orphans because of those protocols," Heidi said, fighting back tears. "We must speak out, even if it's . . . hard." Her voice broke on the last word.

And so, I assisted Shixiong in translating these top secret documents, which we compiled into a 141-page booklet called *Religion and National Security in China* in cooperation with human rights partners at Freedom House, Voice of the Martyrs, Open Doors, Compass Direct, and the UK's Jubilee Campaign. We were all on edge.

These documents demonstrated for the first time in history how China's central party leaders knew of and encouraged the torture of people who belonged to "cults." Their fourteen "cults" were described as a "crawling danger to domestic security and defense," but their definition of "cult" was so ambiguous and arbitrary it could be applied to almost anyone in an unregistered group. Also, the documents showed how extensively the Communists spy on members of these groups—both in China and abroad.

This rang true to me. Since we'd moved to Philadelphia, I noticed Chinese people sitting in cars outside my house for hours. Sometimes Heidi was afraid of running errands with the children. Were we imagining things? Or was it possible that

China had sent agents to Philadelphia in an effort to kidnap me . . . or even worse?

One rather chilling sentence encouraged local police to "purify the area" after religion had been introduced. Also, the documents detailed the use of secret government agents to infiltrate Protestant house churches, as well as ordering "forceful measures" against the Falun Gong, a relatively new spiritual discipline first introduced in China in 1992 that focuses on morality, meditation, and slow-moving qi gong exercises. In addition to the documents, we identified more than twenty-three thousand people arrested since 1983, and collected statements from five thousand torture and persecution victims in twenty-two provinces and two hundred cities.

Jonathan Chao helped write all the detailed footnotes for the documents, so I tried to credit his effort by making an editorial note at the end of the booklet. "Footnotes by Chinese church historian, Dr. J. C."

"Why did you use my initials in here?" he said, when he first read the hard copy of our report. "The PSB will figure out that's me in no time!"

To calm Jonathan's nerves, I reprinted all of our materials without attributing him in any way. We were all afraid. Friends and even people associated with the United States government had warned us about what we were about to do. "China has assassinated people for much less," one said.

● ● ●

In spite of our apprehension, we pressed ahead. On the morning of Monday, February 11, we held a press conference at West 51st Street in New York City, which not coincidentally was ten days before President Bush was to meet with Chinese President Jiang Zemin. We chose to hold the press conference in New York City instead of Washington, DC, because it was just months after the September 11 attacks. New Yorkers hadn't wanted to know so much about terrorism, but now they had stared it in the face and were resolved to fight it.

Shixiong approached the podium and cleared his throat. The reporters packed several rows of seats, and cameras flashed when he began speaking. "Today, we disclose confidential Chinese documents that were brought to us by brave people at the risk of their lives. We'd like to let these bloody documents speak for themselves, so that you can see what today's religious freedom really means to the Chinese Communist Party!"

The reporters typed furiously on their laptops as he stepped away from the podium and I approached. I wished I'd brought some water. My mouth had gone dry, and I feared I might open my mouth and no sound would come out. I'd never held a press conference before. *Who will deliver the news if not me?* I thought, so I took a deep breath and began.

"We want to further push for religious freedom for the Chinese people," I said before explaining the Chinese government was engaging in "double talk" by saying they had religious freedom while issuing secret orders to crush religious groups. I encouraged President Bush to shine a bright light on the human rights abuse when he visited China, to send a message to President Jiang: America values freedom.

It all felt a little crazy, to be sure. Here I was, a guy with poor English trying to direct the conversation of the leaders of the most powerful countries on the planet. Though we'd hoped our efforts would get attention and we made sure President Bush received a copy of our report, we weren't prepared for what happened next.

Our document release made the front page of the *New York Times*, the *Washington Post*, the *Financial Times*, the *London Times*, *Agence France Presse*, and *South China Morning Post* in Hong Kong.

"Listen to this," I said to Heidi in the aftermath of the release, when I'd retrieved a copy of the *Washington Post*. "A China specialist in London examined our documents and said this 'could be among the most significant internal documents on religious persecution in China seen in the West.'"

"I'm proud of you," Heidi said, as she paused at the door. "I really am." She was leaving to go fill some prescriptions with her mother, father, and babies in tow.

When I finished reading, I looked up to see that Heidi was already out the door, and I was alone in the house for a few moments. There, in the rare silence of our home, I was overwhelmed with gratitude over what we'd been able to accomplish. I knew my father didn't know about any of this, but I just wanted to hear his voice. I picked up the phone, dialed the number, and waited for his familiar voice. He'd never felt so far away. Qinghua answered the phone.

"Hello, sister!" I greeted. "I just wanted to check on you."

"Everything is fine," she said, raising her voice. "We are all very fine at home." She paused, and I could hear the phone being muffled. She was weeping.

"Is Father okay?" I asked, to which she repeated, almost robotically, "We are all very fine at home."

I knew. They'd gotten to them. After phone calls to family friends, I found out the PSB had gone back to my hometown after the document dump. No one was willing to explain the details, but I knew that my aged, disabled father was in trouble, and I needed to get him out of China. But how? I was barely able to escape as a relatively young man. How could he escape with agents monitoring his every move?

As I agonized over my father's predicament, I flipped on the television to see a joint press conference between President Bush and President Jiang in Beijing. Human rights advocates were wondering if Bush would risk ruining the goodwill of the visit by bringing up religious freedom. Though I had to run to campus for my Greek class, I sat down on the sofa and turned up the volume on CSPAN. Bush and Jiang were standing behind flower-decorated podiums on a stage with both American and Chinese flags. Jiang spoke first in Chinese, explaining several issues on which the two countries agreed. Then Bush gave his own review of their visit. "Our talks were candid, and that's very positive. The United States shares interests with China, but we also have some disagreements. We believe we can discuss our differences with mutual understanding and respect."

Disagreements? The word caught my attention.

"China's future is for the Chinese people to decide," he said. "Yet no nation is exempt from the demands of human dignity."

I couldn't believe my ears. Right there, in front of President Jiang, President Bush was bringing up the plight of the persecuted. I held my breath as he continued. "All the world's people, including the people of China, should be free to choose how they live, how they worship, and how they work. Dramatic changes have occurred in China in the last thirty years, and I believe equally dramatic changes lie ahead. The United States will be a steady partner in China's historic transition toward greater prosperity and greater freedom."

ABC journalist Terry Moran asked a follow-up question. "President Jiang, if I may, with respect, could you explain to Americans who may not understand your reasoning why your government restricts the practice of religious faith; in particular, why your government has imprisoned more than fifty bishops of the Roman Catholic Church?"

President Jiang didn't respond to the reporter, and instead stood aloof behind his podium. There was a slight pause, when everyone—including President Bush—looked at him to respond. He didn't. To eliminate the awkward silence, a Chinese Foreign Ministry official jumped in and let a Chinese reporter ask a different question. A little later, another American reporter, Bob Deans of Cox Newspapers, asked the same question about religion. Once again, President Jiang ignored the question and the official pivoted to a Chinese reporter.

However, just as the news conference was wrapping up, President Jiang indicated he wanted to answer the questions of the American journalists. He presented it as if it were an oversight, laughing as he said, in English, that he was not as familiar with press conferences as President Bush.

He reiterated the old Chinese claim that the nation does, in fact, have religious freedom, but added, "Whatever religion people believe in, they have to abide by the law. So some of the lawbreakers have been detained because of their violation of the law, not because of their religious belief."

My phone began ringing off the hook. Though President Bush didn't directly challenge President Jiang over his false claims—at least not publicly—we'd forced human rights onto the summit agenda, an issue that China desperately wanted to avoid. And the questions from the two American reporters had obviously rattled President Jiang.

I was pleased to see President Bush had the moral courage to stand up to President Jiang on a global stage. And I was a little amused that the son of a disabled man and a former beggar had affected the international dialogue at this high level.

All of these great accomplishments aside, however, something significant still haunted me. Deep down, I worried they'd retaliate by killing my father.

25

It was well past dinnertime, and my stomach felt uneasy. Bangkok International Airport was bustling with businessmen with briefcases and tourists with cameras. I stood in one corner of the terminal, my eyes glued to the arrival board. The flight from Qingdao was delayed until almost midnight. I forced my feet to stay firmly where they were planted, even though I felt like pacing . . . even though I felt like running. I couldn't look suspicious. I casually glanced at my watch, unfolded a newspaper, and didn't make eye contact with my American friends standing in opposite corners of the terminal. They would provide reconnaissance and reinforcement if we were apprehended. Another friend, a former member of Congress, and I would soon make our move. None of us were action heroes. What had I gotten us into?

Outside, my friend Paul sat idling in a pick-up truck, our getaway car. He'd circled around so many times that he knew precisely how many seconds it would take for him to get from his position to the terminal gate.

If all went as planned, we could snatch my father and have him in the truck in less than a minute. If it took any longer, Chinese authorities would certainly detain us. I hadn't slept for two days and nights after over thirty hours in the air in flights from the United States to Bangkok, with two stops along the way. I almost totally lost my voice. The chances of this scheme working, however, were admittedly slim. I'd thought it up as I sat in Philadelphia, trying to figure out a way to get my dad out of China.

"Don't tell your mother," I told my nephew over the phone, knowing my elder sister was already in trouble back home because of her relationship with me. "But I need your help. Tell my father he's won a vacation, six days in the tropics, including an automatic visa, and take him to Thailand. We'll take it from there."

Amazingly, the plan had worked so far. My father believed he was headed out on a vacation, but I doubted the PSB agents were fooled. They certainly were on the plane as well, watching my father's every move. They probably anticipated shenanigans and had prepared for a possible rescue attempt by a poolside, from a hotel, or near a tiki bar. I hoped they didn't anticipate a move as soon as he got off the plane. It was very risky to snatch him from right under their noses, in front of the surveillance and security of an international airport.

But we needed the element of surprise.

If this went wrong, I would definitely be arrested and thrown into Chinese prison for the rest of my life. However, I could no longer sleep at night and it was a chance I had to take.

Finally, I looked up from my paper and saw a tourist group walking toward us, following their guide. My nephew, who was pulling a suitcase near the front of the line, had his eyes fixed on me. He motioned with his head to the back of the line, where I saw a very small, stooped, elderly man shuffling through the airport. I hadn't seen my father in seven years, and my throat tightened. But this was no time for sentimentality. What if he didn't willingly go with us? What if the surprise was too much for him? What if he tried to fight us off, alerting the agent who was no doubt hidden among the tourists in the group?

I looked at my accomplices, who alerted Paul. At my signal,

one friend walked toward the line of tourists from the west corner of the airport and I walked from the east. We sidled up right next to my father, put our hands on his elbows, and said, "Come with us. We're here to help."

In one fast move, we grabbed my father, rushed him straight out of the terminal, and practically threw him into the pick-up truck that arrived at precisely the right moment. From start to finish, it took thirty seconds.

"Go, go, go!" I yelled as we got into the truck, and my friends looked back to see if there was any response. Sure enough, one of the "tourists," wearing a camera and a floral necklace, suddenly emerged from the line, furious when he realized my father was gone. We slammed the door and drove away just as the PSB agent dropped his tourist ruse and apprehended my nephew.

"We want to get you out," I said to my father, who was absolutely bewildered as we sped away. "These are my friends and we're trying to help you."

He looked at me in the dark pick-up truck, and recognition flashed across his face. "Pianyi?"

My childhood nickname. He grabbed my hand, squeezed it, and then repeated—more softy and to himself—"Pianyi."

• • •

Our rescue could not have gone more smoothly. Within four days, the United Nations office in Bangkok recognized my father as a refugee, a process that sometimes takes months or even years. Then, in a US Department of Justice building in Bangkok, we met officials who would process immigration issues for individuals set to resettle in America after receiving UN refugee status.

Oddly, however, he refused to answer their questions. He sat in his chair, his head turned away from the official and his interpreter, defiantly. After a while, the immigration officer looked at me and said, "Your father's not cooperating. If he doesn't start answering our questions, we'll cancel this meeting."

"Dad," I said, in Chinese, trying to hide my frustration. I'd done so much maneuvering to make this meeting happen, I couldn't imagine canceling it. It might take months to get back on the docket. "You *must* respond to this man."

"His interpreter is from Taiwan," he said. "I can't understand his accent."

The officer sighed, shuffled his papers, and looked warily at the interpreter.

"Let's try this again," he said. "Mr. Fu, can you please tell me what happened when—"

Just then, my father twisted in his chair and exploded in anger.

"Go ahead and beat me!" he yelled. "I have nothing to say to you!"

Suddenly, it dawned on me. We were in a plain white room with metal chairs, a desk, and a man asking him detailed questions. My father believed he was back in China being interrogated by the PSB.

"Don't worry, Dad," I said, very gently. "This man is here to help you. We're not in China anymore, and we're trying to make sure you're safe."

My dad looked at the interviewer and narrowed his eyes suspiciously.

The Department of Justice officer pulled me out of the room for a private word.

"Listen, this is against protocol, but I'm really sorry your father couldn't understand our interpreter and thought he was in danger. I'm going to let you interpret for him."

"Thank you," I said, knowing that relatives cannot normally interpret for relatives during immigration hearings. "I think it'll help him feel more comfortable."

"Please raise your right hand, and repeat after me," he said, in a no-nonsense way. "I solemnly swear . . ."

"I solemnly swear," I repeated.

"That I will translate my father's words faithfully and accurately, to the best of my knowledge," he finished. I repeated his sentence, and was impressed that he wanted to make sure I took my responsibility seriously.

When I came back into the room, I placed my hand on my dad's shoulder. "Go ahead and tell this man what happened."

Reluctantly, he did.

On February 25, 2002, police from the Wangwu Branch of the Gaomi Public Security Bureau took him in for interrogation. They threatened to imprison him unless he could persuade me to stop my "anti-China activities." On March 4, the same officers took him back to the station, where they kicked him, cursed him, and tortured him.

"I told them my son was a good boy," he said. "That he wouldn't betray his motherland, but this only infuriated them. They forced my head down to my knees and made my hands stick straight up in the air and hold that position. They hit my head so much I felt dizzy for days after they released me."

I had to leave the room. I needed air. I needed water. I was the one who should've endured those beatings. I was the one who'd chosen to stand up for the rights of the persecuted church. My dad was just an innocent bystander, a disabled, elderly man who still called me "boy" even though I was thirty-five.

A few months later, we were allowed to leave Thailand and travel to Philadelphia. When nationally syndicated talk radio host Nancy DeMoss heard about our rescue efforts, she paid for our entire trip, which was very expensive. She also gave me a laptop, on which I finished my studies for a language test.

Once my father arrived at our American home, he finally got to meet Daniel and Tracy. As I made the rather awkward introductions, I couldn't help but think, *This is not how it's supposed to happen. Grandfathers should be able to hold their grandchildren, to play with them, to pass on knowledge natu-*

rally as a part of their lives from birth. They shouldn't need to be introduced.

America baffled Dad. Our home was situated on a busy four-lane road, so the loud traffic and activity were quite different from our old peasant village. He didn't understand why so few people walked on the sidewalk in front of our home, or why we used the garden under the windows for ornamental flowers instead of food. Since he couldn't understand English, American television was incomprehensible. Yet he dutifully sat and watched cartoons with the children. During the days, however, Dad and I would take long walks around my home. These were wonderful times of visiting and making up for lost time. I was thankful to be living with my father for the first time since high school, even if we now had seven people living in our two bedrooms.

Our cramped living quarters would certainly make anyone agitated, especially an older man yanked from his homeland and thrown into a completely foreign environment. As time passed, my dad didn't seem to be doing well—but it was more than agitation. He'd stop talking in the middle of a sentence without finishing his thoughts. He seemed nervous around strangers. Even though I warned him not to walk around the area by himself, he'd sneak off and get lost in north Philly. *Could it be Alzheimer's?* I wondered.

In the fall, I took my father to see a neurologist.

"Your father has two tumors the size of eggs in his brain," the doctor told me, looking at the MRI. Then he paused for me to translate the news to my father. I didn't. I wanted to know the whole story before relaying the information to him. He'd already been through so much. I was actually relieved to hear about the tumors, which were benign. Though they needed to be surgically removed, the doctor assured me he'd be fine.

After his surgery at the University of Pennsylvania Hospital, however, he was in terrible shape. I stayed there with him around the clock, making sure he understood what was happening to him. The nurses bound his legs and arms so he wouldn't pull out his stitches during recovery.

• • •

Even though he was expected to survive the surgery, I had the strong feeling that this was his deathbed. Suddenly, I realized I never really knew if my father was a Christian. He'd written me in a letter that he met with the elder Christian man in the village who was known as a wise fortuneteller. Did that mean Dad was a Christian as well? When I went home from college to visit him, he had his own house church. My father was so proud when I attended services, read the Bible with his house church, and did my best to explain the passages. He was proud of my biblical knowledge, even though it was as deep as a thimble. Dad's house church grew, and one of the members became very zealous for the Lord. He rode his bicycle all over town telling people about Jesus, which got the church in trouble. The PSB said he could be a Christian, but he'd have to be more discreet. He couldn't keep his Bible on the table, for example. He had to hide it in the closet.

Soon after, the government broke up my father's house church and his only option was to attend a government-sanctioned church an hour from his home. Though it was very inconvenient, he made the journey every week. He even asked to be baptized there, but the church officials denied his request.

"They said I was too old." He laughed. "But my age should've added a certain urgency to the procedure."

Of course, the truth was they didn't deem him fit for baptism because of me. But even though I knew he had participated in all this religious activity, I had never directly asked him if he was a believer.

I held his hand and tried to engage him in conversation.

"Is your suffering going to make you deny Jesus?" I asked. "Do you really believe in Him as your Savior and Lord?"

My frail dad, who probably weighed eighty pounds, looked up at me. He only had one eye that worked. His head was bandaged from the surgery, he was connected to IVs, and his arms and legs were tied to the hospital bed.

"How could I deny Jesus?" he answered joyfully. "He has done so many good things for me!"

This was the first time I had heard an assurance of his faith.

After the surgery, we knew we couldn't properly care for my father, who needed feeding tubes and constant care. We admitted him to a nursing home, where he fell one morning as he was getting out of bed. A few weeks later, he fell again.

"I have a headache," he told the attendants.

As I monitored his situation, I could tell he was slipping away from us. Had I taken him away from those village barefoot doctors and all the way to the best medical care in America only for him to die of complications from surgery? Did the beatings exacerbate his condition? Was the airport rescue—which at least momentarily felt like a "kidnapping" to him—too much to bear?

One Sunday morning in January, we came home from church to see a blinking light on the answering machine. The nursing home had admitted my father to the hospital. He died just a few days later.

It all felt a little unfair. We'd been separated for so many years and had risked so much to reunite. I'd hoped a new home in America might make up for lost time and restore what the Communists had taken from him. After all, my father was generous, loving, intelligent, and brave, but he was also disfigured, damaged, and limited by cruel circumstances. After he died, I was comforted by the scriptural promise that one day we'll have a reunion that won't require a getaway car or dodging special agents. We'll be restored in a world that doesn't know disability and pain. In a word, we'll finally be home—the kind not made with hands—and I guess we'll all have to wait until then to truly be free.

26

"I don't know what percentage of me is Midland," George W. Bush said during the presidential campaign of 2000. "But I would say if people want to understand me, they need to understand Midland."

Suddenly, reporters from all over the world descended on this oil-rich town in West Texas halfway between Fort Worth and El Paso. No longer was it best-known as the home of "Baby Jessica," who was rescued from a narrow well in 1987. Suddenly it was the cradle of a possible president, and the world wanted to understand his roots.

It wasn't your typical town. Sitting on America's second largest oil reservoir, residents make—and lose—phenomenal amounts of money there. Almost everyone's been both fabulously wealthy and barely able to survive. Whether it's boom or bust, however, their entrepreneurial spirit keeps them going back into the fields to try, one more time, to get every last drop of oil out of the otherwise dry land. Dipping up and down, the perpetually moving pump jacks are the heartbeat of the town.

As rich as the town is in oil, it is poor in vegetation. Shrubby mesquite crawls along the ground and few scraggly trees impede the view of the "tall skies." In fact, the town's motto is "The sky's the limit," a phrase Bush used during his speech to the GOP convention that year. With hard work and perseverance, Midlanders believe, nothing's out of reach. The churches believed this too, and decided to leverage their location's newfound cache to make some impact on the world. This prompted Deborah Fikes, a self-described "Midland housewife," to present an idea to the Midland Ministerial Alliance, a network of more than two hundred churches in the city.

"I want to encourage you to use your platform on international religious freedom issues," she said. "Let's see if we can help people suffering for their beliefs in other countries."

Of course, Midland didn't know any members of the persecuted church. But the Alliance listened to Deborah and began to pray. After Bush was elected, Sudan was on the front page of every newspaper. And so, the Alliance sent a letter to the leaders of Sudan on stationery that read, "Ministerial Alliance of Midland, Texas: Hometown of President Bush and First Lady Laura Bush." It definitely got the attention of the Sudanese government. Sudan's Minister of Foreign Affairs, Mustafa Osman, instructed their ambassador to talk with the Alliance. Deborah was invited to have dinner at the Sudanese ambassador's residence, and she was the only evangelical Christian who had the trust of the Muslim government. Over the course of several months, the Ministerial Alliance of Midland had access to and influence on all four parties key to the peace negotiations: the Sudanese government, the People's Liberation Army, the Kenyan mediator, and the United States.

Minister Osman at one point contacted the Sudanese ambassador and asked, "What do these people from the tribe of George Bush think?"

Suddenly, this alliance of Christian churches in Texas became a major player on the global stage, and our paths were about to cross.

One day Deborah Fikes led a delegation of Ministerial Alliance pastors and priests from different Midland churches to lobby for the Sudanese persecuted. Pastor Kevin York, a friend and associate of Pastor Ronny Lewis, was one of Deborah's delegation. Their meeting was just a few weeks after 9/11, and Washington, DC, was in the throes of an anthrax panic. In fact, on that day there was another anthrax scare that caused all of the senate buildings to be shut down. Senator Brownback cancelled all of his other meetings, but combined the Midland Ministerial Alliance's meeting with one he'd scheduled with me and other house church leaders. We all met in an underground bunker in one of the senate buildings.

"You're the man we've heard so much about?" Deborah said, shaking my hand. She had heard about our escapades in China through Kevin and Ronny.

"You were expecting someone taller?" I asked.

"You've been through so much, I just thought you'd be . . . older." She laughed. As I told them of my advocacy work on behalf of the persecuted Christians in China, Deborah leaned in closer so she wouldn't miss any of the details.

I'd brought some underground house church leaders to meet with Congressman Frank Wolf as well, and the Midland Alliance decided to join our meeting after the Brownback event. Our time together went very smoothly, and Congressman Wolf was interested in learning more about the specific cases of persecution.

"I'll definitely send them to you," I told him, "but it will take me a while to get to it."

"Why don't you just ask your secretary to do it?" he asked.

"Secretary?" I laughed. "I'm the only one."

Later, Kevin and Deborah pulled me aside.

"Is there anything we can do to help?" Kevin asked. "I couldn't help but overhear you saying you didn't have a secretary."

"Your organization has been all over the media lately," Deborah said. "How are you doing all this without help?"

Unbeknownst to me, their Alliance had been praying for opportunities to help Christians in other countries. Unbeknownst to them, I was on the verge of a nervous breakdown. My seminary work was as challenging as ever, the eyes of the world were on me after releasing the top-secret Chinese documents, my kids still were not sleeping through the night, and my father had died. I must've looked haggard and disheveled, because I could see the concern in the eyes of my new friends.

"I do need help," I said to them, in a moment of complete transparency.

"What is your most pressing need?" Kevin asked. He was probably expecting a request for money or connections to government officials.

"I need help answering emails."

"Emails?" He looked at me incredulously.

"Ever since we got on the national stage, my inbox has been flooded." I almost couldn't contain my emotion. I'd been using every ounce of energy to advocate for—and protect—the persecuted church. I had no energy to pretend things were easy. "I do everything out of the attic of my house in Philly, and I've gotten a little behind."

"Don't you have a wife and children?" Deborah asked. As a mother and a wife of a busy oilman, her mind instantly went to my family. "Let us help you."

Suddenly I had two new advocates. First, Kevin contacted his church secretary back in Midland, and said, "You have a new job. From now on, you will be responsible for sorting through Bob's emails." I gave her my log-on information and password, and she immediately called us back.

"Pastor Kevin," she exclaimed, "he has over seven thousand unread emails!"

Kevin looked at me, his eyes wide with disbelief.

"I told you!"

For months, she did no work for the church. She answered emails from journalists whose deadlines had long passed and to Christian leaders who'd offered speaking opportunities that had come and gone. Meanwhile Deborah reached out to her amazing network of high-profile friends that included think-tank members, activists, non-government organization leaders, congressmen, senators, and human rights advocates. She not only told them about ChinaAid, she set up meetings between us and encouraged them to help me in my work. It was touching to have these amazing people come alongside me.

● ● ●

"You ought to visit Midland," Kevin said to me one day.

And so that summer, Heidi, Daniel, Tracy, and I drove to Midland from Oklahoma after a visit with the Voice of the Martyrs. Heidi was pregnant with our third child, an unimaginable blessing since we'd met and married under China's draconian child laws. When we told Deborah we were expecting, she laughed and said, "Well, I'm going to prophesy that this baby will be born in Texas."

They had floated the idea that our family might move to Midland, which I almost couldn't wrap my mind around. A Chinese human rights organization based in Texas? However, our spirits soared at the thought of it. Though we loved being in Philadelphia, we never quite felt safe. Moving would give us more space, more freedom, and more peace of mind.

There was one complication.

After discovering Heidi was pregnant—and we already had many people tucked into our little home—Charlie surprised us with a four-bedroom house even closer to Westminster. His amazing generosity humbled us, but it also made me hesitant to pack up and leave it all behind.

"Charlie," I said to him during our next weekly breakfast. I'd waited to tell him the news until his second cup of coffee was dry. For years, we'd met every week for a time of prayer and encouragement, and I hated seeing that end. "We're moving," I finally spit out.

Instead of being bitter or upset, Charlie and his family held a farewell dinner at their home. Before we left, Charlie handed me a check for thirteen thousand dollars . . . the down payment for a house in Midland.

• • •

Even though we were relocating our family to a city two thousand miles away, I never lost sight of the fact that there were five pastors in China on death row whose execution date was drawing near. We continued to take up donations for their legal defense and provided much-needed context to the media. For example, we explained that the pastor accused of collecting tens of thousands of dollars for a "Bank of Heaven" was actually just collecting tithes during church. We also explained that the leader accused of making messianic claims by saying, "Christ is I, and I am Christ" was really quoting the apostle Paul in Galatians when he wrote, "It is no longer I who live but Christ who lives in me."

Public outcry grew louder as we furiously advocated on the church members' behalf. As the execution date grew closer, however, the South China Church prepared for the inevitable. They sent me a photo of five identical coffins, ready to bestow at least a little dignity to their pastors' martyred bodies. With even more fervor, we called out to God on their behalf.

Then, on October 10, 2002, a miracle happened. In a turn-around the *New York Times* described as "rare," the Supreme Court in the province of Hubei overturned the death sentences. Claiming the convictions weren't based on enough evidence, all of the sentences were commuted. Not coincidentally, this happened just a few weeks before Jiang Zemin visited President Bush at his ranch near Midland. Reporters called this a "gift" to Bush, who'd pressed for religious freedom during their last summit, but the South China Church refers to this incident as their "Festival of Purim." (In 2006, we regrettably learned after extensive investigation that Gong Shengliang did commit sexually immoral behavior with some congregants, and had taught some things that were contrary to Scripture. Although his behavior never justified the severe torture against him and other members of South China Church by the Chinese government, we were devastated by this news.)

• • •

In 2012, I received a letter from Ms. Li Ying, one of the five South China Church leaders whose death sentence had been commuted in 2002. After spending a total of thirteen years in jail, she wrote me a letter that pierced my soul.

"I'm sister Li. I heard your name just when the church-persecuting authority was going to execute the five of us. At that time, I decided if I was ever released the first thing I would do is ask my family how you had helped me, my teacher, and my church. On December 25, 2011, I was released and went home, and my brothers and sisters had endless things to say about you. Every time they talked to you on the phone, they felt deeply connected with you, as if you were a family member connected with a blood tie that could never be severed."

She explained many of the ways they were tortured: beatings, cigarette burns, torture positions, electric shock batons, bricks on their backs, alcohol poured into their mouths, forced drug ingestion, starvation, seared flesh, and much more.

"My teacher was put in the shackles for death row prisoners from the moment he was arrested. His persecutors exhausted all methods and ways available during his interrogation, which caused him to stop breathing many times, and they dumped water on him to wake him up. He was hospitalized for over a month for emergency care. It is not an overstatement that he endured all forms of torture and suffering."

Then one day, she heard about ChinaAid's efforts.

"As I was praying, I heard someone call the name of one of

our sisters and say, 'You'll be saved!' In a miraculous way, God let us know that you had made our experiences known to the whole world. Now the whole world is watching Huanan Church. We also learned that the US President Bush was a pious Christian who loved the Lord and cared about our church greatly. And we learned that our family had found us a lawyer."

• • •

Not long after the October 2002 retrial, I also became aware of thirty-three-year-old Liu Xianzhi (her English name is Sarah Liu), who was one of four women declared innocent in the retrial verdict. However, she and the other women were sent to "reeducation through labor" camp, a fate worse than prison. They stripped her, used three electric shock batons on her simultaneously, torturing her on all parts of her body. When she cried out, they put the flesh-searing shock baton in her mouth. It burned her mouth so that she couldn't eat for several days. They also used this baton on her genitals, which caused so much pain that she eventually was sent to the hospital unconscious. The doctors and nurses asked her torturers, "How could you treat a girl like this?"

After Sarah was released from labor camp, we rescued her through an underground railroad system stretching from China through Southeast Asia. We arranged for local Christians to cover her with leaves in the back of a truck, where she stayed for hours, completely still. Then they drove that truck, with her in the back under the wet, heavy leaves, across the border to Burma. There, local people created fake identification for her, which identified her as a member of a minority tribal group. To make her appearance match that story, they fixed her hair, put makeup on her face, and sent her into an underground railroad of believers who were willing to risk their lives to save hers. Then, after successfully navigating that maze, she swam across a river to make it into Thailand.

Still, she wasn't free. Once she was in a remote area of Thailand, she was in more danger than ever. She needed to get to Bangkok, but the windy roads were dotted with police checkpoints. Without a passport, she'd certainly be sent back to China and put right back into jail. I sent a friend of mine from Hong Kong to help her. After exhausting every other option, they realized the only option was to go to the nearest airport and fly. Even though she didn't have a passport or valid identification, they did just that. Miraculously, none of the airport officials asked her to show any identification.

After Sarah had managed an escape worthy of a James Bond movie, she had yet to face the mountains of bureaucracy the United Nations would throw at her. They presented so much red tape that we wondered if she'd ever be allowed to leave. The US Ambassador-at-Large for International Religious Freedom, John Hanford, who was appointed by President Bush, personally took our phone calls, called the UN, and demanded they speed up the process to grant her refugee protection. Sarah got her approval within a month because of his direct and decisive intervention, and she finally arrived in America in 2005.

When she was safely in America, Sarah Liu and two other refugees from the South China Church all resettled in Midland. The Midland community helped provide support for their living expenses under ChinaAid. We invited them over to our home during the Christmas season. We watched as Sarah walked ever so slowly up to our Christmas tree and stared at the lights twinkling on and off, absolutely mesmerized.

"Those are just decorations," I explained. "They're on a string."

I pulled out a package and handed them to her, so she could see what they looked like before being draped over the tree.

She took the string of lights out of the package faster than I could blink, her hands untangling them like she was knitting a blanket. Within seconds, she had completely unwrapped and disassembled the lights. Then she looked up at me with the various parts in her hands.

"I assembled these in my labor camp for sixteen hours a day," she explained. "We made Christmas lights and put them in packages that look just like this one."

She then reassembled them just as quickly. The whole process took only seconds.

• • •

Sarah was the first person to make it through our underground railroad, and through the many months it took to get her to Texas, ChinaAid grew into a much more formidable effort for religious freedom. Not only did Pastor Kevin give me his secretary for several months, he even allowed ChinaAid to operate out of their church offices. They made sure we were set up properly, helped organize our tax information, and created a board of amazingly generous Midlanders. I was hired as a part-time pastor at Mid-Cities Community Church, where I brought Chinese dissidents to tell their stories of persecution and torture to the local Midland congregations. Immediately, the churches were captured by their stories, and the dissidents won everybody's hearts. Midland was in a "boom," with oil prices above a hundred dollars a barrel, and their residents opened their hearts and wallets to help fight for freedom.

A community of believers had embraced us, and moving to Midland was like coming home to a family I'd never met.

"Hurry up," Deborah had said to Heidi, whose belly had been growing bigger as the end of 2004 approached. "I want you to have a real Texas cowgirl!"

When we moved to Midland, Deborah's main focus had been to make Heidi's life more comfortable, and she'd really stepped into a role of mother-in-law. She'd made sure Heidi adjusted to West Texas, helped provide childcare, and even bought little birthday gifts for the children, who soon were calling her "Grandma."

• • •

On Christmas Eve, 2004, Heidi went into labor. This time we left the other two children with Christian neighbors, and I was free to be by my wife's side as she delivered a beautiful baby girl, whom we named Yining, which means "beautiful peace." Her English name would be Melissa. Once we brought her home, we received endless casseroles and babysitting offers from our new Texas friends.

I don't know what percentage of ChinaAid's success is due to Midland. But I know that the generosity of their churches helped prepare us to fight for the plight of the persecuted on an even grander scale.

Sadly, we'd have many more opportunities.

27

"This is China's most expensive drink," Ye Xiaowen, director of the State Administration for Religious Affairs said, as he prepared to make a toast. "And it just happens to also come from my hometown."

Deborah watched as the clear alcohol, Maotai, was poured into her little glass, and braced herself. Maotai, which dates back to the Qing Dynasty, is an enormous part of Chinese history. Ever since Mao and his Long March comrades used it to cleanse their war wounds, it's been a part of Chinese lore and a staple at state banquets. Mao famously offered it to Richard Nixon in 1972, who—against the advice of his aids—freely imbibed.

Deborah had made a special trip to Beijing in January 2008 so she could speak face-to-face with the world leaders. As a member of the famed Midland Ministerial Alliance, she was escorted to meet Minister Ye, who was responsible for implementing all of China's religious policy—good or bad. He treated her with much dignity and prepared a lavish feast in her honor.

That's when she was faced with a glass of 106 proof alcohol. She knew she shouldn't drink much of it, but she put her lips on the glass and tried not to choke. Dan Rather famously described the drink as "liquid razor blades," but Deborah knew this was one of the highest demonstrations of respect. Distilled from fermented sorghum, the alcohol has a lingering aroma of soy sauce. The cheapest bottle costs over three hundred dollars, and a 1980 bottle sold last year for $1.3 million.

After she had successfully managed Minister Ye's toast, he made another. And another. Deborah, however, couldn't drink as much as was expected of her. When Minister Ye noticed that she was merely sipping her drink, he took her glass and poured most of it into his own cup. Culturally, only very close friends—or a subordinate for his supervisor—would do that in China.

The feast was elaborate and festive, as the Chinese government spared no expense. Deborah assumed this was all done to impress the "housewife" from the "tribe of the President." However, between courses, Minister Ye turned to Deborah and said, very innocently, "Do you happen to know a man named Bob Fu?" Suddenly, all of the attention and luxurious food made sense. He was trying to buy Deborah's influence over me.

"Yes," she said. "We're very close."

"Really?" He acted shocked that she'd associate with such a man. "I wish I could have a close friendship with you like Bob Fu."

"His children call me Grandma," she added.

"Well, he's reporting ugly things about China."

"I know Bob's heart," Deborah said. "He doesn't want to misrepresent China. He loves his motherland." This "Texas housewife" was not going to yield an inch. "In fact, Bob Fu wants all of these persecution cases to disappear so he'll have nothing left to report. Only you can make that happen."

At the end of the banquet, Minister Ye and Deborah had developed a strong trust. Right before she left, with much flourish, he presented Deborah with two bottles of Maotai. In China, officials aren't supposed to give bribes, so Maotai is a well-known substitute. "This is for you to take back to America."

She accepted the lavish gift, and said, "Let's build a protocol on how to handle those 'ugly things' Bob reports about you. In the next few months, there will be some cases. A house church leader might be sent to labor camp or a new believer to prison. When that happens, we won't go to the media. Instead, we'll come straight to you."

In exchange for our moratorium on media exposure, the director promised to handle the human rights violations. And so, Deborah became ChinaAid's diplomatic go-between, privately communicating with China's Bureau of Religious Affairs when the inevitable violations occurred. And they definitely happened. In the two months of our good faith effort, however, we never got a positive result. In fact, Minister Ye never even followed up.

• • •

Later, when Minister Ye came to the United States for a visit, Deborah hosted a lavish dinner for him at a very nice restaurant in a five-star hotel in Washington, DC. Since he had given her such an extravagant gift of Maotai, she wanted to present him with something even more valuable. She bought a bilingual Bible and had me highlight all of the Scriptures about loving each other. When he came to the table, he saw the gift and flipped through the pages. Suddenly, his face contorted with rage.

"Love is not proud," he read from one of the Scriptures in 1 Corinthians. "It does not dishonor others . . . it is not self-seeking? Bob Fu doesn't follow these writings!"

Suddenly, everyone in the room got quiet as he went on a political diatribe against me. The Chinese embassy diplomats were shocked that he was expressing such disgust with Deborah's gift. When his anger subsided, he looked around the room and was immediately embarrassed. "You are the host and here I am doing a political speech," he said, his face splotchy from his diminishing anger. "I'm so sorry."

Deborah also handed him a letter I'd written him, inviting him to come to Midland to talk about the issues with me face-to-face. Needless to say, he didn't accept the invitation.

However, I still lived in Ye's mind. This became evident when John Hanford, who led the Office of International Religious Freedom in the State Department, held a private, friendly dinner for Minister Ye. During the dinner, John turned to him and said, "Let's talk about persecution in your country. Last year alone . . ." Then, John proceeded to list the names of many persecuted Christians.

As soon as Minister Ye heard this, he exclaimed, "This is from Bob Fu!"

I'm sure he was thinking, *I can't even get into the White House, yet this poor guy from Shiziyuan Village feeds them all this terrible information.* And certainly, as Minister Ye undoubtedly knew, this was not the first time I had made President Bush aware of such "terrible information."

* * *

In 2004, my old friend Zhuohua Cai—who set up the illegal training center in the China countryside and ran the illegal printing press—had gotten in trouble. By this time, he was a prominent Beijing house church leader, still printing Bibles and giving them away free of charge. He kept a stash of Christian literature in a warehouse, far from the eyes of the Public Security Bureau. However, on September 11, he was waiting at a bus stop when state security agents drove up in a van, arrested him, and charged him with "illegal business practices." He was fined 150,000 yuan ($18,500) and sentenced to three years in prison. Apparently, the police had discovered his warehouse, which had over two hundred thousand pieces of printed Christian literature and Bibles—the largest "foreign religious infiltration" in the history of the People's Republic of China. While Pastor Cai was in jail, along with his wife and brother-in-law, he was tortured with electric cattle prods. I immediately hired Zhang Xingshui, a prominent attorney at Beijing's Jingding Law Firm, to defend my old friend.

• • •

In April 2005, I had an amazing opportunity to bring up Pastor Cai's case in an internationally significant way. The United Nations Commission on Human Rights invited me to deliver a formal speech during the General Assembly on Religious Intolerance. I was very honored, because the UNCHR was the highest authority on this earth with the stated mission to protect and promote human rights for all. I traveled to Geneva with a team of people, including Deborah Fikes, my assistant Melissa Rasmussen, and our first underground railroad survivor, Sarah Liu. The non-governmental organization (NGO) A Woman's Voice International was kind enough to sponsor me at the conference, a requirement for all of the guest speakers. They also set up a special briefing in one of the UN's smaller conference rooms, where Sarah gave her testimony about how she was sentenced to death as a member of the South China Church, tortured viciously in prison, and escaped.

Later that week, it was time for me to deliver my remarks. As I sat at my desk, I was a little nervous watching people filter in. Gradually the semicircle of desks—in one of the largest conference rooms at the Palais des Nations in Geneva—filled with delegates. I'd spoken at the UN before, but this time the atmosphere was particularly lively. There were many NGO representatives, government delegates, and more than sixty UNCHR elected members lined up to speak during that two weeks. Each NGO rep was only allotted about eight minutes, so I made sure to pack as much information into my speech as possible.

"Mr. Chairman, A Woman's Voice International would like to draw to the attention of this commission the plight of three leaders of the Chinese house church movement who have experienced persecution at the hands of state authorities in the People's Republic of China," I began. It felt a little awkward to be detailing the abuses of the Chinese government right in front of their delegation; however, they refused to meet with me personally in advance. I plunged ahead, describing several cases of abuse and torture of Christians in China, beginning with my friend Cai.

The room was filled with hundreds of people, who all spoke in different languages and were arranged by country. While I talked, there was a lot of action in the room, people milling around, looking at notes, making connections with old friends, laughing, preparing for their own speeches. No one was really paying attention to my speech.

"Though China has amended its constitution to protect human rights," I continued, leaning close to the microphone to allow my voice to carry, "these cases exemplify both the arbitrary nature of what passes for justice in the People's Republic of China and the sad state of religious freedom there."

Still, no one was listening.

"Mr. Chairman, I'd now like for you to pay special attention. I'm holding an electric shock baton identical to those used to torture Christians, including Pastor Cai."

Then I pulled out the electric shock baton, about the size of a flashlight, that I'd smuggled out of China. I didn't smuggle it into the UN, however. Deborah and I had gotten permission from the Secretariat's office before my speech. Also, I'd brought the baton through several layers of security. In other words, the UN had already approved of my electric baton demonstration.

Nonetheless, when I held the baton above my head and pressed the button, the cacophony of elbow rubbing and mingling suddenly stopped. For six seconds, people heard the staticky, unmistakable sound of an electric current. No one said a word. Were they wondering what that current might feel like against their own skin? Were they angry with the Chinese for employing this against the innocent? Were they remembering the previous testimony of Sarah, about how the agents put a similar baton into her mouth and private parts? I'm not sure.

However, I was remembering the times I saw this device used against prisoners in my own jail cell so many years ago. The whole room was frozen. Stunned. And I felt something significant was happening for my suffering brothers and sisters.

As soon as I turned off the current, the room erupted again in conversation, but this time the chattering was anxious. All eyes were on me as UN Security surrounded me and grabbed the shock baton off the desk while I continued speaking.

"We feel threatened!" a delegate from the Chinese government yelled out. I'm not sure how she made the claim with a straight face. The Chinese delegation immediately pressured the Secretariat of the Human Rights Commission to expel me and all of the Woman's Voice International delegates. Although he refused to expel the others, the security guards standing next to the angry Chinese delegation grabbed me.

I was escorted to the security room, where a female Chinese diplomat was standing next to me to register their complaint. "We feel threatened by this man."

At that very moment those torture devices were being widely used against hundreds of thousands of victims of conscience in their country—especially women. Even the manufacturer described its product as "an ideal tool for the Chinese law enforcement officials."

"How can you be threatened by just six seconds of demonstration when your government shoves that into the mouths of people like Sarah Liu?" I said.

Without any sort of investigation or hearing, they yanked my UN badge off my neck, forced me out of the room, and threw me into a UN police car.

China, of course, had manipulated the whole procedure. After I left, their delegation virtually ground the Commission proceedings to a halt for nearly an hour by making excessive demands upon the Secretariat's time and immobilizing the regular proceedings of the Commission.

Later, I was asked to testify before Congress about this incident, and I summed up my UN experience by saying, "About nine years ago, I was forced into a police car and taken from my home to prison by the Chinese Public Security Bureau in Beijing for alleged illegal religious activities. Sadly, this is the second time I have been put into a police car, and the UN security guards did it. The only reason I was treated like that was because of a complaint filed by representatives of torturers."

Sadly, my testimony at the United Nations ended up getting A Woman's Voice International suspended for one year and did nothing to help save Pastor Cai. In fact, he and his attorney had been informed that the government told the court to prepare to sentence him for fifteen years, which was five times the original sentence.

● ● ●

Meanwhile, in China, far away from the false outrage of the well-heeled UN delegates, a PSB agent apprehended the attorney we'd hired to defend Pastor Cai. President Bush was coming to Beijing to discuss the upcoming Olympics, and China was doing everything it could to make sure their human rights violations wouldn't factor into their talks. Our attorney was forced to temporarily relocate to a town a hundred miles from Beijing. Even though Pastor Cai was in jail and his attorney was forced into hiding, they were still in the heart and on the mind of the leader of the free world.

"What I say to the Chinese is . . . a free society is in your interests," President Bush said during his speech with Japan's Prime Minister Koizumi. He said that China should let people "worship without state control and to print Bibles and other sacred texts without fear of punishment." In fact, the theme of his Asian tour was religious freedom. When he went to China, he visited Gangwashi Church, my former church whose seventy-year-old pastor had been yanked from the pulpit during that near-riot. After listening to a translation of the sermon through a headset, President Bush and the First Lady stood on the steps of the church and said, "The Spirit of the Lord is very strong inside your church. It wasn't all that long ago that people were not allowed to worship openly in this society. My hope is that the government of China will not fear Christians who gather to worship openly."

It didn't take long for the media of the Chinese government to connect Bush's comments about religious freedom and Bible printing to Pastor Cai. He was released after serving only three years.

• • •

President Bush proved time and time again that he had a heart for religious freedom.

In April 2006, I invited seven Chinese human rights activists to Washington, DC, for the Freedom in China Summit 2006 conference. Four were able to attend the conference: attorney Guo Feixiong, known as a "barefoot lawyer" from the Guangdong province, because of his efforts on behalf of marginalized groups; legal scholar Li Baiguang, who had taught house church leaders about their legal rights and demanded the government comply with its own religious policies; law professor and blogger Wang Yi; and one of China's most prominent essayists, Yu Jie. Lawyer Gao Zhisheng, constitutional law scholar Dr. Fan Yafeng, and lawyer Zhang Xingshui were unable to accept the invitation, as Chinese security forces blocked their travel. After the conference, the four dissidents traveled with me back to Midland to spend some time at China Aid. That's when I received a very important telephone call from the White House.

"President Bush would like to meet you and your fellow dissidents in the Oval Office to discuss religious freedom," I was told.

I was elated. Although I'd formally requested to meet with the president before the conference and had several high-level meetings in the White House, I didn't receive any indication that a meeting with President Bush would actually occur.

I was asked to provide a list of the names of the people I would like included in the meeting, and when I hung up the phone I immediately began formulating my list. I couldn't suppress a smile as I wrote down the names of my four guests, knowing their lives would be forever changed by this official White House invitation.

The three Christian dissidents were having a Bible study with my staff in our ChinaAid office. The fourth, Mr. Guo, was not a believer and had chosen to skip the Bible study session. When I got back to the office, I excitedly told Wang Yi, Yu Jie, and Li Baiguang the news.

"Who's going?" Yu Jie and Wang Yi asked.

"All of you and Guo," I said happily. When I said Guo's name, however, Yu Jie's and Wang Yi's faces fell. During our trip to DC, I had noticed some tension between the dissidents—namely, Yu and Wang didn't seem to like Guo, but I couldn't tell exactly why. I was bothered and puzzled by their reaction, but the extent of their disapproval wasn't apparent until Yu and Wang pulled me aside before lunchtime, ushering me out for a walk and a more private conversation.

"If Guo goes," they told me, "we won't."

"What do you mean?" I asked anxiously. I was very confused and even felt a little threatened.

"We'll boycott the meeting at the White House if Guo remains on the guest list."

Apparently, I had unwittingly waded into a schism. Christian activists Yu and Wang had a more modest approach of working within the government system, whereas nonChristian Guo was a human rights defender who fought to reform the system. In fact, Guo, along with Gao Zhisheng, was a pioneer of the lawyers' human rights movement in China.

Later I learned from the other dissident, Dr. Li Baiguang,

that Yu and Wang had lobbied him to join their boycott if Guo was included, but Dr. Li had declined. He said he wanted to respect my decision as host.

I returned to my office and agonized over what to do next. This wonderful opportunity was being marred by squabbles and turf wars. On one hand, it would've been very offensive to disinvite Guo. On the other hand, it would be even more awkward to show up at the White House and have to explain a boycott.

Yu Jie, Wang Yi, and Taiwanese pastor and lawyer David Cheng, who also happened to be visiting Midland, entered the room, and I suggested that we pray over the decision.

After the prayer, Wang Yi and I went to Guo, who was in another room in the ChinaAid office. It was the most awkward moment in my whole life. Wang seriously told him that after our prayer, we felt he should not go to the meeting with President Bush. This might sound very holy—bringing concern over a decision to God for his guidance—but it actually was pretty cowardly. In a sense, we used this prayer to cover a decision I didn't feel comfortable making. Guo was furious and even called Dr. Fan, lawyer Gao Zhisheng, and Zhang Xingshui to help persuade us to change our minds.

I hesitantly spoke directly to Guo.

"Feixiong," I said. "I have something to tell you." With great reluctance and a heavy heart, I began explaining I was no longer inviting him to meet with President Bush.

This was a decision I'd come to regret.

The next day, before I sent Guo to a previously scheduled New York appointment, I explained to him the true circumstances around my decision. Though he seriously disagreed, he respectfully didn't mar the event with any sort of protest. He simply handed me a letter after I resubmitted a new invitation list to the White House.

And so, after our dispute, the three dissidents, Deborah Fikes, and I traveled to DC to experience an unprecedented historical moment for the Chinese house church movement. I tried to push the squabble out of my mind, and to focus on the real significance of the event at hand. The leader of the free world was sending an unambiguous message to China: he was aware of the crackdown on the religious groups, but America valued freedom.

• • •

"The president isn't quite ready to see you," said Pat Davis, an official from the National Security Council. She was the one who had originally notified me about the Oval Office meeting, and she seemed a little anxious. "My apologies."

We were sitting outside the Oval Office, uncomfortable in our best suits, and the meeting had been delayed several times. Apparently, there was a faction of advisors in the State Department who passionately opposed our visit. They argued if we were welcomed into the Oval Office—the inner sanctum of power—it would unnecessarily inflame America's carefully cultivated relationship with China. For several days prior to our arrival, they'd been going back and forth about how to best handle us. National Security Advisor Steve Hadley finally put his foot down and we received our invitation. However, there now seemed to be a last-minute complication.

"Would you like some coffee or tea while you wait?" an aide asked.

Earlier that morning, the White House had received a confidential, urgent memo from US Ambassador to China Clark T. Randt: if these dissidents were honored by an Oval Office meeting with the president, Chinese senior officials had threatened that they could not guarantee the dissidents' safety upon their return to China. The White House took this to mean they'd be arrested or executed, and knew that they were perhaps placing these men in grave danger.

Michael Gerson, Senior Advisor to the President, who met with our delegation in his office in the West Wing of the White

House during our time in DC, later recounted the behind-the-scenes activity in his book *Heroic Conservatism*:

> This development raised ethical questions. Should we cancel the meeting and prevent these dissidents from risking their lives? I considered some analogies. In a previous time, would I have advised Solzhenitsyn or Sakharov to lower their risky profile? Of course not. On a battlefield, would I prevent a soldier from taking on a heroic but risky mission to save others? Not if the soldier knew the odds of failure. A deep reverence for human life does not require us to oppose life-risking heroism.*

Instead of making the decision for us, an official entered our waiting area and told us what had been going on behind the scenes. He left the decision up to us. "Do you still want to meet with the president?"

It wasn't even a question in our minds. We knew the tactics of the Chinese government more than anyone; all of us had already either been imprisoned or under constant surveillance. We decided long ago that we would not bend our knee to China. "Of course," we all said. "We're already here."

When President Bush heard our response, he immediately sent for us. I was so humbled by the opportunities God had given me as we walked through the hallowed halls of the White House. Born in such humble beginnings, I was teasingly called "Prime Minister Fu" by my classmates who believed I could only rise so far into the social strata. Yet, here I was, about to meet the leader of the free world.

"Wait right here," a woman said, putting her hand gently on my shoulder. I was quite sure we were only a few steps away from the Oval Office, and my heart was racing. I'd read so much about this very place, even when I was a child in my peasant village, and here I stood.

*Michael J. Gerson, *Heroic Conservatism: Why Republicans Need to Embrace America's Ideals* (New York: HarperOne, 2008), 97.

"I'm sorry," she said to me, very quietly. "You won't be allowed in." Evidently, part of the last-minute negotiations included two concessions. First, the meeting would not take place in the Oval Office, but in a room called the "Yellow Oval," located in the president's personal residence. Second, one member of our group would not be allowed to meet with the president in the White House: troublemaker and whistleblower Bob Fu.

I was incredibly disappointed, but stepped aside as my friends went in to meet with President Bush, Vice President Cheney, the National Security Advisor, Gerson, and other staff. After all, I hadn't done any of this to elevate myself, and it was clear that the Chinese government still had me in their crosshairs. After the meeting, my friends gave me a complete rundown of all that happened. They said President Bush had welcomed them by saying, "I've been told you all love freedom as house church movement members." After they told him about their struggles, they shared a very poignant moment. Gerson describes the scene from his perspective best:

> Near the end of the meeting, the president was told the dissidents wanted to pray with him. Everyone stood, and the president asked people to join hands—the vice president looking momentarily stricken with awkwardness. (Clearly, where Vice President Cheney comes from, prayerful hand holding isn't so common.) After a short prayer for mercy, blessing, and protection, the president asked the dissidents to join him in a picture. As they were leaving, the president told them: "Now I've seen your faces and know your names. From now on, whenever I talk about human rights in China, I'll be thinking about you."*

Afterward, the White House took precautions to protect these dissidents. According to a senior Bush official, the president sent a back channel message to the Chinese government: "I,

*Ibid., 98.

President Bush, am personally invested in the welfare of these three dissidents, and if anything happens to them, then this would cause a severe disruption in US-China relations." When they arrived home at the Beijing airport, American diplomats met them and kept in close contact with them. In fact, a Chinese agent later approached Dr. Li Baiguang and said, "Now that you are called a friend by the President of the United States, we won't hurt you physically anymore. But you still need to be careful as a Chinese citizen."

Though the meeting went wonderfully, Guo was still angry at them for his mistreatment. Eight days after the event, he published the letter he'd written protesting his exclusion on a Chinese website. Understandably, it caused quite an uproar in the Chinese human rights activist community. Right after his statement went public, I issued an apology, but nothing could undo the damage I'd inflicted on this man. After all, my decision meant Guo didn't experience the elevated status of having "friends in high places."

Within just a few months of being disinvited from the Bush event, he was arrested.

• • •

In God's good timing, I did eventually get to meet the president. On July 29, 2008, just before noon, I met with President Bush and four other human rights leaders to discuss human rights in advance of the 2008 Olympic Games. They were beginning in Beijing the following week, and the president's meeting sent a very strong message to China about American priorities. In our visit, he said he wanted to talk to President Hu Jintao about human rights violations, to explain that Christians in his country are peace-loving and caring people, and to urge China not to be afraid of us. He also planned on speaking with the Chinese people about the importance of religious liberty. I gave him some gray wristbands with "Pray for China" printed in black letters in both English and Chinese, which ChinaAid had made in conjunction with the Voice of the Martyrs. The bracelets were made to remind people that Chinese believers were still being punished for their faith through beatings, imprisonment, and even death—even as the eyes of the world were fixed on the super-fast athletes, the new Olympic arena, and all the expensive advertisements.

It was touching that President Bush cared so much about religious freedom, a passion he demonstrated all the way to the last hours of his term. During roughly the same time frame, the two attorneys with remarkably similar names, Gao and Guo, were persecuted, and their families were forced to escape China and seek asylum in the United States.

● ● ●

Guo Feixiong worked with Gao Zhishen, who was one of the most successful Chinese human rights lawyers. He was part of the legal defense team for a house church network in Beijing and had advocated for the freedom of nonChristian religious sects, including the much maligned and persecuted Falun Gong, and had helped in Pastor Cai's defense. Because of his activities, Gao's law license had been revoked and his firm shut down. When he continued to give legal advice to the persecuted, agents began living in their home, leaving the lights on at all times for sleep deprivation, and even starving their young son to extract information out of the parents. Agents followed their daughter to school, where they beat her in front of her classmates.

Through ChinaAid's encouragement, Congress passed a resolution demanding the Chinese government stop harassing Gao's family. Gao was arrested, interrogated, tortured mentally, stripped naked, and shocked with electric batons on his private parts before he was released. After his release—knowing his time of freedom would be short—he hatched a plan to enable his family to cross the mountainous border, with the help of many believers in the underground railroad for the religiously persecuted.

About that time, Guo Feixiong was also arrested in the southern Chinese city of Guangzhou and was falsely charged with "running an illegal business," a retaliation against him for his work in publicizing the arrest of his co-worker Gao to the outside world.

One morning, I learned through a friend with Radio Free Asia that Gao's family had arrived in Bangkok. I got assurance from the White House and the State Department, then bought a ticket to Bangkok that afternoon. It was the most expensive ticket I'd ever purchased, but time was of the essence. When I arrived, I went to the small home where Gao's family was hiding out; a Falun Gong family had offered shelter to Gao's family because of his advocacy for religious freedom. The tiny house was a one-bedroom with no mattresses, and everyone slept on the floor. I spent the Chinese New Year with the Gao family there.

Through our underground church efforts, Guo's son had also been rescued, and he arrived in Bangkok as well. While I was in Thailand, I met with the little boy and arranged for him to stay with the Gao family.

Because these were such high-profile cases, the Chinese government was probably already in hot pursuit. Consequently, I moved the family from the Falun Gong home to a hotel, then to another hotel. We made sure they were Western hotel chains to avoid being compromised. Finally, I rented an apartment in an international community full of Westerners. None of us had very much sleep, and they were frazzled at having to relocate every few days.

One day, my phone rang. It was Gao!

He was attending a relative's wedding in the Shanxi province, which was his hometown, and could tell he was being followed. He borrowed a phone, went to a toilet room, and called his family from the stall. It was the last conversation they would have with him before he disappeared.

"I want to see you guys in heaven," he said.

I had brought the Jesus movie with me and showed it to his family. The children were young and full of pure faith. As they watched the movie and saw Jesus crucified and resurrected, tears ran down their faces and they believed. After the movie, the little boy came to me and placed some Thai coins in my hands.

"This is for Jesus," he said. Even though he'd only been a Christian for a few minutes, he already made an offering to his Lord.

Gao's wife, however, was not so sure about Christianity. "My kids can believe in Jesus," she told me, "but the Falun Gong has helped me so much. I can believe in that religion."

But during her last conversation with Gao, he had said, "I don't want to be forever separated from you. If the Communists take me from you now, I at least want to be reunited with you after my death."

It was a heartwrenching conversation. At the end of it, Gao spoke to me. "I entrust my family to you," he said.

"Don't you want us to rescue you too?" I asked. I could tell that he was torn. However, he felt his calling was to stay in China and continue the fight for religious freedom. On January 16, 2009, I called the White House and the State Department to try to get his family out of the country. "We need to get Gao's family political asylum in the United States."

"Don't you realize that today is the last working day before Barack Obama's inauguration?" the person said. "We're in the middle of a transition of power."

"Can't you help them anyway?"

The person on the other end of the phone paused.

"All right," he said. "But if you'd called just a few hours later, all of our computers would've been shut down and we'd no longer have access to them."

Once again, the religious dissidents got the full cooperation of the White House, which set the process in motion and accepted his family directly as refugees without going through the UN. They were processed as political refugees in the most urgent manner because of the potential threat and danger they could face in Thailand.

This allowed their immigration paperwork to be completed in eleven days. In the realm of government bureaucracy, this was a total miracle.

However, even though they had the go-ahead from the American government, Thailand refused to give the Gao family exit privileges because they didn't have passports. With the Chinese government hot on our trail, I had to fly back to Washington, DC, to pressure the Thai government to issue exit permits for Gao's family. While I was there, I also tried to persuade the State Department to process the Guo family in the same urgent way the Gao family was processed. However, the White House had already transitioned over to the new administration, and things became much more difficult for China's persecuted.

After I left Bangkok, Guo's wife and daughter were also rescued and made it to Thailand. The State Department, however, refused to accept the Guo family directly. Instead, they insisted that they go through the UN, an entity under such influence of the Chinese government. While I was in Texas, I prepared their application and emailed it to them. Then they went to the UN to file their application. It didn't work, just as we'd predicted. The UN denied their application for refugee protection, and even urged them to go back to China.

I learned of this when I was traveling with my family back from Oklahoma, where we'd been visiting friends. We were heading down the interstate, listening to music and chatting while the kids dozed in the back. Heidi and I had been talking about errands that needed to be run. Specifically, she was reminding me that when we got back to Texas, I needed to apply for visas for her and the children because they wanted to make a trip to Hong Kong.

"I put everyone's passports in your suitcase," she said, gently nudging me, "in case you want to take care of that when we get back to Texas."

I smiled. No matter how much I was fighting for the persecuted church, I was still a husband with a "honey-do" list. I also needed to mow the lawn. Just then, my cell phone rang.

"The United Nations rejected refugee protection for the Guo family," I was told.

• • •

When I got off the phone, I looked at my family. They were all tucked safely in our blue van, thankfully oblivious to the terrible circumstances of believers on the other side of the world. However, they'd paid a price for my advocacy. For my children's entire lives, I'd been fighting for human rights, traveling to rescue the persecuted, and speaking out on behalf of the voiceless. In other words, I'd been busy. In America, this was parental taboo. "It's both quality and quantity," I heard pastors say from the pulpit to an auditorium full of parents trying to make the most of their family life. In fact, Pastor Kevin York became a wonderful counselor to Heidi and me once we moved to Midland. At first, he correctly encouraged me to find a good work/family balance. In Philadelphia especially, I didn't say no to even the most obscure speaking engagement. This left Heidi alone with the children weekend after weekend, an unsustainable situation for everyone.

"Pastor Kevin," I remember saying, "imagine this scenario. I'm sleeping, when one of my seven phones rings in the middle of the night because of the time difference from China. It's a woman screaming, because agents are in her house beating her children. She needs legal help, so she calls me. What do I do?" I asked. It was a real question. In American Christianity, a "good parent" is the one who attends every violin recital and volleyball practice. "Her phone call means that I need to get out of bed and make sure she gets a lawyer immediately. I need to find out the details of the case and write a press release—in English and in Chinese—to send to the senators and the congressmen who care about human rights. And that's just the beginning."

Kevin had looked at me with tears in his eyes. He'd been a pastor for several years and had encouraged men to be more "available" to their families. "Put career second," he had told them. "Just turn the phone off."

"Or recently," I added, "a pastor in Guangxi Province called me, right after his wife had been dragged to the hospital by agents to be forced to have an abortion. She was seven months pregnant. When they got there, they found eighty mothers being forced to abort within the next forty-eight hours. So I called NPR and other reporters, trying to shed light on this incident. But by the time the reporters got there, the agents had already poisoned her and the baby was dead." I held up my phone. "It's no exaggeration to say every time this thing rings, it could be a matter of life and death."

Kevin looked at me. "I don't know what to advise," he said. "I've used up all of my American put-your-family-before-work counseling techniques, and I've got nothing left. But the one thing I know is that you simply can't turn off your phone, and we'll try to make sure you get the help you need to make it as easy as possible on your family."

I remember that conversation well, because my family has had to eat many meals alone, celebrate birthdays without me, and frequently fear for my safety. God asks us to pick up our cross and follow Him . . . even parents. That means one father might follow Him to the school Christmas play and another might follow Him into a war zone, making him miss all the soccer games. Following God looks different for every family, and there was no easy answer to how I could enjoy my family as much as I wanted while also fighting for the persecuted. Midland made it easier, but there were some moments—like when we were driving home from a family vacation—when it hurt to do the right thing.

"Guo's family needs help," I sighed. Heidi knew Guo, since we had hosted him in Midland in May 2006 and attended meetings with him at the Hudson Institute and in Washington.

Heidi smiled a weary smile. The kids were still sleeping. "What happened?"

"The United Nations told them to go back to China. They said Guo's political activity was his problem, not the family's. They said China might sentence them to a few years in prison, anyway," I said, incredulous. "Not because they're political prisoners, but because they illegally crossed the border."

Heidi looked at me. "I assume you have to get there?"

We drove straight to the airport in Dallas, where Heidi dropped me off and continued home without me. As I walked through the airport, lugging my suitcase to the international departure gate, I couldn't shake the feeling that I was at least partially responsible for Guo's arrest. Had I not disinvited him from the White House event, surely China would not have brazenly trumped up false charges and imprisoned him. I resolved to do all I could to help his family.

Little did I know this promise would lead me to commit a felony.

28

I walked around the corner of a hotel in Bangkok and stopped when I came face-to-face with two men. They had closely cropped black hair and, I detected, bad breath. Though they had on street clothes, I could tell instantly I was inches away from colliding with two members of China's secret police.

"Excuse me," I said, looking down at my feet and walking through the hallway of the hotel, directly passing my destination, room 610. Without a sideways glance, I walked back to the elevator and out the lobby.

Had we been compromised? Chinese secret police scour the streets of Bangkok looking for dissidents. They've been known to kidnap people—even those granted US asylum—transport them back to China, accuse them of breaking the law, and make them disappear forever into the prison system. I was taking a huge risk helping Guo Feixiong's family, and I wanted to make sure I could get back to my own.

Guo's wife was a lady named Zhang Qing. She, along with her thirteen-year-old daughter, Sara, and her six-year-old son, Peter, were hidden in room 610, assisted by some believers from Thailand and a missionary from Britain named Catherine. It was ironic to me that their room number was 610, because the "610 Office" is a Chinese security agency that persecutes the

Falun Gong. It was named because it was created on June 10, 1999, but I tried not to take the hotel number coincidence as a bad omen for our mission.

After all, they wouldn't be there long. Every three days, the family walked out of their hotel room without any bags and checked into another hotel across town. At night, Catherine would go to their old room, get their luggage, and carry it to their new location. Though the mother already had a visa, the two children didn't. This meant they needed to hide from the Thai police as well as the Chinese.

After walking around the hotel, I determined my run-in with the secret police agents was coincidental. Had they known who I was, I'd certainly be in the back of their van on my way back to prison. Slowly, I ambled back to the hotel and knocked on the door of the family's room.

"It's me!" Guo's family was sitting in the small room, wondering why it had taken me so long to arrive. "We have to get you all out of here."

I told them about the security agents who might be on their tail. Qing told me about a suspicious incident they'd had recently when they went out in public.

"After we were rejected by the UN, Catherine and I were in a cab when another car slammed right into us," she said. "I knew we had to get out before the police showed up. I don't think it was really an accident."

I'd already consulted with one of Britain's Christian refugee lawyers, who'd flown to Bangkok from London to meet with me. We interviewed Qing multiple times and went without much sleep for several days and nights. Then, we met with a high-ranking official from the Office of the United Nations High Commissioner for Refugees at the UN compound to talk about appealing their rejection.

"We never know if an appeal will be successful, or how long it will take," the official told us in a monotonous voice.

"But we have a family in terrible danger," I said. "We need to get them to safety as soon as possible."

"It might take months, it might take years," she said, and then she looked up at us as if to say, *Is there anything else?*

"Two of them are children!" I said. "Please!"

"There's nothing I can do," she said.

Because we knew it would take a long time to process, we didn't even file the appeal. The family didn't have the luxury of waiting for the appeals process, because every day presented new chances of arrest. Plus, I'd already been gone a week and needed to travel back to America to keep ChinaAid running, to tend to my family, and to make my scheduled appointments. If Guo's family was going to be stuck there for years, there's no way I could live in Thailand until their release. I extended my trip for a few more days, but eventually my time ran out.

"I'm so sorry," I told the family, standing in their hotel room with my suitcase. "I want to get you guys out of here, but we've exhausted every option and I have to leave." Immediately, Sara's eyes seemed full of fear. Even Catherine didn't make eye contact with me. I didn't blame them. We'd lost.

"They'll capture us!" Qing said.

Peter, though he was only six, had stopped banging on the floor with a stick long enough to look up sadly. I felt like I was abandoning my own family. After all, I had a wife, a daughter, and a son. If I were in Guo's shoes, to what extent would I want someone to fight for my family? How long would I want them to stay? How far would I want them to go?

Then, it hit me. Right before Heidi dropped me off at the airport, she'd reminded me I needed to get the kids visas for an upcoming trip. I hadn't run that errand yet, so I had all my family's passports in my suitcase. Right there, as I stood in a hotel room with this family and the British missionary staring at me, I had a moment of conscience. My limited knowledge of US refugee law told me that if a person could set foot on American soil, they could be considered eligible for political asylum. The asylum officer should not care about how that person arrived. What if I gave my kids' passports to Guo's kids and tried to pass them off as my own? If the security agents at the airport bought the ruse, we'd be in America the next day.

When I presented my idea privately to Qing and Catherine, they were hesitant.

"How old is your daughter?" Qing said, examining my daughter Tracy's passport.

"She's ten."

"Sara's thirteen. Do you think she'll pass for such a young child?"

I reached into my suitcase and pulled out Daniel's passport. He was twelve already, which was a much larger age gap to overcome since Peter was only six.

"I'm not saying this is a good option," I admitted. "I'm saying this is our only option."

We sat in sober silence. "Using another person's passport is a serious crime," Catherine said.

"God," I prayed. "What is the moral thing to do in this circumstance?"

If the Guo family were caught, they'd certainly be taken back to China and put in prison. If I were caught, there's no telling what China would do to me. After all, I'd so publicly revealed their state secrets. I'd never see my family again. However, there was no way I was going to abandon this family.

I sat down with the children and taught them my family background: my father's name, my mother's name, my hometown province, where I went to school, where I'd been employed. Since Catherine and Qing both had legal passports, they'd travel together as vacationers to the United States. I'd be a father traveling with my two children back to our American home.

"Quick," I said to Sara. "What was your grandfather's name?"

"Fu Yubo?"

"Perfect!" Then, I got down on the floor where Peter was still holding his stick. "Listen," I said to him very gently. "You must not speak. Just pretend that you don't know English and don't say anything no matter what they ask you. Pretend to be shy."

"How on earth will they believe Peter is twelve?" Catherine asked. "He barely comes up to my waist!" She bit her lip in thought, then said, "I have an idea! Let's put him in a wheelchair. We can pretend he's disabled, and they won't be able to tell how short he is."

The next morning, we wrapped his legs with bandages and I prepared to take the biggest gamble of my life.

● ● ●

"I can push him wherever you need to go," a dark-haired Thai college student named Kasem smiled as he rolled a wheelchair around for us. He had volunteered to work at the Bangkok airport that day and had been assigned wheelchair duty. "Did you have a fall?"

Peter looked at me, opened his mouth slightly, remembered our stern instructions, and frowned.

Good boy, I thought.

"So where are you from?" I asked, engaging Kasem in small talk. "This is Tracy," I pointed to Sara. "And this is Daniel," I said, pointing to Peter. We chatted through customs and in the immigration line.

There, time died.

Catherine and Qing, who were about fifteen people in front of us, easily got past the immigration agents and casually walked off to the side. Sara and Peter didn't say a word as Kasem chatted about his new job at the airport.

As I stood in the airport, I remembered the fear I felt when Heidi and I were escaping Beijing during her pregnancy. In a weird way, this was more horrifying. Now, I had so much more to lose—Heidi, three children, a nonprofit organization fighting injustice, and a home in America. Plus, I was responsible for another family's well-being. The line in front of me grew shorter.

We were up.

Kasem pushed Peter up to the immigration officers as they took the three passports from me. Mine was on top of the stack. They looked at me, then at the passport, and nodded. Then they opened Tracy's passport, looked at the little picture of my daughter, back at Sara, and back at the passport. After about two seconds, the immigration agent nodded. I tried not to look relieved or excited.

When she opened the last passport and looked at Daniel's photo, I felt my heartbeat in my ears and neck. Daniel was six years older than Peter, and they looked nothing alike. I'd banked on having a careless agent, but I could tell this lady meant business. Her uniform was perfectly pressed, her shoes were shiny. Her bun was pulled so tightly it made her face taut.

"What's wrong?" I asked, very casually. "There are no problems?"

She shook her head, and said something to her co-worker in Thai. Though I couldn't understand her language, her tone of incredulity told me she was probably saying, "Does this boy look like his picture?" She held the passport in front of her co-worker's face. He squinted, then nodded slightly.

"What is your name?" she asked him, but Peter—true to form—didn't answer. We'd told him to act shy, but he was taking it even further by acting dumb. "Grhumph," he said.

"Name?"

"Grhumph!"

"My son's not well," I explained.

The agent took out a flashlight and shined a light on Peter's ears, like she was inspecting him after he took a bath.

"See, these ears just don't match." The minute hand on a giant clock in the terminal had gone around about ten times since we'd first approached this agent. They were onto us, but the agent hadn't yet ordered the officers to arrest us. I smiled and said, "Just let us through," I said. "My children are tired."

"Why are you in a wheelchair?" She knelt down before Peter. He mumbled unintelligibly, and—had I not been so terrified—I would've been impressed by his acting skills. Even at his young age, he seemed to understand what was going on.

"What happened?" she asked me.

"Oh, we had a terrible vacation," I said. "He fell." Instead of telling a detailed story, which I thought might make me look guilty, I didn't elaborate. She lifted up his blanket, looked at his short, six-year-old legs, and examined his bandages.

It's over, I thought. *No one could think this kid is a twelve-year-old.* I wondered how my demise would happen. Would these officers arrest us immediately? Would we be separated? Would Catherine and Qing explain to Heidi what happened to me?

Just then, Peter did something so gross—so brilliant—I couldn't believe my eyes. He began to foam at the mouth. Perhaps, when she began to inspect his legs, he suddenly felt the peril we were in. The entire time we'd been held there, he must've been saving up saliva in his mouth. When she got close to his bandages, he started drooling all over himself.

The officer immediately stood up, her eyes wide in disgust. They handed up tissues, while they brought other officers over for their opinion. While they examined the documents, I didn't say anything. I just prayed.

Save us.

After about thirty minutes, I'd practically sweated through my shirt and was thankful I was wearing a jacket. "Come on," I said, finally. "There's no problem."

The immigration officer turned to Kasem, who'd been standing there the whole time silently, his hands on Peter's wheelchair. "What do you think?" she said, handing him the passport. "Do you think the little boy matches this photo?" She pointed to the picture.

"Absolutely!" Kasem said, with a big smile. I was thankful I'd built up a rapport with him.

"Okay," the agent said, biting her lip. I didn't wait for her to finish her sentence. As she was handing me the stack of passports, I walked past her as quickly as possible without looking guilty.

"Thank you," I said to Kasem, as I took control of Peter's wheelchair. "I'll take it from here."

I didn't breathe until we were safely in the air. The fact that we made it this far was nothing short of miraculous. When we landed in the Dallas airport, I wanted to stand up and cheer. We'd made it! We were free! I couldn't wait to be reunited with Heidi to tell her all we'd managed to pull off. I wanted to rustle Daniel's hair, to hug Tracy, and to kiss Melissa's little feet. However, the customs agent took one look at our passports and said, very sternly, "All of you. Come with me."

I should've realized our arrival would raise red flags in their system. After all, how could "Daniel Fu" and "Tracy Fu" land in Dallas if there's no record of their departure? We were led into a special room, where there was one long table. I'd managed to keep the kids out of Chinese prison only to deliver them to an American detention center.

"We need you to come with us," they said to Sara. She stood silently, and walked out of the room like a gladiator going into the Coliseum. *If she's not out in twenty minutes*, I thought, *I'll surrender*. I'd prepared all of the documentation for their asylum papers and was carrying them in my suitcase.

Sara knew some English, but not much. The officers from the Customs and Border Protection used an AT&T operator on the phone to translate for her. She insisted repeatedly I was her father, but I didn't feel right about letting her be questioned by American police all alone. After twenty minutes, I went to the little window where an officer was standing and said, "I have a story to tell."

The officers gathered around and I told them everything. "Well, it all started in China, when . . ."

Immediately, the whole office began scrambling.

"Where's the mother, sir?" an enormous officer barked at me. He wasn't interested in my tale of religious persecution. About halfway through my explanation, I was accused of child trafficking.

"She's already through customs," I said. "She might be in the luggage area or the pick-up area."

He wheeled away from me and spoke into his walkie-talkie. The entire airport police force scoured the airport in search of an Asian woman who matched the description I gave them. When the airport police surrounded Qing, they also apprehended Catherine.

For seven hours, I sat in that room as they asked me questions dripping with the kind of contempt reserved for a kidnapper.

"This is a high-profile case," I warned them. "You should handle it very professionally."

I heard one of the senior officers in an adjacent room say, "Okay, guys, let's do everything by the book. This is big."

To add credibility to my story, I pulled out their petitions for asylum, then showed them some of my state department contacts who were familiar with the case. Eventually I was released, Guo's family was placed in immigration detention, and Catherine's passport was stamped "Seven Years No Return" and her green card was confiscated. She was punished the most severely, and still can't return to the United States even though her brother lives here. Guo's family finally got their political asylum approved a few months later, after the Manhattan-based Human Rights First enlisted the pro bono help of a law firm in Dallas. My children's passports were confiscated, and it took two years and nine trips to Houston to get new passports. The Dallas prosecutor's office dropped their charge against me for child trafficking. Qing, Sara, and Peter settled into Midland very seamlessly. The kids attend a private Christian school where Sara, a couple of years later, was even elected Homecoming Queen.

Guo, who is not a believer in Christ, was amazed when he heard the story of how we protected his family. Ten days after he was released from prison, he wrote me a letter.

"I believe the sacred cause of Christianity will play a crucial part in the spiritual life of a free Chinese society to come. Inspired by your virtue and holiness, I will always preserve in my heart my best wishes to you and to Christ-followers all over the world."

The letter blessed me so much.

Jesus once asked, "What do you benefit if you gain the whole world but lose your soul?" During this experience I learned the opposite is also true: if you've rescued one soul, it means more than the whole world.

29

One of our most recent cases made my iPhone famous.

The case centered around Chen Guangcheng, a blind man from Linyi County, Shandong Province, which also happens to be Heidi's hometown. He lost his sight as a young child, and was illiterate until he was in his twenties. After teaching himself to read braille, he taught himself the law, and began successfully advocating for the rights of the disabled. But when he started interviewing people in Linyi County about their experience with forced abortions, local officials grew incensed.

Chinese political structure—from the national level all the way down to the village level—has family planning commissions with almost unlimited power. If a woman manages to hide her illegal pregnancy and has an "extra child," the commission can make her pay fines worth three to five times the family's income, confiscate property, or throw her in prison. (China collects more than ten billion US dollars in "family planning" fines every year.) But if the woman is unable to hide her illegal pregnancy, officials will inject her with a poison regardless of how far along she is. Every day, thirty thousand women are forced to have abortions, no doubt contributing to Chinese women's astronomical suicide rates. China boasts that it has successfully prevented four hundred million children from being born, more than the entire population of the United States.

This commitment to the eradication of so many children requires the complicity of the whole community. In Chen's area, a newly married couple's neighborhood, both sets of grandparents, and the couple's parents all must sign a joint family planning covenant that makes them liable for the couple's fertility. If the couple violates the "family planning" policies, these friends and family members are held responsible. This means that a woman must hide her pregnancy from everyone or she'll be reported. She must also submit to embarrassing monthly exams to make sure she's not pregnant.

When Chen began interviewing his neighbors, it caused a huge stir. No one dared question this sacred core of Communist Party doctrine, which is actually written in the constitution and is called "State Basic Policy." No court in China is even allowed to take cases related to the issue. But when this blind man began walking around and simply asking women about their experiences, he heard chilling stories.

One woman told him she was forced to have an abortion in her seventh month of pregnancy, then was forced to be sterilized. He learned of an elderly villager who was kidnapped, starved, and beaten when his daughter failed to show up for a tubal ligation sterilization check. He learned of officials breaking brooms over elderly people's heads. One woman who became illegally pregnant told him that twenty-two of her relatives were seized, including three children, one pregnant woman, and an elderly grandma. He learned of elderly siblings—a brother and a sister—who were forced to beat each other after the woman's daughter-in-law got pregnant. He learned of a farmer who committed suicide when his family and neighbors were tortured because his son had an "extra child."

Chen documented that, in 2005, there were 130,000 forced abortions and sterilizations in his area alone.

His research, of course, put him on a collision course with the Communist Party. In 2007, he was arrested for "blocking traffic" and spent four years and three months in jail. Chen was associated with the human rights attorneys with whom ChinaAid worked closely, so we immediately advocated for his release. Certainly prison was worse for Chen, who couldn't even see his torturers. After his release, we'd hoped conditions would improve for Chen. Instead they actually got worse. He was immediately put under house arrest with his wife, young daughter, and mother who was close to eighty years old. The government hired over sixty officers who took turns surrounding his home every hour of every day. They also jammed his cell phone signal, built walls around his house, and beat any visitors. When Guo, for example, insisted on seeing him, the guards overturned his car.

In fact, for five months, no one really knew what had happened to Chen. Then, in November of 2011, Chen and his wife, Yuan Weijing, managed to secretly record a video showing the condition of their house arrest. They showed their dilapidated farmhouse, their dwindling supply of food and firewood, and a man peering over a wall into their living area.

ChinaAid smuggled out the video, which immediately went viral. A website asked people to send in photos of themselves wearing sunglasses like Chen's, as a sign of solidarity with Chen's family. People sent thousands of photos from all over the world—from Provo to Paducah, from China to Uganda, from New Zealand to New York. "Free Chen" bumper stickers began showing up on the cars of people concerned about human rights.

"Chen Guangcheng is a hero to many people around the world, a peaceful advocate for human rights and a defender of society's most vulnerable, its women and children," I told the press. "The world community should act to secure his unconditional release."

Chen's guards were perplexed—how did this blind man make

a video that drew attention to his plight when he had no internet, no cell service, and no ability to even leave the house? To dissuade this kind of behavior, they mercilessly beat him and his wife. Additionally, the guards put hundreds of glass bottles around Chen's bed. If the blind man tried to get out of bed, he'd certainly push over the bottles and alert the police.

But even as they clamped down on him in the house, awareness of his saga still grew throughout America and the world. Actor Christian Bale, star of the recent Batman film trilogy, called Chen his personal hero. In fact, when the actor was in China for the debut of the biggest-budget Chinese movie ever made, he and a CNN film crew drove eight hours to Chen's hometown. As soon as they got close to his house, however, thugs stopped them. The men were in plain clothes, showed no identification, and wouldn't let them pass. When the actor and the film crew tried to force themselves through, a scuffle ensued. They drove away, but the Communists chased them in a van for half an hour.

"This doesn't come naturally to me; this is not what I actually enjoy. It isn't about me," Bale said as the Communists chased his vehicle. "But this was just a situation that said I can't look the other way. The local people who are standing up to the authorities, who are visiting Chen and his family and getting beaten for it, I want to support what they're doing."*

It's not often that Batman gets punched by a Communist thug. So when it happened, it made headlines all over the world. The CNN video of the scuffle of Christian Bale and the thugs who guarded Chen's house went viral. It was a public relations nightmare for China; they needed to promote the movie, which featured a celebrity now inextricably linked to the blind dissident.

---

*"Batman Star Christian Bale Attacked Stopped in China from meeting a Blind Activist Lawyer," YouTube video, 2:46, posted by TibetArchive on Dec. 15, 2011, http://www.youtube.com/watch?v=X-NGweWIQqc.

— • • • —

Meanwhile, Chen hatched a plan of escape. For two months, he pretended to be sick and stayed in bed every day. When he was sure the guards no longer saw him as a mobility threat, he made his move. Somehow, he managed to navigate through the glass bottles, escape the house, jump eight tall walls, and walk through the fields and small roads for nineteen hours. The blind man evaded over a hundred guards—those who were stationed near his bedroom, along the major roads, and even in the village. During his late-night journey, he fell many times and even broke several bones in his foot. Yet he kept going.

When the Communists discovered he'd escaped, they were furious and embarrassed. Even after spending 20 million yuan, or $3.5 million, they were foiled by a man who couldn't even see his captors.

Chen walked until he reached a friend, who harbored him. For days, he moved amongst several homes within the underground network of safe houses to avoid detection. Eventually, he suspected police were on his trail, so he decided to go to the safest place imaginable: the United States Embassy.

That's when I got a call.

"Go to Washington, DC," my friend in Beijing told me, before saying other sentences that included the code word "blind."

I knew from her language that something big was going on, and it related to Chen. As I decided whether to travel to DC on such meager information, Chen and his friends made their way to the embassy, pursued by unmarked Beijing police cars. After a brief car chase, Chen walked into the United States Embassy.

It was an escape worthy of a Christian Bale movie.

Chen sought refuge, not political asylum. That meant he was only protected while inside the embassy. The moment he stepped outside of the building, he'd be arrested.

I was still in Midland when news of Chen's escape broke,

causing worldwide speculation about his whereabouts. Because I was his only spokesperson in the West, ChinaAid phones rang constantly. Every employee dropped what they were doing, fielded calls, and scheduled my interviews on three calendars—one for radio interviews, another for TV interviews, and the last for newspaper interviews. Though we didn't have a nice studio or fancy equipment, we hung a red blanket which had "ChinaAid" printed in white letters on the wall.

I stepped back to look at it, and asked, "What do you think about my backdrop?"

My staffers weren't so sure, so I paraphrased a psalm. "Some trust in chariots and some in horses, and some in high-tech, soundproof television studios." I smiled. "But we trust in the name of the Lord our God."

I spoke to reporters from all over the globe—Chile, Mexico, the Philippines, Taiwan, Israel, Europe, and the United States. The more publicity Chen received, the better. I knew he still wasn't safe. During my hundreds of interviews, I was repeatedly asked the same question: Where is Chen?

"Chen is in the most secure location," I said, with purposeful ambiguity. I couldn't reveal that he was at the United States Embassy just yet. Secretary of State Hillary Clinton happened to be heading to the embassy on other business, and Chen released a video appeal to Premier Wen Jiabao in which he asked for an admission that he and his family were wrongfully persecuted for the last seven years, a guarantee of his family's safety, and prosecution of those who had abused him.

When the media finally discovered he was at the US Embassy, their attention became an absolute frenzy. How had a blind man orchestrated such a political nightmare for China? How would America handle this sort of situation?

We'd soon find out. On the day Hillary Clinton arrived, US Embassy officials told Chen that his family could be in grave danger. Reluctantly, Chen walked out of the embassy. That day, I got a phone call from the Assistant Secretary of State.

"We had a good negotiation with the Chinese officials. China agreed to let Chen attend a university and even pay his tuition. They even agreed to investigate Chen's abusers at the local level."

"Where is he now?"

"He walked out."

Since I hadn't heard from Chen, I gave the United States government the benefit of the doubt. Soon, however, I got two messages from friends who'd talked to Chen and told me a very different story. After he walked out of the embassy, his wife told him thugs had bound her to a chair, beaten her, threatened to kill her, and said they wanted to use her as a hostage to get Chen out of the embassy. That night, Chen was crying. He knew China would never keep their end of the bargain.

• • •

I flew to Washington, DC, to testify in an emergency session of Congress to get to the bottom of Chen's situation. Congressman Chris Smith was waiting for a call from Chen, which was supposed to have been arranged by the State Department. Sadly, the call never came. We didn't know what had happened to Chen—but it couldn't have been good.

"Maybe you can meet me at the hearing a few minutes early and we can try to talk to Chen," Congressman Smith said.

I dialed the number, but we weren't able to get through.

Many people testified about their interpretation of the events in China, but no one could definitively speak to Chen's state of mind. As the last speaker was testifying, Congressman Smith texted me. "Want to try again?"

I went back out into the hall and realized that the phone number I'd dialed previously was incorrect. Somehow we had transposed two numbers. When I hurriedly dialed the right number, Chen answered! I motioned to Congressman Smith, who immediately adjourned the hearing. He and Congressman Frank Wolf came out to a side room to have a talk with Chen.

"Ask him if he'd like to testify," Congressman Smith said.

"I'm not sure if that's the best idea," I said. This incident already had international implications. First, it overshadowed the China-US Economic and Strategic Dialogue for which Hillary Clinton had visited China. Second, China had publicly lambasted the United States' dealing with the matter.

"Why don't we ask Chen?" asked Rep. Wolf. "Let him decide."

Chen had been in prison for over four years and locked in his house for three. Suddenly throwing him into the spotlight of a congressional hearing sounded risky, but it only made sense. If China was trying to silence him, America should let the man speak.

I translated the question for Chen: "Would you like to testify during this hearing before the Congressional-Executive Commission on China?"

"Sure," Chen responded. "No problem."

When Congressman Smith dramatically returned to his dais, leaned into the microphone, and announced, "Bob Fu has made contact with Chen Guangcheng—in his hospital room," the room got quiet.

In order for the phone to be better positioned to the microphones, I sat beside the congressman and held up my phone. All of the major media networks were taking photographs of the closest thing to Chen in that room—my iPhone. I didn't want to speak too much or too little, but it seemed God had prepared the moment to address the confusion surrounding whether Chen had left the embassy voluntarily, whether he wanted to stay in China as a reformer, or whether he'd rather seek asylum in America.

"I want to go to the United States," he said, which I translated into the microphone. "I want to make the request to have my freedom of travel guaranteed."

Then, I elaborated on Chen's message. "He said he wants

to come to the United States for some time of rest. He has not had any rest in the past ten years."

After the hearing, a huge crowd of reporters followed me and I was very intimidated. Over the next few days, I was on John King's program, *PBS NewsHour*, and many other shows.

Thirteen days later, Chen was called to testify once again before Congress from his hospital bed. Before the hearing, I was briefed by the US chief negotiator, who was a State Department legal counselor, and the Assistant Secretary of State.

"I'd just like to remind you that today there's not only a hearing but high-level negotiations going on between China and the United States." He paused, before adding the obvious. "Be very careful." However, this time I didn't feel nervous. Again, it was only right for Chen to speak for himself.

Through my translation, he told about how the local authorities in his hometown were exacting revenge on members of his family. Officials broke into one relative's house in the middle of the night and began beating everyone. When Chen's nephew grabbed a kitchen knife to defend himself, they accused him of murder. Even though he was simply trying to defend himself—and no one had actually been killed—Chen was worried his nephew could be tortured and faced a severe sentence. Also, several other relatives had been arrested.

After these two hearings, Hillary Clinton told China's national leader that Chen had testified in Congress and made his wish clear. He now lives in New York with his wife, though his nephew is still in prison.

Recently, Chen was named *GQ*'s "Rebel of the Year." The accompanying article featured Chen wearing a long red scarf, standing on a pier. Suddenly, this blind Chinese man who couldn't speak a word of English had made it fashionable to fight against China's forced abortion policies. That couldn't have been what the Chinese government had anticipated when they decided to surround his small house with hundreds of Communist thugs.

Chen did, incidentally, end up meeting Christian Bale. In 2012, the actor gave the dissident the Human Rights Award at the annual gala of Human Rights First, during which he called Chen a "giant among men." A tear rolled down from beneath Chen's now-famous sunglasses as the movie star embraced him.

Once Chen was safely in New York, Heidi was the only Chinese guest allowed to meet with Chen and his family in their New York University apartment. I was in Asia engaging in another major rescue mission, but did get to meet up with them a few days later. As I listened to the story of his miraculous escape, Chen said, "God must've helped me escape."

● ● ●

Stories like Chen's make me so thankful I started ChinaAid in my hot Philadelphia attic. I've always felt the organization was a natural progression of the work of my mentor Dr. Jonathan Chao, who encouraged me to be a "missionary scholar" while we were in China. I listened so intently to his plans for the church in China that I was able to write pages and pages about it for my prison interrogators so many years ago. Even though they weren't impressed by the "three huas," Jonathan's vision has impacted my ministry ever since and I think he would've been proud to see Chen's saga unfold on primetime television.

Sadly, Jonathan died of lymphoma in 2004 after a lifetime of Bible smuggling and other covert "religious infiltration." This year, as I was writing this book, I too went to the doctor and received some bad news.

"We found a tumor," the doctor told me, and Heidi squeezed my hand.

Yet God is good.

Sometimes, people ask me how I've lived without being immobilized by fear, especially considering some of my more harrowing experiences. The question, however, is easily answered by a story I heard from a friend in the Chinese countryside—the

Anhui Province—back when I was a "double agent," teaching future Communist leaders during the day and training pastors of illegal countryside churches during the nights and weekends.

This man was sent to a labor camp for running a house church. On the first day of his imprisonment, the guards lined up all the new prisoners to shave their heads. His young daughter was watching him through the iron gate, crying.

"Oh, Daddy, you didn't commit a crime!" she protested. "Even if you're released, people will see your shaved head and think you're a criminal."

"Remember what the Bible says?" he said in the gentlest voice possible. "Every piece of hair is counted. Without His permission, not a single piece can fall to the ground."

When he got back into line, resigned to his fate, his daughter pressed her face against the cold bars. But when it was the man's turn to get his head shaved, the clippers malfunctioned. The guard angrily examined the device, found it to be functioning, and tried again.

"There's a problem," he told the other guard, because—once again—when he placed the clippers on his head, they didn't work. The second guard angrily walked over to my friend, placed his clippers on his head, and flipped the switch. Nothing.

The guards scrambled, now that both sets of clippers didn't appear to be working with a long line of prisoners yet to shave. Finally, they sent him away, grumbling about how there must be something wrong with the man's hair. As he walked away, the clippers began working again. The father caught his daughter's eye and smiled. Not a single piece of his hair had fallen to the ground.

As a forty-four-year-old man, I still feel very much like the prisoner's daughter must've felt on that day: delighted and thankful our lives are totally in God's hands. Without His permission no one can reduce one second of our life, nor can we add a single hour to our lives by worrying.

It frees us to work tirelessly and courageously for the cause of Christ, without fearing what will become of us. In fact, Chen's saga could easily be the climax of my story, the capstone of a career of fighting for justice. And, indeed, if God had prepared me from childhood to advocate for this one man, it would've been enough.

However, I know one day soon my phone will ring again. On the other end will be a person needing help, a child of the Lord being mistreated by the powerful and the corrupt.

After Chen's high-profile victory, it's tempting to slow down, to spend more time with my family and on myself.

But I'm still here, I'm still fighting, and—by the grace of God—I'm still going to answer the call.

For we do not want you to be unaware, brothers, of the affliction we experienced in Asia. For we were so utterly burdened beyond our strength that we despaired of life itself. Indeed, we felt that we had received the sentence of death. But that was to make us rely not on ourselves but on God who raises the dead. He delivered us from such a deadly peril, and he will deliver us. On him we have set our hope that he will deliver us again. You also must help us by prayer, so that many will give thanks on our behalf for the blessing granted us through the prayers of many.

2 CORINTHIANS 1:8–11 ESV

Epilogue

A Letter to American Readers

Dear American readers;

"China is a sleeping giant," Napoleon said. "When she awakes, she will shake the world." And we have seen this prescient nineteenth-century observation come true. After occupation, division, isolation, famine, and plenty, the nation has definitely awakened. Sometimes Americans are confused about how exactly to perceive modern China. Is it a military threat? How do we deal with their currency manipulation? Is it immoral to purchase products made in China? While the politicians debate these issues, people of all political parties and religious beliefs should emphatically agree on this: China's human rights violations should not be tolerated, overlooked, or swept under the rug.

I created ChinaAid in the attic of my Philadelphia home many years ago. Our organization is still going strong, and I'd love for you to join us in our efforts to promote freedom and the rule of law in China. All Americans should be able to rally around freedom. Chen Guangcheng is the perfect example of this great country supporting and celebrating someone who had enough courage to stand up to his oppressors. Though he is not a Christian, Guangcheng knew that forced abortion policies are hurtful to women, morally corrosive to society, and deadly to the most innocent of victims. Americans have embraced him since he arrived in New York, and he has been honored on many occasions.

Recently, at the National Cathedral in Washington, DC, Chen said, "I'm often asked what the international community can do to help promote democracy and rule of law in China. I sincerely hope that people around the world will lose their fear of offending China because it's rich and powerful. I want people to stop turning a blind eye to the abuses that people throughout China are suffering. . . . Don't do anything on the basis that China's rulers will be pleased or not pleased."

ChinaAid provides training, financial support, and legal defense for people like Chen. In fact, in the past ten years we have supported over a thousand persecuted prisoners of faith and freedom. Our associated attorneys travel thousands of miles across China, file legal challenges, provide criminal defense, and even file applications to stage public protests. They do this at huge security and political risk to themselves.

Are we always successful? No. In fact, we lose most of these cases. Since China is still ruled by the Communist Party, judicial independence simply does not exist. However, if you ask those who were defended, they will tell you our success rate is 100 percent.

Let me give you one example. On July 29, 2012, Pastor Jin Yongsheng, a house church leader in Inner Mongolia (a region in northern China), and twenty-four other believers, including his wife and two daughters, were providing health education to the public when local authorities intervened. Pastor Jin was viciously manhandled, beaten, and injured, then fined and sentenced to fifteen days administrative detention. The authorities claimed that pastor Jin "was engaged in proselytizing in the name of rendering medical service by measuring people's blood pressure." The authorities also raided his church and confiscated many items of church property, including Sunday offerings. ChinaAid sent an attorney to request administrative review in accordance with Chinese law. The government denied the request. We lost the first round.

But ChinaAid continued to support Jin. The attorney filed an administrative lawsuit against the local Public Security Bureau officials for violating the law and failing to protect citizens' religious freedom. In November, Jin informed us they had encountered significantly less persecution after the media exposure resulting from ChinaAid's reports and the attorney's legal defense work. Moreover, provincial and municipal PSB officers made a trip to his home and apologized for violating the rights of Pastor Jin and his house church. They even returned about $2,000 USD that was confiscated in the raid!

In a bold step toward building goodwill and trust with the PSB and local government, Pastor Jin decided to withdraw the pending administrative lawsuit against the PSB. Pastor Jin and his church have been greatly encouraged by this battle and now have much more freedom to worship both in their village and in the surrounding area. More importantly, the persecutors now understand that Pastor Jin is not alone, that harassing him means people all over the world will fight back.

This story effectively demonstrates, I think, why the conventional way of measuring success might not apply in China. It is also an example of the kind of action atheists, Buddhists, Hindus, Falun Gong, and Christians should all support. Religious freedom, it can be argued, is our first freedom, and it lays the foundation for all other basic human rights.

• • •

If you are a fellow brother or sister in Christ, however, you realize ultimately the Chinese people need our Lord and Savior Jesus Christ. I want to make some observations that may be helpful as we go about the work of spreading the gospel in China.

First, it's important to slow down. Americans like to see things get done instantly—instant food, Twitter, and "shock and awe" military campaigns. I once saw an ad in a major Christian magazine with the slogan "one dollar, one soul." Apparently it cost one dollar to purchase a Bible in China, which could convert one Chinese soul—or so the equation of instant gratification went. Some Americans go to China for a "short-term mission" and leave behind a kind of Americanized Chinese Christianity—with believers who can only pray in English. Unfortunately, the fast-food approach will not work when talking about life-and-death decisions of salvation. It's even counterproductive. The "Four Spiritual Laws" (a very helpful tool used by Campus Crusade for Christ) is not a magic marketing book or business model to harvest souls. Instead of looking for a quick fix, I encourage you to learn about the Chinese people and their culture. China's history is almost twenty times longer than America's, so it may take some time, but it's worth it. It took my American teachers years before their living and interacting with Chinese students bore spiritual fruit.

Second, genuineness is a valuable social currency with the Chinese. Chinese culture, especially after sixty years of communism and wave after wave of class struggle, is desperate for trust. Many of my classmates were more willing to share their personal secrets with American teachers than with fellow Chinese students because they were so caring and seemed to be trustworthy. I will never forget being invited to the foreign expert regiment building where our American teachers lived. We students talked, laughed, and joked like little children.

On one of those weekends, I walked into the apartment of a teacher who'd been in China for at least three years. He was playing his guitar and singing, and he suddenly began crying. He told me he was missing his home and parents in California. I was so touched by his confession and emotion. Chinese professors would never weep in front of their students. Because of our American teachers' honesty and openness, we felt total freedom—including the liberty to grab anything we wanted from their refrigerators. That's love!

Third, let's resist the urge to promote a certain brand of theology. I once met with a famous American evangelist in a five-star hotel in Beijing. "How many Chinese Christians," he asked, "have the spiritual gift of speaking in other tongues?" While I am not personally against that doctrine and practice (and have even had this experience), I could tell that this secondary issue was his main concern, and that made me uneasy. A few years later this minister wrote a book about how to speak in tongues that was distributed by the tens of thousands through underground Chinese printing networks. Now this issue has become one of the most divisive issues in Chinese churches.

When I enrolled at Westminster Theological Seminary in 1997, I was handed a form asking me to declare my Protestant denomination. My eyes glazed over as I looked over the list— there were two hundred options! Fortunately the list included "Independent," which I checked. That was one of my first experiences of culture shock.

Instead of getting bogged down by these little things, choose to live out the true gospel of grace and truth. Show care and concern for others, and present the truth of Jesus in the context of love. Sometimes this can be done with a small handwritten card, a home-cooked meal, or just a visit. My in-laws were very touched when two American teachers showed up at their doorstep in a remote village. These Americans were traveling by bicycle on the dusty roads. They prayed for my wife's family members and other villagers. They might have been the first "big nose" visitors that village had ever seen. After they left, both of my in-laws came to Christ.

The end of the matter is this: Chinese people don't need Christianity without Christ. They need logical and intellectually compelling truth. Don't be afraid of the difficult questions about the purpose of life or how man is going to find it in a materialistic, trustless society. Let us grapple with the claims of Christ on these issues—but don't stop there.

The Chinese heart needs to be touched—brought to life—with magnificent acts of true sacrifice, love, and service. Doing this with sincerity will speak volumes—but don't stop there.

Chinese hands need to experience the good news in practical actions that help others. We have learned to live for our financial well-being. Though we want to help others, this is considered a noble waste of time. The Cultural Revolution stopped our hearts cold, making us hesitant to help others. Why? Because doing so requires trust. When we see the gospel transforming communities large and small, from healing a marriage to helping orphans and those with HIV, we see a vision of true love.

Most of you won't be able to go to China. You can still reach out to the 150,000 Chinese students and scholars on US college campuses. You can do this by demonstrating a healthy marriage, building real friendships, and inviting them to investigate the teachings of Christ for themselves. When the gospel impacts their lives, they will influence their countrymen. This is a great strategic investment, because many of these students will serve in key roles in Chinese society.

Consider visiting ChinaAid.org to find out how you can write letters to the persecuted church, sign petitions for justice, send messages to authorities, and donate money toward spreading the gospel and fighting for the persecuted in China.

Sometimes it's easy to get overwhelmed by the size and strength of the no-longer-sleeping giant of China. Start small. Do something. Be faithful, loving, and courageous. After all, God's people have faced giants before.

Love,
Bob Fu

CHINAaid
对华援助协会

Acknowledgments

I'd like to thank my wise and extremely sacrificial wife Heidi; my three children, Daniel, Tracy, and Melissa; and of course my deceased parents, my two sisters, and my elder brother. I would also like to thank:

My mentor Dr. Jonathan Chao (deceased) and his wife Rebecca Chao; Dr. and Mrs. Stephen Tong, my past theological advisors at Westminster Theological Seminary; Dr. and Mrs. Bill and Barbara Edgar; Dr. Pete Lillback; Dr. Clair Davis; Dr. Sam Logan; Dr. and Mrs. Vern and Dianne Poythress; Rev. Tim Conkling, my current PhD advisor and friend from Durham University; Dr. Robert Song; Mr. and Mrs. Paul and Tina Aldrich; my sponsors Charlie and Karen Erickson; Michael and Susan Erickson; Rev. Ron Lewis and King's Park International Church; "Mummy" Deborah Fikes, her husband Stan, and their caring children Stacey and Lindsey; Rev. and Mrs. Kevin and Renee York, Rev. and Mrs. Daniel Stephens, and Mid-Cities Community Church in Midland; and Rev. and Mrs. Patrick Patton and Stonegate Fellowship.

Past and current board members of ChinaAid and their spouses, including Joe and Terry Torres, Scott and Connie McGraw, Tim and Terry Dunn, former Congressman Beau Boulter and his wife Rosemary, Doug and Angie Robison, Bruce and Martha Lowe, Dr. and Mrs. Stephen Chan, Dr. and Mrs. Yujian Hong, Mr. and Mrs. Paul Gustafson, Rev. and Mrs. Tom and Sue Vermillion, and Rev. and Mrs. Chris Davis. Thanks also to our director in Los Angeles, Rev. and Mrs. Eddie and Rosemary Romero, and the whole Romero family.

Dr. and Mrs. Wayne and Barbara Grudem at Phoenix Theological Seminary, John Politan, and their fellow attendants at Scottsdale Bible Church's Sunday school classes. You always practice deep theological thinking with compassion for the persecuted, which inspires me and my staff to move forward.

My friends Dr. and Mrs. Will and Rana Inboden; Dr. and Mrs. Toney Carnes; Dr. David Aikman and his gifted, hardworking wife Ms. Charlene Fu; Dr. and Mrs. Graham and Lindy Walker; Dr. and Mrs. Steven Garber; Mr. and Mrs. Bill and Traci McConnell and family; Mr. and Mrs. Randy and Torri Delong and family; Judge and Mrs. Dan and Barbara Dane; Mr. and Mrs. Kyle and Jamie Stallings; Mr. and Mrs. Corey and Cheryl Odden; Mr. and Mrs. Hsiao-Wen and Susana Kao; Ms. Emilie Kao; Dr. and Mrs. James Song; Dr. and Mrs. Peter Ko; Dr. Edward Lee; Mr. Bob Maginn and Ms. Ling Chai; Dr. and Mrs. Ken-Peng Jen; Dr. and Mrs. Peter Chow and Rev. Robert Chang; Rev. Stephen Lee; Mr. and Mrs. Rob and Reggie LittleJohn; Ms. Catherine Tien; and "Mummy" Karen Deussing and Rev. David Johnston.

Those who have played critical roles for the timely rescue of Heidi, our three-month-old son Daniel, and me in 1997: Dr. Don Argue, Dr. Carol Lee Hamrin, Dr. Robert H. Schuller, former President Bill Clinton, former Secretary of State Madeleine Albright, former Assistant Secretary of State John Shattuck, Mr. Greg Chen, Mr. Danny Smith and his passionate Jubilee Campaign team members, Dr. Ron Boyd-MacMilan, Dr. Tony Lambert, Mr. and Mrs. John and Karen Short, Mr. and Mrs. Robert and Wayii Stevenson, Rev. Yir-Ming Chu, Rev. Greg O'Connor, and Mr. and Mrs. Merv and Grace Knight. Thanks also to those who helped rescue my father, whose names will be revealed when China is free. Also Mrs. Nancy DeMoss and Dr. John Bechtel of the DeMoss Foundation, for your unspeakable love and encouragement.

Church family members who helped sustain my family through those difficult years in Philadelphia, especially during my father's sickness, including Ms. Sally Cummings (deceased) and deacon committee members of the former Main Line Chinese Christian Church; Trinity Christian Church of Greater Philadelphia; Faith, Hope, and Love Chinese Church; Proclamation Presbyterian Church; and Allentown Chinese Christian Church.

My first spiritual father and teacher Brent and his wife Julie, plus a number of those friends from ELIC and Campus Crusade for Christ who serve in my motherland sacrificially, honorably, and anonymously. Rev. and Mrs. Alan Yuan (deceased), Pastor Shijun Feng, and Elder Moses Xie (deceased) from Beijing. Our loving friendship through China ministry with Mr. and Mrs. Aubin and Joanny Chang has been deepened more from Beijing to Philadelphia. Attorney David Taylor from South Carolina has been an encouragement for justice. To Christian Literatures Crusade (CLC) and WEC International, who provided our refugee family temporary accommodation when we landed in Philadelphia: your kindness and hospitality will never be forgotten. Thanks also to pastor Joshua Lin and my fellow brothers and sisters in Beijing House Church, with whom I am ordained as "Pastor-at-Large."

The staff and volunteers at the Voice of the Martyrs, including Dr. Tom White (deceased) and his wife Ofelia, Jim and Peggy Dau, Klaas Brobbel, Floyd Brobbel, and Edwin Baelde, and also leaders at Release International UK, Christian Solidarity Worldwide (CSW), International Christian Concern, Dr. Richard Land, and Dr. Barrett Duke of the Ethics and Religious Liberty Commission of the Southern Baptist Convention. Thanks also to those friends in public service, including Rep. Frank Wolf, Rep. Chris Smith, Rep. Jim McGovern, Rep. Joe Pitts, Governor Sam Brownback, Vice President of EU Parliament Edward McMillan-Scott, MP Dr. Bastiaan Belder, and Lord David Alton.

Those who have been praying for me and my family and supporting our ministries in China, the United States, and other parts of the world. And thanks to all of my hardworking but low-paid staff and volunteers at ChinaAid, as well as generous partners and sacrificial givers, some of whose names will remain invisible for security reasons.

My smart, loving agent Ms. Chris Park and my DC advisor Dr. Scott Flipse. Without your encouragement and innovative thinking, this book still wouldn't have even begun. To the exceptional team at Baker Books for their passion and work on behalf of this book: Dwight Baker, Elizabeth Kool, Dave Lewis, Rod Jantzen, Rob Teigen, Max Eerdmans, Scott Hurm, Bill Shady, Nathan Henrion, Deonne Lindsey, Brianna DeWitt, Lindsey Spoolstra, and Heather Brewer. I also loved working with Chad Allen and Ruth Anderson, whose enthusiasm about the book was so encouraging. Thanks also to Larry Ross, Kristin Cole, and Steve Yount at A. Larry Ross for helping this story get into the larger culture. And of course, I have to thank my amazing writer Nancy French, who embraced my story and brought it to life, working tirelessly on my behalf, even on Christmas Eve. She went above and beyond the call of duty.

Finally, my fellow persecuted brothers and sisters in China, for their courage on behalf of the gospel, and to those persecuted Chinese rights defenders and lawyers who serve a cause beyond themselves by risking their lives to defend the oppressed on this earth.